Celebration of Discipline

Celebration of Discipline

The Path to Spiritual Growth

Richard Foster

Hodder & Stoughton
LONDON SYDNEY AUCKLAND

Unless otherwise indicated, all scriptural quotations are taken from
the Revised Standard Version of the Bible, copyright © 1946, 1952,
1971 by the Division of Christian Education of the National
Council of the Churches of Christ in the United States of America.

Some of the material from chapter 2 was originally published
in the booklet *Meditative Prayer*.

This revised edition copyright © 1989 by Richard Foster

Celebration of Discipline first published in Great Britain in 1980
This edition published in 2005

The right of Richard Foster to be identified as the Author
of the Work has been asserted by him in accordance
with the Copyright, Designs and Patents Act 1988.

9

British Library Cataloguing in Publication Data

A record for this book is available from the British Library

ISBN 0 340 73521 X

Typeset in Bembo by Avon DataSet Ltd,
Bidford-on-Avon, Warwickshire

Printed and bound in Great Britain by
Clays Ltd, St Ives plc

The paper and board used in this paperback are natural recyclable
products made from wood grown in sustainable forests.
The manufacturing processes conform to the environmental
regulations of the country of origin.

Hodder & Stoughton
A division of Hodder Headline Ltd
338 Euston Road
London NW1 3BH
www.madaboutbooks.com
www.hodderbibles.co.uk

Contents

Foreword

There are many books concerned with the inner life, but there are not many that combine real originality with intellectual integrity. Yet it is exactly this combination that Richard Foster has been able to produce. Steeped as he is in the devotional classics, the author has given us a careful study that may, itself, be valued for a long time. Though the present volume demonstrates indebtedness to the Classics, it is not a book about them; it represents, instead, genuinely original work.

What strikes us at once is the comprehensive character of the current undertaking. Many contemporary books deal with particular aspects of the inner life, but this one is different in that it deals with an astonishing variety of important topics, much of its freshness of treatment arising from its boldness. The author has undertaken to examine a wide spectrum of experience, from confession to simplicity of joy. Since the finished product is the outcome of wide reading and careful thinking, it is not the sort of book that can be dashed off quickly or cheaply.

The sources of insight are varied, the chief ones being the Holy Scriptures, and the recognised classics of devotion, but these are not the only fountains from which the author draws. The careful reader soon recognises a large indebtedness to secular thinkers as well. In view of the fact that the author is himself a Quaker, it is not surprising that the contributions of the classic Quaker writers are prominent. These include the works of George Fox, John Woolman, Hannah Whitall Smith, Thomas Kelly, and many more. The purpose here is not sectarian but genuinely ecumenical, since important insights ought never to be limited to the group from which they arise. What we are given, accordingly, is an example of the catholicity of sharing.

The treatment of simplicity is especially valuable, partly because it is not simple. Indeed the ten 'controlling principles' concerning simplicity, which are explained in Chapter 6, are themselves sufficient justification for the appearance of another book on the spiritual life. The ten principles enunciated, while rooted in ancient wisdom, are made astonishingly contemporary.

The author understands very well that the emphasis upon simplicity may itself become a snare. This is why he will not settle for anything so obvious as the adoption of a plain garb, though he can say tersely, 'Hang the fashions. Buy only what you need.' Here is a radical proposal which, if widely adopted, would be immensely liberating to people who are the victims of the advertisers, particularly those on television. A genuine cultural revolution would ensue if considerable numbers were to obey the trenchant command, 'De-accumulate.'

The greatest problems of our time are not technological, for these we handle fairly well. They are not even political or economic, because the difficulties in these areas, glaring as they may be, are largely derivative. The greatest problems are moral and spiritual, and unless we can make some progress in these realms, we may not even survive. This is how advanced cultures have declined in the past. It is for this reason that I welcome a really mature work on the cultivation of the life of the spirit.

D. Elton Trueblood

Acknowledgments

1978
Books are best written in community. I am deeply indebted to those whose lives have surrounded mine and have given substance to the ideas in this book. It was through the friendship and teaching of Dallas Willard that I first saw the meaning and necessity of the Spiritual Disciplines. For many years he has been my mentor in the Disciplines. His life is the embodiment of the principles in this book.

I owe much to Bess Bulgin, who carefully and prayerfully read each line of this book many times over. Her feel for rhythm has greatly enhanced its readability. Ken and Doris Boyce helped me more than they will ever know by their constant encouragement and enthusiasm. The help of Connie Varce, in typing, grammar, and optimism added a great deal. Mary Myton worked endlessly in typing both rough draft and the final manuscript. Stan Thornburg taught me about the Discipline of service with his words and his life. Rachel Hinshaw graciously offered her skills as a professional proofreader. My special thanks to Newberg Friends Church for releasing me to have time to write in the final weeks of this book, and especially to Ron Woodward, whose pastoral load of necessity increased as mine decreased.

My children, Joel and Nathan, were incredibly patient in allowing their daddy to cut short games and stories more than once. With the completion of this book comes the joy of once again lengthening those games and stories.

1988

It has been ten years since *Celebration of Discipline* was first published. I still find it true that books are best written in community; the only difference now is that the community to which I am indebted is vastly larger. Over the years numerous persons have written to encourage, challenge, correct, and stimulate my thinking. In addition, many have talked with me in person about their own strivings, learnings, and growings. All of these people and more have taught me much about the spiritual life and have contributed to this revision.

I especially want to thank my wife, Carolynn, who over the years has taught me more about walking with God than words can express. The dedication of this book to her has even more relevance now than it did ten years ago. Also, I want to express my appreciation to my administrative associate, Lynda Graybeal, who has worked tirelessly on the many details of this revision.

As I revise *Celebration*, I am struck profoundly by the weakness of words. At best they are broken and fragmented witnesses to God's truth. We do indeed see through a glass darkly. And yet I am struck even more profoundly by the fact that God can take something so inadequate, so imperfect, so foolish as words on paper and use them to transform lives. How this happens I do not know. It is a miracle of grace and points to the fact that, if there is anything in these pages that ministers life to you, it did not come from me. *Soli Deo Gloria!*

1998

Twenty years ago I wrote, 'Books are best written in community.' Ten years ago I reaffirmed that confessional statement, adding, 'the only difference now is that the community to which I am indebted is vastly larger.' So it is today, double and triple.

I would like, however, to add one difference now that was not true before: various ones of our ever-expanding community have since travelled through the Valley of the Shadow. They now live on the other side, overflowing, I have no doubt, with utter joy and complete fulfilment.

The first of these to travel this journey was Bess Bulgin. When I was writing *Celebration*, I met with Bess weekly, and she would critique my work. Bess was a poet and brought a poet's eye to all that I wrote. More than just critique happened though: a friendship was forged, rich and abiding.

Then I moved. I did not know if Bess and I would ever meet again this side of the Valley. We did. We both sensed it would be our last time together and said so. We talked and reminisced. She shared a new poem with me. Then, with trembling voice, I read the closing paragraph from the final book of *The Chronicles of Narnia* to her: 'but the things that began to happen after that were so great and beautiful that I cannot write them. And for us this is the end of all the stories, and we can most truly say that they all lived happily ever after. But for them it was only the beginning of the real story. All their life in this world and all their adventures in Narnia had only been the cover and the title page: now at last they were beginning Chapter One of the Great Story, which no one on earth has read: which goes on forever: in which every chapter is better than the one before.'

I finished reading, and we sat together in perfect silence. Then I left, travelling back to my new home. Not long after Bess left too, travelling to her new home beyond the Valley of the Shadow.

Such loss is a reality we all must face at one time or another, perhaps many times over. Hear, then, these bracing words of Charles Wesley:

If DEATH my friend and me divide,
thou dost not, Lord, my sorrow chide,
or frown my tears to see;
restrained from passionate excess,
thou bidst me mourn in calm distress
for them that rest in thee.

I feel a strong immortal hope,
which bears my mournful spirit up
beneath its mountain load;
redeemed from death, and grief, and pain,
I soon shall find my friend again
within the arms of God.

Pass a few fleeting moments more
and death the blessing shall restore
which death has snatched away;
for me thou wilt the summons send,
and give me back my parted friend
in that eternal day.

Introduction

It is a wonder to me how God uses squiggles on paper to do his work in the hearts and minds of people. How are these squiggles transformed into letters and words and sentences and, finally, meaning? Oh, we may congratulate ourselves on knowing a little about the function of neurotransmitters in the brain or about how endorphin proteins affect learning and memory retention, but if we are honest, we know that thinking itself is a mystery. Doxology is the only appropriate response.

At this writing, it has been two decades since this particular set of squiggles, *Celebration of Discipline*, was first published. After the first decade, the publisher, no doubt puzzled by its longevity and popularity, wanted to celebrate this milestone, and asked me to revise the original text – which I was glad to do. And now, after a second decade, the puzzle continues. Somehow (who can ever explain how?) people continue to find help in their daily walk with God through the pages of this book. To celebrate this twentieth anniversary, the publisher has asked me to write an introduction, and, again, I am glad to comply. And perhaps in fulfilling their request it is appropriate to tell how the book you hold in your hands came into being.

SPIRITUAL BANKRUPTCY

Fresh out of seminary, I was ready to conquer the world. My first appointment was a small church in a thriving region of Southern California. 'Here,' I mused, 'is my chance to show the denominational leadership, nay, the whole world, what I can do.' Believe me, visions of far more than sugar plums were dancing in my head. I *was* sobered a bit when the former pastor, upon learning of my appointment, put his arm on my shoulder and said, 'Well, Foster, it's your turn to be in the desert!' But the 'sobering' lasted only a moment. 'This church will become a shining light set on a hill. The people will literally flood in.' This I thought, and this I believed.

After three months or so I had given that tiny congregation everything I knew, and then some, and it had done them no good. I had nothing left to give. I was spiritually bankrupt and I knew it. So much for a 'shining light on a hill.'

My problem was more than having something to say from Sunday to Sunday. My problem was that what I did say had no power to help people. I had no substance, no depth. The people were starving for a word from God, and I had nothing to give them. Nothing.

THREE CONVERGING INFLUENCES

In the wisdom of God, however, three influences were converging in that little church that would change the direction of my ministry, indeed, of my whole life. Together they would provide the depth and the substance I needed personally and the depth and the substance that, in time, would lead to the penning of *Celebration*. But that is running ahead of my story.

The first thing to happen was precipitated by an influx of genuinely needy people into our small congregation. They simply flowed in like streams after a thunderstorm. Oh, how they hungered for spiritual substance and, oh, how willing they were to do almost anything to find it. These were the castoffs of today's fast-track culture – 'the sat upon, spat upon, ratted on' – and so their neediness was quite obvious. Just as obvious was my inability to give them substantive pastoral care.

This lack of any real spiritual density led me, almost instinctively, to the Devotional Masters of the Christian faith – Augustine of Hippo and Francis of Assisi and Julian of Norwich and so many others. Somehow I sensed that these ancient writers lived and breathed the spiritual substance these new friends in our little fellowship were seeking so desperately.

To be sure, I had encountered many of these writers in academic settings. But that was a detached, cerebral kind of reading. Now I read with different eyes, for daily I was working with heartbreaking, soul-crushing, gut-wrenching human need. These 'saints', as we sometimes call them, knew God in a way that I clearly did not. They experienced Jesus as the defining reality of their lives. They possessed a flaming vision of God that blinded them to all competing loyalties. They experienced life built on the Rock.

It hardly mattered who I read in those days – Brother Lawrence's *The Practice of the Presence of God*, Teresa of Ávila's *Interior Castle*, John Woolman's *Journal*, A. W. Tozer's *The Knowledge of the Holy* – they knew God in ways far beyond anything I had ever experienced. Or even wanted to experience! But as I continued to soak in the stories of these women and men who were aflame with the fire of divine love, I began desiring this kind of life for myself. And desiring led to seeking and seeking led to finding. And what I found settled me, deepened me, thickened me.

The second influence came from an individual in that tiny congregation, Dr Dallas Willard. A philosopher by profession, Dallas was well versed in the classics, and, at the same time, had an uncanny perception into the contemporary scene. He taught our fledgling little group: studies in Romans and Acts and the Sermon on the Mount and the Spiritual Disciplines and more.

But regardless of the specific topic, he constantly drew us into the big picture. It was life-based teaching that always respected the classical sources and always sought to give them contemporary expression. Those teachings gave me the *Weltanschauung*, the worldview, upon which I could synthesise all my academic and biblical training.

But it wasn't just the teaching, or at least it wasn't teaching as we usually think of teaching. It was a heart-to-heart communication that went on between this world-class philosopher and that little ragtag band of Christ's disciples. Dallas taught us right in the midst of our struggles, our hurts, our fears. He had descended with the mind into the heart and taught out of that deep centre.

Today, many years later, I still revel in the impact of those teaching/living/praying sessions. It was, of course, teaching-in-community. We were in each other's homes – laughing together, weeping together, learning together, praying together. Some of the best teaching times grew out of the dynamic of those home settings where we might go late into the night – posing questions, debating issues, applying gospel truth to life's circumstances. Dallas would move among us, teaching, always teaching. A spiritual charisma of teaching, I think. Teaching with wisdom. Teaching with passion. Teaching with heart. And always we experienced a sense of the numinous.

The third influence came initially from a Lutheran pastor, William Luther Vaswig. (With a name like 'William Luther Vaswig' how could he pastor anything but a Lutheran church?) Bill's church, large and influential, overshadowed our tiny Quaker fellowship. But what drew me to Bill had nothing to do with 'large' or 'influential' or even 'Lutheran.' No, what I saw was someone thirsting for the things of God. So I sought him out. 'Bill,' I said, 'you know more about prayer than I do. Would you teach me everything you know?'

Now, the way Bill taught me about prayer was by praying. Lively, honest, heartfelt, soul-searching, hilarious praying. As we did this, over time we began experiencing that 'sweet sinking into Deity' Madame Guyon speaks of. It, very honestly, had much the same feel and smell as the experiences I had been reading about in the Devotional Masters.

This movement into prayer was actually a two-pronged influence. My praying experiences with Bill were augmented by those of a wonderfully determined woman, Beth Shapiro, who was the head of the elders for our little fellowship. Beth was a nurse at a large hospital, and after working the night shift, she would come over to our church building in the early morning and we (Beth and I) would spend an hour or two praying for people. All kinds of people. People in our fellowship and people outside our fellowship. Whomever and whatever, Beth would want to pray for them.

Then we would often discuss issues of theology, of faith, of life. And whatever we talked about Beth tested out at the hospital. If we discussed the Bible's teaching on 'the laying on of hands,' at work Beth would put her hands into the rubber gloves of an incubator and place them on a premature infant, praying silently and lovingly, and watch that little one increase in health and well-being. These were the kinds of things Beth would do, not just now and again, but repeatedly. Through Beth I learned the necessity of bringing spiritual realities into the press of raw humanity.

Now, these three influences converged in those days of my young pastoring, and the result was a quiet revolution, inside and out. And in our fellowship of needy seekers we were experimenting with everything we were learning. Those were heady days, for we sensed we were on to something of enormous significance. We were hammering out on the hard anvil of daily life all that appeared years later in *Celebration of Discipline*. But these influences by themselves did not move me into actual writing. More was needed.

THREE EMPOWERING CATALYSTS

This 'more' came in the form of three separate and quite different catalysts. The first came by the hand of Bill Cathers, a former missionary and a man of unusual discernment and wisdom. It happened in this way. Growing out of three days of fasting and praying, I felt a concern to call Bill and invite him to pray for me. That was the extent of my guidance, only that he pray for me; I had not the slightest idea what he should pray or even why. He agreed to come.

When Bill arrived, the very first thing he did was to begin confessing his sins to me. I sat there astonished. 'What is he doing? He's the spiritual sage.' These were my inner thoughts, but I waited in silence. Finally, he finished, and I spoke over him those liberating words of 1 John 1:9, 'If we confess our sins, he who is faithful and just will forgive us our sins and cleanse us from all unrighteousness.'

Then Bill, looking right at me – and right through me – asked ever so quietly, 'Now, do you still want me to pray for you?' He had seen into my heart! He knew that I had put him high on a pedestal as some spiritual guru, and he was pulling all that down into a crumpled heap. Sobered by his discernment, I replied simply, 'Yes, I do.'

He then laid his hands on me and prayed one of the deepest prayers I have ever received. The power of that prayer is still with me today. I cannot begin to convey to you the height and the depth, the length and the breadth of his prayer, but I will tell you one word he spoke – a power-filled word, a prophetic word. 'I pray,' he said, 'for the hands of a writer.'

There it was. I had longed to write for years. But I had never told a living soul about this secret desiring. I was too shy to tell anyone. On that day I felt empowered for the ministry of writing, and while *Celebration* lay some years in the future, I did begin the necessary apprenticeship by writing numerous magazine articles.

The second catalyst was D. Elton Trueblood, a respected author of some thirty-six books. By now I was serving on an innovative pastoral team in the Pacific Northwest in what church-growth specialists call 'the large church.' It was a place where things seemed to go right no matter what I did. It was also a time for pondering lessons learned and considering whether they had broader application.

During this period I attended a national gathering of Quaker leaders among whom was Dr Trueblood. Following the conference, my co-worker Ron Woodward and I stayed a couple of extra days to do some sermon planning for the months ahead.

So it was that I happened upon Dr Trueblood in the hotel lobby. His genuine interest and kindness toward one totally unknown cannot be overstated. After a few moments of conversation, he turned to me abruptly and asked what book I was writing. The question came as a complete shock, and I stammered out something about not being ready for a book-length effort, but that I was writing several articles. 'Hmmm,' he mused. 'Yes, that is fine. But *soon* you must write a book!' The words carried such authority and weight and I could not get them out of my consciousness. He 'spoke truth to power' into me on that day.

Returning home, I dared to write to Trueblood, indicating that I did indeed have an idea for a book, and I enclosed a brief summary of what today is *Celebration of Discipline*. He wrote back a warm and encouraging response accompanied by one stern counsel: 'Be certain that every chapter forces the reader into the next chapter.' It was a counsel that did indeed inform the order of *Celebration*.

There was a third catalyst. While the other two experiences were sharp and dramatic, this final one was protracted and inconspicuous. It came from Ken and Doris Boyce, longtime friends who had stepped into something of a parenting role in my life after my own biological parents had passed through the Valley of the Shadow.

They helped in innumerable ways. When I was in graduate school, Doris (in those distant days before computers) typed many a term paper for me, including my doctoral dissertation. She was always careful to tell me how wonderful they all were – even the ones so technical that she had little idea what I was writing about.

Through the years Ken talked theology-in-the-marketplace with me, and illustrated it for me. Doris always encouraged me, perhaps to a fault. Both were always careful never to say too much about my writing, but always to reassure me in my writing. They cheered me on from the sidelines and believed in me when I could hardly believe in myself.

At one critical period, Ken and Doris let me use their motor home so that I could have uninterrupted space for writing. There I would sit, shaping ideas, crafting words, striking them out and re-shaping and re-crafting. I wrote the first pages of *Celebration* in that motor home in the driveway of Ken and Doris Boyce.

These three experiences catapulted me into writing. But writing is not publishing. Frankly, I knew nothing about the world of agents and editors, galleys and page proofs. To move from writing to book publishing took a series of events beyond my control.

THREE DIVINE PROVIDENCES

A writer's conference was being held in nearby Portland, Oregon. Prior commitments made it impossible for me to attend, but I paid full tuition for the event solely for the opportunity of a ten-minute interview with a representative from Harper & Row. I knew Harpers to be a general house publisher with a sturdy religion division and a solid reputation for serious literature. One thing that I, quite fortunately, did not know was that it was unheard of for an unpublished writer to approach such a prestigious House.

Thus I met Roy M. Carlisle, religion editor for Harpers. Our time together went well, and he asked me to send him a full book proposal. I did so immediately and boldly stated in my cover letter, 'This book is for all those who are disillusioned with the superficialities of modern culture, including modern religious culture.'

Mr Carlisle replied to my proposal in a timely fashion, and I shall always remember verbatim the opening sentence of his letter: 'In a word we are wildly enthusiastic about your proposal.' Of the more than seven hundred unsolicited manuscripts submitted to Harpers that year, mine was the only one accepted. Why, I could not imagine!

What I did not know was that a second providence was under way. At the very time I was in conversations with Mr Carlisle, Elton Trueblood sent my book summary, along with his hearty recommendation, to Clayton Carlson, Religion Publisher for Harper & Row. Elton had published all of his thirty-six books with the House of Harper and had a long-standing relationship with Mr Carlson. He, no doubt, opened doors that otherwise might have been closed to me. I knew nothing of this detail all these twenty-plus years, only recently learning about it from Mr Carlson. Trueblood never once mentioned it.

But there is more. With the acceptance of the book proposal, I was faced with a difficult dilemma. The responsibilities at the church demanded full attention: sermon preparation, hospital calls, counselling, and more. In addition, the publication deadline threw me into a panic. How could I do it? I, in fact, knew that I could not. So, what should I do? I was baffled. The only option I could imagine was to decide against writing the book.

At this critical juncture the wisdom of our team ministry approach proved itself. Ron Woodward, the head of our team, stepped forward in an act of sheer grace and self-sacrifice, volunteering to cover all preaching assignments until I finished the manuscript. Our elders too recognised this as a crucial opportunity. Thus, for the sake of the larger Christian community, they freed me from virtually all other pastoral responsibilities so I could devote my energies exclusively to writing. This I did, twelve to fifteen hours a day, for thirty-three days. To be sure, more work had to be done, but the basic structure of the book was completed in that concentrated period of writing. Never before or since have I had such complete freedom from all concerns and responsibilities, and it was to my mind an inspired and selfless act on the part of the church elders and Ron and the other team members. So it was that *Celebration of Discipline* came into being.

What then, I ask you, is this book really? Nothing but squiggles on paper. But through the grace of God it has been used, lo these twenty years, as an instrument for human transformation. For this I thank God. And what of its future? That I gladly leave in the hands of Divine Providence. *Soli Deo Gloria.*

1

The Spiritual Disciplines:
Door to Liberation

I go through life as a transient on his way to eternity, made in the image of God but with that image debased, needing to be taught how to meditate, to worship, to think.

— Donald Coggan

Superficiality is the curse of our age. The doctrine of instant satisfaction is a primary spiritual problem. The desperate need today is not for a greater number of intelligent people, or gifted people, but for deep people.

The classical Disciplines* of the spiritual life call us to move beyond surface living into the depths. They invite us to explore the inner caverns of the spiritual realm. They urge us to be the answer to a hollow world. John Woolman counsels, 'It is good

---

* You may be wondering why the Disciplines described in this book are termed 'classical.' They are not classical merely because they are ancient, although they have been practised by sincere people over the centuries. The Disciplines are classical because they are *central* to experiential Christianity. In one form or another all of the devotional masters have affirmed the necessity of the Disciplines.

for thee to dwell deep, that thou mayest feel and understand the spirits of people.'[1]

We must not be led to believe that the Disciplines are only for spiritual giants and hence beyond our reach, or only for contemplatives who devote all their time to prayer and meditation. Far from it. God intends the Disciplines of the spiritual life to be for ordinary human beings: people who have jobs, who care for children, who wash dishes and mow lawns. In fact, the Disciplines are best exercised in the midst of our relationships with our husband or wife, our brothers and sisters, our friends and neighbours.

Neither should we think of the Spiritual Disciplines as some dull drudgery aimed at exterminating laughter from the face of the earth. Joy is the keynote of all the Disciplines. The purpose of the Disciplines is liberation from the stifling slavery to self-interest and fear. When the inner spirit is liberated from all that weighs it down, it can hardly be described as dull drudgery. Singing, dancing, even shouting characterise the Disciplines of the spiritual life.

In one important sense, the Spiritual Disciplines are not hard.* We need not be well advanced in matters of theology to practise the Disciplines. Recent converts – for that matter people who have yet to turn their lives over to Jesus Christ – can and should practise them. The primary requirement is a longing after God. 'As a hart longs for flowing streams, so longs my soul for thee, O God. My soul thirsts for God, for the Living God,' writes the psalmist (Ps. 42:1, 2).

Beginners are welcome. I, too, am a beginner, even and *especially* after a number of years of practising every Discipline discussed in this book. As Thomas Merton says, 'We do not want to be beginners. But let us be convinced of the fact that we will never be anything else but beginners, all our life!'[2]

---

* In another sense, they are hard indeed – that is a theme we will develop later.

Psalm 42:7 reads 'Deep calls to deep.' Perhaps somewhere in the subterranean chambers of your life you have heard the call to deeper, fuller living. You have become weary of frothy experiences and shallow teaching. Every now and then you have caught glimpses, hints of something more than you have known. Inwardly you long to launch out into the deep.

Those who have heard the distant call deep within and who desire to explore the world of the Spiritual Disciplines are immediately faced with two difficulties. The first is philosophic. The materialistic base of our age has become so pervasive that it has given people grave doubts about their ability to reach beyond the physical world. Many first-rate scientists have passed beyond such doubts, knowing that we cannot be confined to a space-time box. But the average person is influenced by popular science, which is a generation behind the times and is prejudiced against the nonmaterial world.

It is hard to overstate how saturated we are with the mentality of popular science. Meditation, for example, if allowed at all, is not thought of as an encounter between a person and God, but as psychological manipulation. Usually people will tolerate a brief dabbling in the 'inward journey,' but then it is time to get on with *real* business in the *real* world. We need the courage to move beyond the prejudice of our age and affirm with our best scientists that more than the material world exists. In intellectual honesty, we should be willing to study and explore the spiritual life with all the rigour and determination we would give to any field of research.

The second difficulty is a practical one. We simply do not know how to go about exploring the inward life. This has not always been true. In the first century and earlier, it was not necessary to give instruction on how to 'do' the Disciplines of the spiritual life. The Bible called people to such Disciplines as fasting, prayer, worship, and celebration but gave almost no instruction about how to do them. The reason for this is easy to see. Those Disciplines were so frequently practised and such a part of the general culture that the 'how to' was common knowledge. Fasting, for example, was so common that no one had to ask what to eat before a fast, or how to break a fast, or how to avoid dizziness while fasting – everyone already knew.

This is not true of our generation. Today there is an abysmal ignorance of the most simple and practical aspects of nearly all the classic Spiritual Disciplines. Hence, any book written on the subject must provide practical instruction on precisely how we do the Disciplines. One word of caution, however, must be given at the outset: to know the mechanics does not mean that we are practising the Disciplines. The Spiritual Disciplines are an inward and spiritual reality, and the inner attitude of the heart is far more crucial than the mechanics for coming into the reality of the spiritual life.

In our enthusiasm to practise the Disciplines, we may fail to practise discipline. The life that is pleasing to God is not a series of religious duties. We have only one thing to do, namely, to experience a life of relationship and intimacy with God, 'the Father of lights with whom there is no variation or shadow due to change' (James 1:17).

THE SLAVERY OF INGRAINED HABITS

We are accustomed to thinking of sin as individual acts of disobedience to God. This is true enough as far as it goes, but Scripture goes much further.* In Romans the apostle Paul frequently refers to sin as a condition that plagues the human race (i.e., Rom. 3:9–18). Sin as a condition works its way out through the 'bodily members,' that is, the ingrained habits of the body (Rom. 7:5ff.). And there is no slavery that can compare to the slavery of ingrained habits of sin.

Isaiah 57:20 says, 'The wicked are like the tossing sea; for it

---

* Sin is such a complex matter that the Hebrew language has eight different words for it, and all eight are found in the Bible.

cannot rest, and its waters toss up mire and dirt.' The sea does not need to do anything special to produce mire and dirt; that is the result of its natural motions. This is also true of us when we are under the condition of sin. The natural motions of our lives produce mire and dirt. Sin is part of the internal structure of our lives. No special effort is needed to produce it. No wonder we feel trapped.

Our ordinary method of dealing with ingrained sin is to launch a frontal attack. We rely on our willpower and determination. Whatever may be the issue for us – anger, fear, bitterness, gluttony, pride, lust, substance abuse – we determine never to do it again; we pray against it, fight against it, set our will against it. But the struggle is all in vain, and we find ourselves once again morally bankrupt, or, worse yet, so proud of our external righteousness that 'whitened sepulchres' is a mild description of our condition. In his excellent little book entitled *Freedom from Sinful Thoughts* Heini Arnold writes, 'We . . . want to make it quite clear that we cannot free and purify our own heart by exerting our own "will".'[3]

In Colossians Paul lists some of the outward forms that people use to control sin: 'touch not, taste not, handle not.' He then adds that these things 'have indeed a show of wisdom in *will worship*' (Col. 2:20–23, KJV, [italics added]). 'Will worship' – what a telling phrase, and how descriptive of so much of our lives! The moment we feel we can succeed and attain victory over sin by the strength of our will alone is the moment we are worshiping the will. Isn't it ironic that Paul looks at our most strenuous efforts in the spiritual walk and calls them idolatry, 'will worship'?

Willpower will never succeed in dealing with the deeply ingrained habits of sin. Emmet Fox writes, 'As soon as you resist mentally any undesirable or unwanted circumstance, you thereby endow it with more power – power which it will use against you, and you will have depleted your own resources to that exact extent.'[4] Heini Arnold concludes, 'As long as we think we can save ourselves by our own will power, we will only make the evil in us stronger than ever.'[5] This same truth has been experienced by all the great writers of the devotional life from St Augustine to St Francis, from John Calvin to John Wesley, from Teresa of Ávila to Julian of Norwich.

'Will worship' may produce an outward show of success for a time, but in the cracks and crevices of our lives our deep inner condition will eventually be revealed. Jesus describes this condition when he speaks of the external righteousness of the Pharisees. 'Out of the abundance of the heart the mouth speaks . . . I tell you, on the day of judgment men will render account for every *careless word* they utter' (Matt. 12:34–36, [italics added]). You see, by dint of will people can make a good showing for a time, but sooner or later there will come that unguarded moment when the 'careless word' will slip out to reveal the true condition of the heart. If we are full of compassion, it will be revealed; if we are full of bitterness, that also will be revealed.

It is not that we plan to be this way. We have no intention of exploding with anger or of parading a sticky arrogance, but when we are with people, what we *are* comes out. Though we may try with all our might to hide these things, we are betrayed by our eyes, our tongue, our chin, our hands, our whole body language. Willpower has no defence against the careless word, the unguarded moment. The will has the same deficiency as the law – it can deal only with externals. It is incapable of bringing about the necessary transformation of the inner spirit.

THE SPIRITUAL DISCIPLINES OPEN THE DOOR

When we despair of gaining inner transformation through human powers of will and determination, we are open to a wonderful new realisation: inner righteousness is a gift from God to be graciously received. The needed change within us is God's work, not ours. The demand is for an inside job, and only God can work from the inside. We cannot attain or earn this righteousness of the kingdom of God; it is a grace that is given.

In the book of Romans the apostle Paul goes to great lengths to show that righteousness is a gift of God.* He uses the term thirty-five times in this epistle and each time insists that righteousness is unattained and unattainable through human effort. One of the clearest statements is Romans 5:17, '. . . those who receive the abundance of grace and the *free gift of righteousness* [shall] reign in life through the one man Jesus Christ [italics added].' This teaching, of course, is found not only in Romans but throughout Scripture and stands as one of the cornerstones of the Christian faith.

The moment we grasp this breathtaking insight we are in danger of an error in the opposite direction. We are tempted to believe there is nothing we can do. If all human strivings end in moral bankruptcy (and having tried it, we know it is so), and if righteousness is a gracious gift from God (as the Bible clearly states), then is it not logical to conclude that we must wait for God to come and transform us? Strangely enough, the answer is no. The analysis is correct – human striving *is* insufficient and righteousness *is* a gift from God – but the conclusion is faulty. Happily there is something we can do. We do not need to be hung on the horns of the dilemma of either human works or idleness. God has given us the Disciplines of the spiritual life as a means of receiving his grace. The Disciplines allow us to place ourselves before God so that he can transform us.

The apostle Paul says, 'he who sows to his own flesh will from the flesh reap corruption; but he who sows to the Spirit

---

* This includes both objective righteousness and subjective righteousness. In this book we are dealing with the issue of subjective righteousness (or sanctification if you prefer another theological term), but it is important to understand that both are gracious gifts from God. And, in fact, the Bible does not make the clear division between objective and subjective righteousness that theologians are accustomed to draw, simply because the biblical writers would find it ludicrous to talk of having one without the other.

will from the Spirit reap eternal life' (Gal. 6:8). Paul's analogy is instructive. A farmer is helpless to grow grain; all he can do is provide the right conditions for the growing of grain. He cultivates the ground, he plants the seed, he waters the plants, and then the natural forces of the earth take over and up comes the grain. This is the way it is with the Spiritual Disciplines — they are a way of sowing to the Spirit. The Disciplines are God's way of getting us into the ground; they put us where he can work within us and transform us. By themselves the Spiritual Disciplines can do nothing; they can only get us to the place where something can be done. They are God's means of grace. The inner righteousness we seek is not something that is poured on our heads. God has ordained the Disciplines of the spiritual life as the means by which we place ourselves where he can bless us.

In this regard it would be proper to speak of 'the path of disciplined grace.' It is 'grace' because it is free; it is 'disciplined' because there is something for us to do. In *The Cost of Discipleship* Dietrich Bonhoeffer makes it clear that grace is free, but it is not cheap. The grace of God is unearned and unearnable, but if we ever expect to grow in grace, we must pay the price of a consciously chosen course of action which involves both individual and group life. Spiritual growth is the purpose of the Disciplines.

It might be helpful to visualise what we have been discussing. Picture a long, narrow ridge with a sheer drop-off on either side. The chasm to the right is the way of moral bankruptcy through human strivings for righteousness. Historically this has been called the heresy of moralism. The chasm to the left is moral bankruptcy through the absence of human strivings. This has been called the heresy of antinomianism. On the ridge there is a path, the Disciplines of the spiritual life. This path leads to the inner transformation and healing for which we seek. We must never veer off to the right or the left, but stay on the path. The path is fraught with severe difficulties, but also with incredible joys. As we travel on this path, the blessing of God will come upon us and reconstruct us into the image of Jesus Christ. We must always remember that the path does not produce the change; it only places us where the change can occur. This is the path of disciplined grace.

There is a saying in moral theology that 'virtue is easy.' But the maxim is true only to the extent that God's gracious work has taken over our inner spirit and transformed the ingrained habit patterns of our lives. Until that is accomplished, virtue is hard, very hard indeed. We struggle to exhibit a loving and compassionate spirit, yet it is as if we are bringing something in from the outside. Then bubbling up from the inner depths is the one thing we did not want, a biting and bitter spirit. However, once we live and walk on the path of disciplined grace for a season, we will discover internal changes.

We do no more than receive a gift, yet we know the changes are real. We know they are real because we discover that the spirit of compassion we once found so hard to exhibit is now easy. In fact, to be full of bitterness would be the hard thing. Divine Love has slipped into our inner spirit and taken over our habit patterns. In the unguarded moments there is a spontaneous flow from the inner sanctuary of our lives of 'love, joy, peace, patience, kindness, goodness, faithfulness, gentleness, self-control' (Gal. 5:22, 23). There is no longer the tiring need to hide our inner selves from others. We do not have to work hard at being good and kind; we *are* good and kind. To refrain from being good and kind would be the hard work because goodness and kindness are part of our nature. Just as the natural motions of our lives once produced mire and dirt, now they produce 'righteousness and peace and joy in the Holy Spirit' (Rom. 14:17). Shakespeare observes that 'The quality of mercy is not strained' – nor are any of the virtues once they have taken over the personality.

THE WAY OF DEATH: TURNING THE DISCIPLINES INTO LAWS

The Spiritual Disciplines are intended for our good. They are meant to bring the abundance of God into our lives. It is possible, however, to turn them into another set of soul-killing laws. Law-bound Disciplines breathe death.

Jesus teaches that we must go beyond the righteousness of the scribes and the Pharisees (Matt. 5:20). Yet we need to see that their righteousness was no small thing. They were committed to following God in a way that many of us are not prepared to do. One factor, however, was always central to their righteousness: *externalism*. Their righteousness consisted in control over externals, often including the manipulation of others. The extent to which we have gone beyond the righteousness of the scribes and the Pharisees is seen in how much our lives demonstrate the internal work of God upon the heart. To be sure, this will have external results, but the work will be internal. It is easy in our zeal for the Spiritual Disciplines to turn them into the external righteousness of the scribes and the Pharisees.

When the Disciplines degenerate into law, they are used to manipulate and control people. We take explicit commands and use them to imprison others. Such a deterioration of the Spiritual Disciplines results in pride and fear. Pride takes over because we come to believe that we are the right kind of people. Fear takes over because we dread losing control.

If we are to progress in the spiritual walk so that the Disciplines are a blessing and not a curse, we must come to the place in our lives where we can lay down the everlasting burden of always needing to manage others. This drive, more than any single thing, will lead us to turn the Spiritual Disciplines into laws. Once we have made a law, we have an 'externalism' by which we judge who is measuring up and who is not. Without laws the Disciplines are primarily an internal work, and it is impossible to control an internal work. When we genuinely believe that inner transformation is God's work and not ours, we can put to rest our passion to set others straight.

We must beware of how quickly we can latch on to this word or that word and turn it into a law. The moment we do so we qualify for Jesus' stern pronouncement against the Pharisees: 'They bind heavy burdens, hard to bear, and lay them on men's shoulders; but they themselves will not move them with their finger' (Matt. 23:4). In these matters we need the words of the apostle Paul embedded in our minds: 'We deal not in the letter but in the Spirit. The letter of the Law leads to the death of the soul; the Spirit of God alone can give life to the soul' (2 Cor. 3:6, Phillips).

As we enter the inner world of the Spiritual Disciplines, there will always be the danger of turning them into laws. But we are not left to our own human devices. Jesus Christ has promised to be our ever-present Teacher and Guide. His voice is not hard to hear. His direction is not hard to understand. If we are beginning to calcify what should always remain alive and growing, he will tell us. We can trust his teaching. If we are wandering off towards some wrong idea or unprofitable practice, he will guide us back. If we are willing to listen to the Heavenly Monitor, we will receive the instruction we need.

Our world is hungry for genuinely changed people. Leo Tolstoy observes, 'Everybody thinks of changing humanity and nobody thinks of changing himself.'[6] Let us be among those who believe that the inner transformation of our lives is a goal worthy of our best effort.

FOR STUDY

As you begin this study of the Christian Disciplines, there are several pitfalls that advance warning may help you to avoid. Briefly, I shall list seven – surely there are more!

The first pitfall is the temptation to turn the Disciplines into law. There is nothing like legalism to choke the heart and soul out of walking with God. The rigid person is not the disciplined person. Rigidity is the most certain sign that the Disciplines have gone to seed. The disciplined person can do what needs to be done when it needs to be done. The disciplined person can live in the appropriateness of the hour. The disciplined person can respond to the movings of divine grace like a floating balloon. Always remember that the Disciplines are perceptions into life, not regulations for controlling life.

The second pitfall is the failure to understand the social implications of the Disciplines. These are not a set of pious exercises for the devout, but a trumpet call to obedient living in a sin-racked world. They call us to wage peace in a world obsessed with war, to plead for justice in a world plagued with inequity, to stand with the poor and disinherited in a world that has forgotten its neighbour.

A third pitfall is to view the Disciplines as virtuous in themselves. In and of themselves the Disciplines have no virtue, possess no righteousness, contain no rectitude. It was this important truth that the Pharisees failed to see. The Disciplines place us before God; they do not give us Brownie points with God.

A fourth and similar pitfall is to centre on the Disciplines rather than on Christ. The Disciplines are for the purpose of realising a greater good. And that greater good is Christ Himself, who must always remain the focus of our attention and the end of our quest.

A fifth pitfall is the tendency to isolate and elevate one Discipline to the exclusion or neglect of the others. The Disciplines are like the fruit of the Spirit – they comprise a single reality. Sometimes we become intrigued with fasting, for example, and we begin to think of that single Discipline as comprising the whole picture. What is only one tree we see as the whole forest. This danger must be avoided at all costs. The Disciplines of the spiritual life are an organic unity, a single path.

The sixth pitfall is to think that the twelve Disciplines

mentioned in *Celebration* somehow exhaust the means of God's grace. I have no exhaustive list of the Christian Disciplines and as far as I know none exists, for who can confine the Spirit of God? *Celebration* is merely one attempt to compile those acts of devotion which the writers of Scripture and the Saints throughout the history of the Church have said were important in experiential faith. But Christ is greater than any attempt to describe His workings with His children. He cannot be confined to any system, no matter how worthy.

The seventh pitfall is the most dangerous. It is the temptation to study the Disciplines without experiencing them. To discuss the Disciplines in the abstract, to argue and debate their nature or validity – these we can do in comparative safety. But to step out into experience, this threatens us at the core of our being. And yet there is no other way. Prayerfully, slowly, perhaps with many fears and questions, we need to move into this adventurous life of the Spirit.

Daily Scripture Readings

Sunday	–	The longing to go deeper. Psalm 42
Monday	–	The slavery to ingrained habits. Psalm 51
Tuesday	–	The slavery to ingrained habits. Romans 7:13–25
Wednesday	–	The bankruptcy of outward righteousness. Philippians 3:1–16
Thursday	–	Sin in the bodily members. Proverbs 6:16–19
Friday	–	Sin in the bodily members. Romans 6:5–14
Saturday	–	The victory of Spiritual Discipline. Ephesians 6:10–20

Study Questions

1 I say that 'Superficiality is the curse of our age.' If you tend to agree list several indicators in our culture that would illustrate this fact. If you tend to disagree list several

indicators in society that would illustrate your conviction. Are there influences in our day that would cause Christian people to be more superficial than Christian folk of other centuries?

2 I refer to the Disciplines discussed in this book as 'classical'. What reason do I give for saying this? Critique my rationale – that is, do you agree or disagree?

3 What is the purpose of the Spiritual Disciplines?

4 What is a primary requirement to embarking on this journey? Are there things that would keep you from fulfilling this requirement?

5 Consider carefully Heini Arnold's statement, 'We want to make it quite clear that we cannot free and purify our own heart by exerting our own will'. Does that ring true in your own experience?

6 I indicate that those who desire to explore the world of the Spiritual Disciplines are faced with two difficulties. What is the 'practical difficulty'? Can this be seen in your own life? What is the 'philosophical difficulty'? How can this be seen in your own life?

7 What do I mean by 'disciplined grace'? What does the concept of 'cheap grace' mean? With which of these two types of grace are you most familiar?

8 If you were walking on the narrow ledge of which I speak, which side would you fall from most often? Explain how this can be seen in your own life.

9 As you read the book, consider what you feel are the most dangerous things about the book. (That is, what elements might lead people away from God, rather than to God?)

10 What struck you most forcefully in this chapter? Were there areas you disagreed with, or were unable to identify with, or perhaps found difficult to understand?

Suggestions for Further Reading

There is a wealth of literature on the Spiritual Disciplines, and the following represent some of the best works in the general field of the spiritual life. They provide an excellent background and framework out of which to study the Christian Disciplines.

Bonhoeffer, Dietrich, *The Cost of Discipleship*, London: SCM Press, 1964. This is the book that gave us the term 'cheap grace' and which so forcefully called us to a more costly form of discipleship.

Caussade, Jean-Pierre de, *The Sacrament of the Present Moment*, trans. by K. Muggeridge, London: Fount, 1981. Written by an eighteenth century French Jesuit; it is sheer delight to read.

Kelly, Thomas R., *A Testament of Devotion*, London: Quaker Home Service, 1979. I can count on one hand the twentieth century classics of devotion – this is one of them.

Kempis, Thomas À., *The Imitation of Christ*, trans. by E. M. Blaiklock, London: Hodder & Stoughton, 1979. A new translation by E. M. Blaiklock adds fresh vitality to this undisputed leader of the classics of Christian devotion.

Law, William, *A Serious Call to a Devout and Holy Life*, ed. Halcyon Backhouse, London: Hodder & Stoughton, 1987. An influential work on the Christian life by the person often called the greatest of the post-Reformation English mystics. Law was the leader of a small spiritual community and included among his disciples John and Charles Wesley.

Lawrence, Brother, *The Practice of the Presence of God*, trans. by E. M. Blaiklock, London: Hodder & Stoughton, 1982. These simple letters and conversations by Nicholas Herman – Brother Lawrence – of France have inspired three centuries of Christians to live in more intimate communion with Christ.

Loyola, St Ignatius of, *The Spiritual Exercises*, ed. Robert Backhouse, London: Hodder & Stoughton, 1989 (May). A programme of 'spiritual exercises', including examination of conscience, meditation and other methods of prayer, with guidelines on adaptation to individual needs and difficulties.

Peterson, Eugene, *A Long Obedience in the Same Direction*, Basingstoke: Marshall Pickering, 1989 (March). Through a study of the 'Songs of Ascents' – Psalms 120–134 – Eugene Peterson helps Christians wrestle with many of the classic Spiritual Disciplines.

Richards, Lawrence O., *A Practical Theology of Spirituality*, Basingstoke: Marshall Pickering, 1988. A clear, fully biblical study of the theology of Spirituality, its inner reality and outward expression.

Sales, Francis de, *An Introduction to the Devout Life*, London: Hodder & Stoughton, 1988. Much of this material is the result of counsel Francis gave to a single individual, Mme Louise Charmoisy, in the early seventeenth century. It covers a wide variety of spiritual matters for those seeking to deepen their devotional life.

Sanford, Agnes, *The Healing Light*, Evesham: James (Arthur), 1981. The classic statement on the healing ministry to which Jesus calls the Church and a book which has influenced my own pilgrimage immensely.

Tozer, A. W., *The Pursuit of God*, Bromley, Kent: STL Books, 1980, and Eastbourne: Kingsway, 1984. A tender, sensitive book filled with insight and a catholicity of outlook that is refreshing.

PART I

The Inward Disciplines

2

The Discipline of Meditation

True contemplation is not a psychological trick but a theological grace.
— Thomas Merton

In contemporary society our Adversary majors in three things: noise, hurry, and crowds. If he can keep us engaged in 'muchness' and 'manyness,' he will rest satisfied. Psychiatrist Carl Jung once remarked, 'Hurry is not *of* the Devil; it *is* the Devil.'[1]

If we hope to move beyond the superficialities of our culture, including our religious culture, we must be willing to go down into the recreating silences, into the inner world of contemplation. In their writings all the masters of meditation beckon us to be pioneers in this frontier of the Spirit. Though it may sound strange to modern ears, we should without shame enrol as apprentices in the school of contemplative prayer.

BIBLICAL WITNESS

The discipline of meditation was certainly familiar to the authors of Scripture. The Bible uses two different Hebrew words (הָגָה and שִׂיחַ) to convey the idea of meditation, and together they are used some fifty-eight times. These words have various meanings: listening to God's word, reflecting on God's works, rehearsing God's deeds, ruminating on God's law, and more. In each case there is stress upon changed behaviour as a result of our encounter with the living God. Repentance and obedience are essential features in any biblical understanding of meditation. The psalmist exclaims, 'Oh, how I love thy law! It is my meditation all the day . . . I hold my feet from every evil way, in order to keep thy word. I do not turn aside from thy ordinances, for thou hast taught me' (Ps. 119:97, 101, 102). It is this continual focus upon obedience and faithfulness that most clearly distinguishes Christian meditation from its Eastern and secular counterparts.

Those who walked through the pages of the Bible knew the ways of meditation. 'And Isaac went out to meditate in the field in the evening' (Gen. 24:63). 'I think of thee upon my bed, and meditate on thee in the watches of the night' (Ps. 63:6). The Psalms virtually sing of the meditations of the people of God upon the law of God: 'My eyes are awake before the watches of the night, that I may meditate upon thy promise' (Ps. 119:148). The psalm that introduces the entire Psalter calls all people to emulate the 'blessed man' whose 'delight is in the law of the LORD, and on his law he meditates day and night' (Ps. 1:2).

The old priest Eli knew how to listen to God and helped the young boy Samuel know the word of the Lord (1 Sam. 3:1–18). Elijah spent many a day and night in the wilderness learning to discern the 'still small voice of Yahweh' (1 Kings 19:9–18). Isaiah saw the Lord 'high and lifted up' and heard his voice saying; 'Whom shall I send, and who will go for us?' (Isa. 6:1–8). Jeremiah discovered the word of God to be 'a burning fire shut up in my bones' (Jer. 20:9). And on march the witnesses. These were people who were close to the heart of God. God spoke to them not because they had special abilities, but because they were willing to listen.

In the midst of an exceedingly busy ministry Jesus made a habit of withdrawing to 'a lonely place apart' (Matt. 14:13).* He

---

* See also Matt. 4:1–11, Luke 6:12, Matt. 14:23, Mark 1:35, Mark 6:31, Luke 5:16, Matt. 17:1–9, and Matt. 26:36–46.

did this not just to be away from people, but so he could be with God. What did Jesus do time after time in these deserted hills? He sought out his heavenly Father; he listened to him, he communed with him. And he beckons us to do the same.

HEARING AND OBEYING

Christian meditation, very simply, is the ability to hear God's voice and obey his word. It is that simple. I wish I could make it more complicated for those who like things difficult. It involves no hidden mysteries, no secret mantras, no mental gymnastics, no esoteric flights into the cosmic consciousness. The truth of the matter is that the great God of the universe, the Creator of all things desires our fellowship. In the Garden of Eden Adam and Eve talked with God *and* God talked with them – they were in communion. Then came the Fall, and in an important sense there was a rupture of the sense of perpetual communion, for Adam and Eve hid from God. But God continued to reach out to his rebellious children, and in stories of such persons as Cain, Abel, Noah, and Abraham we see God speaking and acting, teaching and guiding.

Moses learned, albeit with many vacillations and detours, how to hear God's voice and obey his word. In fact, Scripture witnesses that God spoke to Moses 'face to face, as a man speaks to his friend' (Exod. 33:11). There was a sense of intimate relationship, of communion. As a people, however, the Israelites were not prepared for such intimacy. Once they learned a little about God, they realised that being in his presence was risky business and told Moses so: 'You speak to us, and we will hear; but let not God speak to us, lest we die' (Exod. 20:19). In this way they could maintain religious respectability without the attendant risks. This was the beginning of the great line of the prophets and the judges, Moses being the first. But it was a step away from the sense of immediacy, the sense of the cloud by day and the pillar of fire by night.

In the fullness of time Jesus came and taught the reality of the kingdom of God and demonstrated what life could be like in that kingdom. He established a living fellowship that would know him as Redeemer and King, listening to him in all things and obeying him at all times. In his intimate relationship with the Father, Jesus modelled for us the reality of that life of hearing and obeying. 'The Son can do nothing of his own accord, but only what he sees the Father doing; for whatever he does, that the Son does likewise' (John 5:19). 'I can do nothing on my own authority; as I hear, I judge' (John 5:30). 'The words that I say to you I do not speak on my own authority; but the Father who dwells in me does his works' (John 14:10). When Jesus told his disciples to abide in him, they could understand what he meant for he was abiding in the Father. He declared that he was the good Shepherd and that his sheep know his voice (John 10:4). He told us that the Comforter would come, the Spirit of truth, who would guide us into all the truth (John 16:13).

In his second volume Luke clearly implies that following his resurrection and the ascension Jesus continues 'to do and teach' even if people cannot see him with the naked eye (Acts 1:1). Both Peter and Stephen point to Jesus as the fulfilment of the prophecy in Deuteronomy 18:15 of the prophet like Moses who is to speak and whom the people are to hear and obey (Acts 3:22, 7:37).* In the book of Acts we see the resurrected and reigning Christ, through the Holy Spirit, teaching and guiding his children: leading Philip to new unreached cultures (Acts 8), revealing his messiahship to Paul (Acts 9), teaching Peter about his Jewish nationalism (Acts 10), guiding the Church out of its cultural captivity (Acts 15). What we see over and over again is God's people learning to live on the basis of hearing God's voice and obeying his word.

This, in brief, forms the biblical foundation for meditation,

---

* See also Deut. 18:15–18; Matt. 17:5; John 1:21, 4:19–25, 6:14, 7:37–40; Heb. 1:1–13, 3:7–8, 12:25.

and the wonderful news is that Jesus has not stopped acting and speaking. He is resurrected and at work in our world. He is not idle, nor has he developed laryngitis. He is alive and among us as our Priest to forgive us, our Prophet to teach us, our King to rule us, our Shepherd to guide us.

All the saints throughout the ages have witnessed to this reality. How sad that contemporary Christians are so ignorant of the vast sea of literature on Christian meditation by faithful believers throughout the centuries! And their testimony to the joyful life of perpetual communion is amazingly uniform. From Catholic to Protestant, from Eastern Orthodox to Western Free Church we are urged to 'live in his presence in uninterrupted fellowship.'[2] The Russian mystic Theophan the Recluse says, 'To pray is to descend with the mind into the heart, and there to stand before the face of the Lord, ever-present, all seeing, within you.'[3] The Anglican divine Jeremy Taylor declares, 'Meditation is the duty of all.'[4] And in our day Lutheran martyr Dietrich Bonhoeffer, when asked why he meditated, replied, 'Because I am a Christian.'[5] The witness of Scripture and the witness of the devotional masters are so rich, so alive with the presence of God that we would be foolish to neglect such a gracious invitation to experience, in the words of Madame Guyon, 'the depths of Jesus Christ.'[6]

THE PURPOSE OF MEDITATION

In meditation we are growing into what Thomas à Kempis calls 'a familiar friendship with Jesus.'[7] We are sinking down into the light and life of Christ and becoming comfortable in that posture. The perpetual presence of the Lord (omnipresence, as we say) moves from a theological dogma into a radiant reality. 'He walks with me and he talks with me' ceases to be pious jargon and instead becomes a straightforward description of daily life.

Please understand me: I am not speaking of some mushy, giddy, buddy-buddy relationship. All such sentimentality only betrays how little we know, how distant we are from the Lord high and lifted up who is revealed to us in Scripture. John tells us in his Apocalypse that when he saw the reigning Christ, he fell at his feet as though dead, and so should we (Rev. 1:17). No, I am speaking of a reality more akin to what the disciples felt in the upper room when they experienced both intense intimacy and awful reverence.

What happens in meditation is that we create the emotional and spiritual space which allows Christ to construct an inner sanctuary in the heart. The wonderful verse 'I stand at the door and knock . . .' was originally penned for believers, not unbelievers (Rev. 3:20). We who have turned our lives over to Christ need to know how very much he longs to eat with us, to commune with us. He desires a perpetual Eucharistic feast in the inner sanctuary of the heart. Meditation opens the door and, although we are engaging in specific meditation exercises at specific times, the aim is to bring this living reality into all of life. It is a portable sanctuary that is brought into all we are and do.

Inward fellowship of this kind transforms the inner personality. We cannot burn the eternal flame of the inner sanctuary and remain the same, for the Divine Fire will consume everything that is impure. Our ever-present Teacher will always be leading us into 'righteousness and peace and joy in the Holy Spirit' (Rom. 14:17). Everything that is foreign to his way we will have to let go. No, not 'have to' but 'want to,' for our desires and aspirations will be more and more conformed to his way. Increasingly, everything within us will swing like a needle to the polestar of the Spirit.

UNDERSTANDABLE MISCONCEPTIONS

Whenever the Christian idea of meditation is taken seriously, there are those who assume it is synonymous with the concept of meditation centred in Eastern religions. In reality, the two ideas stand worlds apart. Eastern meditation is an attempt to empty the mind; Christian meditation is an attempt to fill the mind. The two ideas are quite different.

Eastern forms of meditation stress the need to become detached from the world. There is an emphasis upon losing personhood and individuality and merging with the Cosmic Mind. There is a longing to be freed from the burdens and pains of this life and to be released into the impersonality of Nirvana. Personal identity is lost and, in fact, personality is seen as the ultimate illusion. There is an escaping from the miserable wheel of existence. There is no God to be attached to or to hear from. Detachment is the final goal of Eastern religion.

Christian meditation goes far beyond the notion of detachment. There is need for detachment – a 'sabbath of contemplation' as Peter of Celles, a Benedictine monk of the twelfth century, put it.[8] But there is a danger in thinking only in terms of detachment as Jesus indicates in his story of the man who had been emptied of evil but not filled with good. 'When the unclean spirit has gone out of a man . . . he goes and brings seven other spirits more evil than himself, and they enter and dwell there; and the last state of that man becomes worse than the first' (Luke 11:24–26).[9]

No, detachment is not enough; we must go on to *attachment*. The detachment from the confusion all around us is in order to have a richer attachment to God. Christian meditation leads us to the inner wholeness necessary to give ourselves to God freely.

Another misconception about meditation is that it is too difficult, too complicated. Perhaps it is best left to the professional who has more time to explore the inner regions. Not at all. The acknowledged experts in this way never report that they were on a journey only for the privileged few, the spiritual giants. They would laugh at the very idea. They felt that what they were doing was a natural human activity – as natural, and as important, as breathing. They would tell us that we do not need any special gifts or psychic powers. Thomas Merton writes,

'Meditation is really very simple and there is not much need of elaborate techniques to teach us how to go about it.'[10]

A third misconception is to view contemplation as impractical and wholly out of touch with the twentieth century. There is a fear it will lead to the kind of person immortalised in Dostoevski's book *The Brothers Karamazov* in the ascetic Father Ferapont: a rigid, self-righteous person who, by sheer effort, delivers himself from the world and then calls down curses upon it. Many people believe that at its very best meditation leads to an unhealthy otherworldliness that keeps us immune to the suffering of humanity.

Such evaluations are far from the mark. In fact, meditation is the one thing that can sufficiently redirect our lives so that we can deal with human life successfully. Thomas Merton writes, 'Meditation has no point and no reality unless it is firmly rooted in *life*.'[11] Historically, no group has stressed the need to enter into the listening silences more than the Quakers, and the result has been a vital social impact far in excess of their numbers. William Penn notes, 'True godliness does not turn men out of the world, but enables them to live better in it and excites their endeavours to mend it.'[12]

Often meditation will yield insights that are deeply practical, almost mundane. Instruction will come on how to relate to your wife or husband, or how to deal with this sensitive problem or that business situation. It is wonderful when a particular meditation leads to ecstasy, but it is far more common to be given guidance in dealing with ordinary human problems. Meditation sends us into our ordinary world with greater perspective and balance.

Perhaps the most common misconception of all is to view meditation as a religious form of psychological manipulation. It may have value in dropping our blood pressure or in relieving tension. It may even provide us with meaningful insights by helping us get in touch with our subconscious mind. But the idea of actual contact and communion with the God of Abraham,

Isaac, and Jacob sounds unscientific and faintly unreasonable. If you feel that we live in a purely physical universe, you will view meditation as a good way to obtain a consistent alpha brain-wave pattern. But if you believe that we live in a universe created by the infinite-personal God who delights in our communion with him, you will see meditation as communication between the Lover and the one beloved.

These two concepts of meditation are complete opposites. The one confines us to a totally human experience; the other catapults us into a divine-human encounter. The one talks about the exploration of the subconscious; the other speaks of 'resting in him whom we have *found*, who loves us, who is near to us, who comes to us to draw us to himself.'[13] Both may sound religious and even use religious jargon, but the former can ultimately find no place for spiritual reality.

How then do we come to believe in a world of the spirit? Is it by blind faith? Not at all. The inner reality of the spiritual world is available to all who are willing to search for it. Often I have discovered that those who so freely debunk the spiritual world have never taken ten minutes to investigate whether or not such a world really exists.

Let me suggest we take an experiential attitude towards spiritual realities. Like any other scientific endeavour, we form a hypothesis and experiment with it to see if it is true or not. If our first experiment fails, we do not despair or label the whole business fraudulent. We re-examine our procedure, perhaps adjust our hypothesis, and try again. We should at least have the honesty to persevere in this work to the same degree we would in any field of science. The fact that so many are unwilling to do so betrays not their intelligence but their prejudice.

DESIRING THE LIVING VOICE OF GOD

There are times when everything within us says yes to the words of Frederick W. Faber:

Only to sit and think of God,
  Oh what a joy it is!
To think the thought, to breathe the Name
Earth has no higher bliss.[14]

But those who meditate know that the more frequent reaction is spiritual inertia, a coldness and lack of desire. Human beings seem to have a perpetual tendency to have somebody else talk to God for them. We are content to have the message second-hand. One of Israel's fatal mistakes was their insistence upon having a human king rather than resting in the theocratic rule of God over them. We can detect a note of sadness in the word of the Lord, 'They have rejected me from being king over them' (1 Sam. 8:7). The history of religion is the story of an almost desperate scramble to have a king, a mediator, a priest, a pastor, a go-between. In this way we do not need to go to God ourselves. Such an approach saves us from the need to change, for to be in the presence of God is to change. We do not need to observe Western culture very closely to realise that it is captivated by the religion of the mediator.

That is why meditation is so threatening to us. It boldly calls us to enter into the living presence of God for ourselves. It tells us that God is speaking in the continuous present and wants to address us. Jesus and the New Testament writers clearly state that this is not just for the religious professionals – the priests – but for everyone. *All* who acknowledge Jesus Christ as Lord *are* the universal priesthood of God and as such can enter the Holy of Holies and converse with the living God.

To bring people to believe that *they* can hear God's voice seems so difficult. Members of the Church of the Saviour in Washington, DC, have been experimenting in this area for some time. Their conclusion: 'We think that we are twentieth- and twenty-first-century people; nonetheless, we have hints that one can receive directions as clear as those given Ananias, . . . "Rise and go to the street called straight".'[15] Why not? If God is alive and active in the affairs of human beings, why can't his voice be heard and obeyed today? It can be heard and is heard by all who will know him as present Teacher and Prophet.

How do we receive the desire to hear his voice? 'This desire to turn is a gift of grace. Anyone who imagines he can simply begin meditating without praying for the desire and the grace to do so, will soon give up. But the desire to meditate, and the grace to begin meditating, should be taken as an implicit promise of further graces.'[16] Seeking and receiving that 'gift of grace' is the only thing that will keep us moving forward on the inward journey. And as Albert the Great says, 'The contemplation of the saints is fired by the love of the one contemplated: that is, God.'[17]

SANCTIFYING THE IMAGINATION

We can descend with the mind into the heart most easily through the imagination. In this regard the great Scottish preacher Alexander Whyte speaks of 'the divine offices and the splendid services of the Christian imagination.'[18] Perhaps some rare individuals experience God through abstract contemplation alone, but most of us need to be more deeply rooted in the senses. We must not despise this simpler, more humble route into God's presence. Jesus himself taught in this manner, making constant appeal to the imagination, and many of the devotional masters likewise encourage us in this way. St Teresa of Ávila says, '. . . as I could not make reflection with my understanding I contrived to picture Christ within me.'[19] Many of us can identify with her words, for we too have tried a merely cerebral approach and found it too abstract, too detached. Even more, the imagination helps to anchor our thoughts and centre our attention. Francis de Sales notes that 'by means of the imagination we confine our mind within the mystery on which we meditate, that it may not ramble to and fro, just as we shut up a bird in a cage or tie a hawk by his leash so that he may rest on the hand.'[20]

Some have objected to using the imagination out of concern

that it is untrustworthy and could even be used by the Evil One. There is good reason for concern, for the imagination, like all our faculties, has participated in the Fall. But just as we can believe that God can take our reason (fallen as it is) and sanctify it and use it for his good purposes, so we believe he can sanctify the imagination and use *it* for his good purposes. Of course, the imagination can be distorted by Satan, but then so can all our faculties. God created us with an imagination, and as Lord of his creation he can and does redeem it and use it for the work of the kingdom of God.

Another concern about the use of the imagination is the fear of human manipulation and even self-deception. After all, some have an 'overactive imagination,' as we say, and they can concoct all kinds of images of what they would like to see happen. Besides, doesn't the Bible warn against 'the vain imaginations' of the wicked (Rom. 1:21)? The concern is legitimate. It is possible for all of this to be nothing more than vain human strivings. That is why it is so vitally important for us to be thrown in utter dependence upon God in these matters. We are seeking to think God's thoughts after him, to delight in his presence, to desire his truth and his way. And the more we live in this way, the more God utilises our imagination for his good purposes. In fact, the common experience of those who walk with God is one of being *given* images of what can be. Often in praying for people I am given a picture of their condition, and when I share that picture with them, there will be a deep inner sigh, or they will begin weeping. Later they will ask, 'How did you know?' Well, I didn't know, I just saw it.

To believe that God can sanctify and utilise the imagination is simply to take seriously the Christian idea of incarnation. God so accommodates, so enfleshes himself into our world that he uses the images we know and understand to teach us about the unseen world of which we know so little and which we find so difficult to understand.

PREPARING TO MEDITATE

It is impossible to learn how to meditate from a book. We learn to meditate by meditating. Simple suggestions at the right time, however, can make an immense difference. The practical hints and meditation exercises on the following pages are given in the hope that they may help in the actual practice of meditation. They are not laws nor are they intended to confine you.

Is there a proper *time* for meditation? When a certain proficiency has been attained in the interior life, it is possible to practise meditation at any time and under almost every circumstance. Brother Lawrence in the seventeenth century and Thomas Kelly in the twentieth both bear eloquent testimony to this fact. Having said that, however, we must see the importance for beginners and experts alike to give some part of each day to formal meditation.

Once we are convinced that we need to set aside specific times for contemplation, we must guard against the notion that to do certain religious acts at particular times means that we are finally meditating. This work involves all of life. It is a twenty-four-hour-a-day job. Contemplative prayer is a way of life. 'Pray without ceasing,' Paul exhorts (1 Thess. 5:17, KJV). With a touch of humour Peter of Celles notes that 'he who snores in the night of vice cannot know the light of contemplation.'[21]

We must come to see, therefore, how central our whole day is in preparing us for specific times of meditation. If we are constantly being swept off our feet with frantic activity, we will be unable to be attentive at the moment of inward silence. A mind that is harassed and fragmented by external affairs is hardly prepared for meditation. The church Fathers often spoke of *Otium Sanctum*, 'holy leisure.' It refers to a sense of balance in the life, an ability to be at peace through the activities of the day, an ability to rest and take time to enjoy beauty, an ability to pace ourselves. With our tendency to define people in terms of what they produce, we would do well to cultivate 'holy leisure.' And if we expect to succeed in the contemplative way, we must pursue 'holy leisure' with a determination that is ruthless to our diaries.

What about a *place* for meditation? This will be discussed under the Discipline of solitude so for now a few words will be sufficient. Find a place that is quiet and free from interruption. No telephone should be nearby. If it is possible to find some place that looks out on to a lovely landscape, so much the better. It is best to have one designated place rather than hunting for a different spot each day.

What about *posture*? In one sense posture makes no difference at all; you can pray anywhere, any time, and in any position. In another sense, however, posture is of utmost importance. The body, the mind, and the spirit are inseparable. Tension in the spirit is telegraphed in body language. I actually have witnessed people go through an entire worship service vigorously chewing gum without the slightest awareness of their deep inner tension. Not only does outward posture reflect the inward state, it can also help to nurture the inner attitude of prayer. If inwardly we are fraught with distractions and anxiety, a consciously chosen posture of peace and relaxation will have a tendency to calm our inner turmoil.

There is no 'law' that prescribes a correct posture. The Bible contains everything from lying prostrate on the floor to standing with hands and head lifted towards the heavens. I think the best approach would be to find a position that is the most comfortable and the least distracting. The delightful fourteenth-century mystic, Richard Rolle, favoured sitting, '. . . because I knew that I . . . longer lasted . . . than going, or standing or kneeling. For [in] sitting I am most at rest, and my heart most upward.'[22] I quite agree, and find it best to sit in a straight chair, with my back correctly positioned in the chair and both feet flat on the floor. To slouch indicates inattention and to cross the legs restricts the circulation. Place the hands on the knees, palms up in a gesture of receptivity. Sometimes it is good to close the eyes to remove distractions and centre the attention on Christ. At other times it is helpful to ponder a picture of the Lord or to look out at some lovely trees and plants for the same purpose. Regardless of how it is done, the aim is to centre the attention of the body, the emotions, the mind, and the spirit upon 'the glory of God in the face of Christ' (2 Cor. 4:6).

THE FORMS OF MEDITATION

Christians throughout the centuries have spoken of a variety of ways of listening to God, of communing with the Creator of heaven and earth, of experiencing the eternal Lover of the world. The accumulated wisdom of their experience can be immensely helpful as we, like them, seek intimacy with God and faithfulness to God.

For all the devotional masters the *meditatio Scripturarum*, the meditation upon Scripture, is the central reference point by which all other forms of meditation are kept in proper perspective. Whereas the study of Scripture centres on exegesis, the meditation of Scripture centres on internalising and personalising the passage. The written Word becomes a living word addressed to you. This is not a time for technical studies, or analysis, or even the gathering of material to share with others. Set aside all tendencies toward arrogance and with a humble heart receive the word addressed to you. Often I find kneeling especially appropriate for this particular time. Dietrich Bonhoeffer says, '. . . just as you do not analyse the words of someone you love, but accept them as they are said to you, accept the Word of Scripture and ponder it in your heart, as Mary did. That is all. That is meditation.'[23] When Bonhoeffer founded the seminary at Finkenwalde, a one-half hour silent meditation upon Scripture was practised by everyone.

It is important to resist the temptation to pass over many passages superficially. Our rushing reflects our internal state and our internal state is what needs to be transformed. Bonhoeffer recommended spending a whole week on a single text! There-fore, my suggestion is that you take a single event, or a parable, or a few verses, or even a single word and allow it to take root in you. Seek to live the experience, remembering the encour-agement of Ignatius of Loyola to apply all our senses to our task. Smell the sea. Hear the lap of water along the shore. See the crowd. Feel the sun on your head and the hunger in your stomach. Taste the salt in the air. Touch the hem of his garment. In this regard Alexander Whyte counsels us, '. . . the truly Christian imagination never lets Jesus Christ out of her sight . . . You open your New Testament . . . And, by your imagination, that moment you are one of Christ's disciples on the spot, and are at His feet.'[24]

Suppose we want to meditate on Jesus' staggering statement, 'My peace I give to you' (John 14:27). Our task is not so much to study the passage as it is to be initiated into the reality of which the passage speaks. We brood on the truth that he is now filling us with his peace. The heart, the mind, and the spirit are awakened to his inflowing peace. We sense all motions of fear stilled and overcome by 'power and love and self-control' (2 Tim. 1:7). Rather than dissecting peace we are entering into it. We are enveloped, absorbed, gathered into his peace. And the wonderful thing about such an experience is that the self is quite forgotten. We are no longer worried about how we can make ourselves more at peace, for we are attending to the impartation of peace within our hearts. No longer do we laboriously think up ways to act peacefully, for acts of peace spring spontaneously from within.

Always remember that we enter the story not as passive observers, but as active participants. Also remember that Christ is truly with us to teach us, to heal us, to forgive us. Alexander Whyte declares, 'with your imagination anointed with holy oil, you again open your New Testament. At one time, you are the publican: at another time, you are the prodigal . . . at another time, you are Mary Magdalene: at another time, Peter in the porch . . . Till your whole New Testament is all over autobiographic of you.'[25]

Another form of meditation is what the contemplatives of the Middle Ages called 're-collection,' and what the Quakers have often called 'centring down.' It is a time to become still, to enter into the recreating silence, to allow the fragmentation of our minds to become centred.

The following is a brief exercise to aid you in 're-collection' that is simply called 'palms down, palms up.' Begin by placing your palms down as a symbolic indication of your desire to turn over any concerns you may have to God. Inwardly you may pray, 'Lord, I give to you my anger toward John. I release my fear of my dentist appointment this morning. I surrender my anxiety over not having enough money to pay the bills this month. I release my frustration over trying to find a baby-sitter for tonight.' Whatever it is that weighs on your mind or is a concern to you, just say, 'palms down.' Release it. You may even feel a certain sense of release in your hands. After several moments of surrender, turn your palms up as a symbol of your desire to receive from the Lord. Perhaps you will pray silently: 'Lord, I would like to receive your divine love for John, your peace about the dentist appointment, your patience, your joy.' Whatever you need, you say, 'palms up.' Having centred down, spend the remaining moments in complete silence. Do not ask for anything. Allow the Lord to commune with you, to love you. If impressions or directions come, fine; if not, fine.

A third kind of contemplative prayer is meditation upon the creation. Now, this is no infantile pantheism, but a majestic monotheism in which the great Creator of the universe shows us something of his glory through his creation. The heavens do indeed declare the glory of God and the firmament does show forth his handiwork (Ps. 19:1). Evelyn Underhill recommends, '. . . begin with that first form of contemplation which the old mystics sometimes called "the discovery of God in his creatures." '[26]

So give your attention to the created order. Look at the trees, really look at them. Take a flower and allow its beauty and symmetry to sink deep into your mind and heart. Listen to the birds – they are the messengers of God. Watch the little creatures that creep upon the earth. These are humble acts, to be sure, but sometimes God reaches us profoundly in these simple ways if we will quiet ourselves to listen.

There is a fourth form of meditation that is in some ways quite the opposite of the one just given. It is to meditate upon the events of our time and to seek to perceive their significance. We have a spiritual obligation to penetrate the inner meaning of events, not to gain power but to gain prophetic perspective. Thomas Merton writes that the person '. . . who has meditated on the Passion of Christ but has not meditated on the extermination camps of Dachau and Auschwitz has not yet fully entered into the experience of Christianity in our time.'[27]

This form of meditation is best accomplished with the Bible in one hand and the newspaper in the other! You must not, however, be controlled by the absurd political clichés and propaganda fed us today. Actually, newspapers are generally far too shallow and slanted to be of much help. We would do well to hold the events of our time before God and ask for prophetic insight to discern where these things lead. Further, we should ask for guidance for anything we personally should be doing to be salt and light in our decaying and dark world.

You must not be discouraged if in the beginning your meditations have little meaning to you. There is a progression in the spiritual life, and it is wise to have some experience with lesser peaks before trying to tackle the Mt Everest of the soul. So be patient with yourself. Besides, you are learning a discipline for which you have received no training. Nor does our culture encourage you to develop these skills. You will be going against the tide, but take heart; your task is of immense worth.

There are many other aspects of the Discipline of meditation that could be profitably considered.* However, meditation is not a single act, nor can it be completed the way one completes the building of a chair. It is a way of life. You will be constantly learning and growing as you plumb the inner depths.

FOR STUDY

The purpose of meditation is to enable us to hear God more clearly. Meditation is listening, sensing, heeding the life and light of Christ. This comes right to the heart of our faith. The life that pleases God is not a set of religious duties; it is to hear His voice and obey His word. Meditation opens the door to this way of living. Jean-Pierre de Caussade wrote, 'There remains one single duty. It is to keep one's gaze fixed on the master one has chosen and to be constantly listening so as to understand and hear and immediately obey his will.'

Meditation is a more passive Discipline. It is characterised more by reflecting than by studying, more by listening than by thinking, more by releasing than by grabbing. In the Discipline of meditation we are not so much acting as we are opening ourselves to be acted upon. We invite the Holy Spirit to come and work within us – teaching, cleansing, comforting, rebuking. We also surround ourselves with the strong light of Christ to protect us from any influence not of God.

Since some have asked, I might just as well come clean and tell you that I have *no* interest at all, or experience, in astro-travel or any of the other rather exotic forms of meditation. Perhaps that reflects my own prejudice but such approaches, it seems to me, do not resonate well with the biblical witness. I find little ethical content or concern for moral transformation in these

---

* Two topics that closely impinge upon meditation will be discussed under the Discipline of solitude: the creative use of silence and the concept developed by St John of the Cross that he graphically calls 'the dark night of the soul.'

forms of meditation. I am much more interested in the kind of hearing that Abraham, Moses and Elijah knew, which brought forth a radical obedience to the one true God.

In *Celebration* I gave only a brief description of the meditation upon Scripture, assuming that people were quite familiar with this form of meditation. In this assumption I was wrong, and so I should like here to provide a brief meditation upon John 6 as an example of one approach to the *meditatio Scripturarum*. It is my hope that this will encourage all of us to drink deeply and extensively at this, the most central and important form of Christian meditation.

The story is a familiar one – Jesus' feeding of the five thousand. Begin by imagining yourself the child who gave his lunch, or perhaps the child's parents: at any rate, try to place yourself in the actual scene. Following the counsel of Ignatius of Loyola, attempt to use all of the senses as you slowly read the passage. Try to see the story – the grass, the hills, the faces of the people. Try to hear the story – the sound of the water, the noise of the children, the voice of the Master. Try to feel the story – the texture of your clothing, the hardness of the ground, the coarseness of your hands. Finally, try to feel with your emotions – hesitancy at bringing your lunch, astonishment at the miracle of multiplied food, joy at the gracious provision of God. At first this approach may necessitate several readings of the text.

Then in your imagination watch the crowd leave and Jesus go up into the hills. You are left alone. You sit on a rock overlooking the water re-experiencing the events of the day. You become quiet, and after a little while Jesus returns and sits on a nearby rock. For a time you are both silent, looking out over the water perhaps, and enjoying one another's presence. After a bit, the Lord turns to you and asks this question, 'What may I do for you?' Then you tell Him what is in your heart – your needs, your fears, your hopes. If weeping or other emotions come, do not hinder them.

When you have finished, you become quiet for a little while.

Then you turn to the Lord and ask, 'What may I do for you?' And then you listen with the heart quietly, prayerfully. No instruction needs to come, for you are just glad to be in Christ's presence. If some word does come to you, take it with utmost seriousness. More often than not, it will be some utterly practical instruction about seemingly trivial matters, for God wants us to live out our spirituality in the ordinary events of our days. And I have often found them to be wonderful words of life. What I have shared here is, of course, only an example – God will, I am sure, give you many other ways to enter into the life of Scripture.

Beyond this, may I make a plea for the memorisation of Scripture.* Through memorisation the biblical witness becomes rooted deep in the inner mind and begins to mould and adjust our world view almost without our realising it. Then too, as we submit ourselves to this small discipline, God is able to teach us through the word of Scripture at any given moment, even in sleep. It is a helpful means to enhance our meditation upon Scripture.

Daily Scripture Readings

Sunday   – The glory of meditation. Exodus 24:15–18
Monday   – The friendship of meditation. Exodus 33:11
Tuesday   – The terror of meditation. Exodus 20:18–19
Wednesday   – The object of meditation. Psalm 1:1–3
Thursday   – The comfort of meditation. 1 Kings 19:9–18
Friday   – The insights of meditation. Acts 10:9–20
Saturday   – The ecstasy of meditation. 2 Corinthians 12:1–4

---

* Contrary to popular myth, memorisation is quite easy once one catches on to the idea. The Navigators have published numerous aids which make the task even more possible.

Study Questions

1 What are some of your first reactions to the idea of meditation? What is your background experience in this area?
2 What is the basic difference between Eastern meditation and Christian meditation?
3 What are some of the things that make your life crowded? Do you think you have a desire to hear the Lord's voice in the midst of all the clutter?
4 Experience the following words of Frederick W. Faber for fifteen minutes. Record what you learn from the experience.

> Only to sit and think of God,
>   Oh what a joy it is!
> To think the thought, to breathe the Name
>   Earth has no higher bliss.

5 What threatens you most about meditation?
6 What do you think about dreams as a means of hearing from God? Have you had any experience in this area?
7 List the five forms of meditation which I give. Ponder the fifth form and what it might mean today given the contemporary political scene.
8 What do you see as the value of thinking through the specifics of time, place and position in regard to the experience of meditation?
9 What are the dangers in concentrating on time, place and position?
10 Do 'Palms down, Palms up' today. Note anything you learn about yourself.

Suggestions for Further Reading

Kelsey, Morton T., *The Other Side of Silence*, London: SPCK, 1977. The most important single book on the theology and psychology behind the experience of Christian meditation.

Marshall, Michael, *A Change of Heart*, London: Collins, 1989. A book of meditations focusing on people whose meetings with Jesus proved a turning point in their lives.

McAlpine, Campbell, *The Practice of Biblical Meditation*, Basingstoke: Marshall Pickering, 1981. Step by step instructions for meditating upon the Scriptures.

Merton, Thomas, *Contemplative Prayer*, London: Darton, Longman & Todd, 1973. A powerful analysis of the central nature of contemplative prayer. A 'must' book.

Merton, Thomas, *Spiritual Direction and Meditation*, Wheathampstead, USA: Clarke (Anthony) Books, 1979. Written mainly with the monastic life in mind but filled with a discernment and practical wisdom which all can appreciate.

Stinissen, Wilfred, *Deep Calls to Deep*, trans. by David C. Pugh, Basingstoke: Marshall Pickering, 1988. This book explores our inner life and what it means to live in meditation. There is practical help on using the Jesus prayer, and twenty pieces for meditation.

Toon, Peter, *Meditating upon God's Word: Prelude to Prayer and Action*, London: Darton, Longman & Todd, 1988. An introduction to daily meditation on the Bible, emphasising its true nature as dialogue with God rather than monologue.

3

The Discipline of Prayer

*I am the ground of thy beseeching; first, it is my will thou shalt have it;
after, I make thee to will it; and after I make thee to beseech it and thou
beseechest it. How should it then be that thou shouldst not have thy
beseeching?*

– Julian of Norwich

Prayer catapults us on to the frontier of the spiritual life. Of all
the Spiritual Disciplines prayer is the most central because it
ushers us into perpetual communion with the Father. Meditation
introduces us to the inner life, fasting is an accompanying means,
study transforms our minds, but it is the Discipline of prayer
that brings us into the deepest and highest work of the human
spirit. Real prayer is life creating and life changing. 'Prayer –
secret, fervent, believing prayer – lies at the root of all personal
godliness,'[1] writes William Carey.

To pray is to change. Prayer is the central avenue God uses to
transform us. If we are unwilling to change, we will abandon
prayer as a noticeable characteristic of our lives. The closer we
come to the heartbeat of God the more we see our need and
the more we desire to be conformed to Christ. William Blake
tell us that our task in life is to learn to bear God's 'beams of
love.' How often we fashion cloaks of evasion – beam-proof
shelters – in order to elude our Eternal Lover. But when we

pray, God slowly and graciously reveals to us our evasive actions and sets us free from them.

'You ask and do not receive, because you ask wrongly, to spend it on your passions' (James 4:3). To ask 'rightly' involves transformed passions. In prayer, real prayer, we begin to think God's thoughts after him: to desire the things he desires, to love the things he loves, to will the things he wills. Progressively, we are taught to see things from his point of view.

All who have walked with God have viewed prayer as the main business of their lives. The words of the gospel of Mark, 'And in the morning, a great while before day, he rose and went out to a lonely place, and there he prayed,' stand as a commentary on the life-style of Jesus (Mark 1:35). David's desire for God broke the self-indulgent chains of sleep: 'Early will I seek Thee' (Ps. 63:1, KJV). When the apostles were tempted to invest their energies in other important and necessary tasks, they determined to give themselves continually to prayer and the ministry of the word (Acts 6:4). Martin Luther declares, 'I have so much business I cannot get on without spending three hours daily in prayer.' He held it as a spiritual axiom that 'He that has prayed well has studied well.'[2] John Wesley says, 'God does nothing but in answer to prayer,'[3] and backed up his conviction by devoting two hours daily to that sacred exercise. The most notable feature of David Brainerd's life was his praying. His Journal is permeated with accounts of prayer, fasting, and meditation. 'I love to be alone in my cottage, where I can spend much time in prayer.' 'I set apart this day for secret fasting and prayer to God.'[4]

For those explorers in the frontiers of faith, prayer was no little habit tacked on to the periphery of their lives; it *was* their lives. It was the most serious work of their most productive years. William Penn testified of George Fox that 'Above all he excelled in prayer ... The most awful, living, reverend frame I ever felt or beheld, I must say was his in prayer.'[5] Adoniram Judson sought to withdraw from business and company seven times a day in order to engage in the holy work of prayer. He began at dawn; then at nine, twelve, three, six, nine, and midnight he would give time to secret prayer. John Hyde of India made prayer such a dominant characteristic of his life that he was nicknamed 'Praying Hyde.' For these, and all those who have braved the depths of the interior life, to breathe was to pray.

Many of us, however, are discouraged rather than challenged by such examples. Those 'giants of the faith' are so far beyond anything we have experienced that we are tempted to despair. But rather than flagellating ourselves for our obvious lack, we should remember that God always meets us where we are and slowly moves us along into deeper things. Occasional joggers do not suddenly enter an Olympic marathon. They prepare and train themselves over a period of time, and so should we. When such a progression is followed, we can expect to pray a year from now with greater authority and spiritual success than at present.

In our efforts to pray it is easy for us to be defeated right at the outset because we have been taught that everything in the universe is already set, and so things cannot be changed. And if things cannot be changed, why pray? We may gloomily feel this way, but the Bible does not teach that. The Bible pray-ers prayed as if their prayers could and would make an objective difference. The apostle Paul gladly announces that we are 'co-labourers with God'; that is, we are working with God to determine the outcome of events (1 Cor. 3:9). It is Stoicism that demands a closed universe not the Bible.

Many people who emphasise acquiescence and resignation to the way things are as 'the will of God' are actually closer to Epictetus than to Christ. Moses prayed boldly because he believed his prayers could change things, even God's mind. In fact, the Bible stresses so forcefully the openness of our universe that, in an anthropomorphism hard for modern ears, it speaks of God constantly changing his mind in accord with his unchanging love (see Exod. 32:14; Jon. 3:10).

This comes as a genuine liberation to many of us, but it also sets tremendous responsibility before us. We are working with

God to determine the future! Certain things will happen in history if we pray rightly. We are to change the world by prayer. What more motivation do we need to learn this loftiest human exercise?

Prayer is such a vast and multifaceted subject that we instantly recognise the impossibility of even lightly touching on all its aspects in one chapter. There is a whole host of important philosophical questions. Why is prayer necessary? How does prayer work; that is, how can a finite human being enter into dialogue with the infinite Creator of the universe? How can an immaterial reality like prayer affect the material world? And many similar questions. There are also the many forms of prayers that have nurtured Christians throughout the centuries. There is discursive prayer, mental prayer, and centring prayer. There is the prayer of quiet, the prayer of relinquishment, and the prayer of guidance. And many more.

A myriad of genuinely good books have been written on prayer, one of the best being Andrew Murray's classic, *With Christ in the School of Prayer*. We would do well to read widely and experience deeply if we desire to know the ways of prayer. Since restriction often enhances clarity, this chapter will be confined to the prayer of intercession; that is, learning how to pray effectively for others. Modern men and women so desperately need the help that we can provide that our best energies should be devoted to this task.

LEARNING TO PRAY

Real prayer is something we learn. The disciples asked Jesus, 'Lord, teach us to pray' (Luke 11:1). They had prayed all their lives, and yet something about the quality and quantity of Jesus' praying caused them to see how little they knew about prayer. If their praying was to make any difference on the human scene, there were some things they needed to learn.

It was liberating to me to understand that prayer involved a learning process. I was set free to question, to experiment, even to fail, for I knew I was learning. For years I had prayed for many things and with great intensity, but with only marginal success. But then I saw that I might possibly be doing some things wrong and could learn differently. I took the Gospels and cut out every reference to prayer and pasted them on to sheets of paper. When I could read Jesus' teaching on prayer at one sitting, I was shocked. Either the excuses and rationalisations for unanswered prayer I had been taught were wrong, or Jesus' words were wrong. I determined to learn to pray so that my experience conformed to the words of Jesus rather than try to make his words conform to my impoverished experience.

Perhaps the most astonishing characteristic of Jesus' praying is that when he prayed for others he *never* concluded by saying 'If it be thy will.' Nor did the apostles or prophets when they were praying for others. They obviously believed that they knew what the will of God was before they prayed the prayer of faith. They were so immersed in the milieu of the Holy Spirit that when they encountered a specific situation, they knew what should be done. Their praying was so positive that it often took the form of a direct, authoritative command: 'Walk,' 'Be well,' 'Stand up.' I saw that when praying for others there was evidently no room for indecisive, tentative, half-hoping, 'If it be thy will' prayers.

There is, of course, a proper time and place to pray, 'If it be thy will.' First, in the prayer of guidance it is the great yearning of our hearts to know the will of God. 'What is your will?' 'What would please you?' 'What would advance your kingdom upon the earth?' This is the kind of searching prayer that should permeate our entire life experience. And then in the prayer of relinquishment, we are committed to letting go of our will whenever it conflicts with the will and way of God. Obviously, our goal is to learn always to think God's thoughts after him, but we all have times when our human desires get in the way. At such times we must follow the lead of our Master who in the garden prayed, 'Nevertheless not my will, but thine, be done' (Luke 22:42).

As I was learning I sought out persons who seemed to experience greater power and effectiveness in prayer than I and asked them to teach me everything they knew. In addition, I sought the wisdom and experience of past masters of prayer by securing and reading every good book I could find on the subject. I began studying the pray-ers of the Old Testament – Moses and Elijah and Hannah and Daniel – with new interest.

At the same time, I began praying for others with an expectation that a change should and would occur. I am so grateful I did not wait until I was perfect or had everything straight before praying for others, otherwise I would never have begun. P. T. Forsythe says, 'Prayer is to religion what original research is to science.'[6] I felt I was engaging in 'original research' in the school of the Spirit. It was thrilling beyond description. Every seeming failure led to a new learning process. Christ was my present Teacher so that progressively his word was being confirmed in my experience; 'If you abide in me, and my words abide in you, ask whatever you will, and it shall be done for you' (John 15:7).

To understand that the work of prayer involves a learning process saves us from arrogantly dismissing it as false or unreal. If we turn on our television set and it does not work, we do not declare that there are no such things as electronic frequencies in the air or on the cable. We assume something is wrong, something we can find and correct. We check the plug, switch, circuitry until we discover what is blocking the flow of this mysterious energy that transmits pictures. We know the problem has been found and fixed by seeing whether or not the TV works. It is the same with prayer. We can determine if we are praying correctly if the requests come to pass. If not, we look for the 'block'; perhaps we are praying wrongly, perhaps something within us needs changing, perhaps there are new principles of prayer to be learned, perhaps patience and persistence are needed. We listen, make the necessary adjustments, and try again. We can know that our prayers are being answered as surely as we can know that the television set is working.

One of the most critical aspects in learning to pray for others is to get in contact with God so that his life and power can flow through us into others. Often we assume we are in contact when we are not. For example, dozens of radio and television signals went through your room while you read these words, but you failed to pick them up because you were not tuned to the proper frequencies. Often people pray and pray with all the faith in the world, but nothing happens. Naturally, they were not tuned in to God. We begin praying for others by first quieting our fleshly activity and listening to the silent thunder of the Lord of hosts. Attuning ourselves to divine breathings is spiritual work, but without it our praying is vain repetition (Matt. 6:7). Listening to the Lord is the first thing, the second thing, and the third thing necessary for successful intercession. Søren Kierkegaard once observed: 'A man prayed, and at first he thought that prayer was talking. But he became more and more quiet until in the end he realised that prayer is listening.'[7]

Listening to God is the necessary prelude to intercession. The work of intercession, sometimes called the prayer of faith, presupposes that the prayer of guidance is perpetually ascending to the Father. We must hear, know, and obey the will of God before we pray it into the lives of others. The prayer of guidance constantly precedes and surrounds the prayer of faith.

The beginning point then in learning to pray for others is to listen for guidance. In the beginning it is wise to set aside Aunt Susie's arthritis for which you have been praying for twenty years. In physical matters we always tend to pray for the most difficult situations first: terminal cancer or multiple sclerosis. But when we listen, we will learn the importance of beginning with smaller things like colds or earaches. Success in the small corners of life gives us authority in the larger matters. If we are still, we will learn not only who God is, but how his power operates.

Sometimes we are afraid that we do not have enough faith to

pray for this child or that marriage. Our fears should be put to rest, for the Bible tells us that great miracles are possible through faith the size of a tiny mustard seed. Usually, the courage actually to go and pray for a person is a sign of sufficient faith. Frequently our lack is not faith but compassion. It seems that genuine empathy between the pray-er and the pray-ee often makes the difference. We are told that Jesus was 'moved with compassion' for people. Compassion was an evident feature of every healing in the New Testament. We do not pray for people as 'things,' but as 'persons' whom we love. If we have God-given compassion and concern for others, our faith will grow and strengthen as we pray. In fact, if we genuinely love people, we desire for them far more than it is within our power to give, and that will cause us to pray.

The inner sense of compassion is one of the clearest indications from the Lord that *this* is a prayer project for you. In times of meditation there may come a rise in the heart, a compulsion to intercede, an assurance of rightness, a flow of the Spirit. This inner 'yes' is the divine authorisation for you to pray for the person or situation. If the idea is accompanied with a sense of dread, then probably you should set it aside. God will lead someone else to pray for the matter.

THE FOOTHILLS OF PRAYER

We should never make prayer too complicated. We are prone to do so once we understand that prayer is something we must learn. It is also easy to yield to this temptation because the more complicated we make prayer, the more dependent people are upon us to learn how to do it. But Jesus taught us to come like children to a father. Openness, honesty, and trust mark the communication of children with their father. The reason God answers prayer is because his children ask. Further, there is an intimacy between parents and children that has room for both seriousness and laughter. Meister Eckhart notes that 'The soul will bring forth Person if God laughs into her and she laughs back to him.'[8]

Jesus taught us to pray for daily bread. Have you ever noticed that children ask for lunch in utter confidence that it will be provided. They have no need to stash away today's sandwiches for fear none will be available tomorrow. As far as they are concerned, there is an endless supply of sandwiches. Children do not find it difficult or complicated to talk to their parents, nor do they feel embarrassed to bring the simplest need to their attention. Neither should we hesitate to bring the simplest requests confidently to the Father.

Children also teach us the value of the imagination. As with meditation, the imagination is a powerful tool in the work of prayer. We may be reticent to pray with the imagination, feeling that it is slightly beneath us. Children have no such reticence. Neither did St Teresa of Ávila: 'This was my method of prayer; as I could not make reflections wth my understanding, I contrived to picture Christ within me . . . I did many simple things of this kind . . . I believe my soul gained very much in this way, because I began to practise prayer without knowing what it was.'[9] In the play *Saint Joan* by George Bernard Shaw, Joan of Arc insists that she hears voices that come from God. She is informed by sceptics that the voices come from her imagination. Unmoved, Joan replies, 'I know, that is how God speaks to me.'

Imagination often opens the door to faith. If God shows us a shattered marriage whole or a sick person well, it helps us to believe that it will be so. Children instantly understand these things and respond well to praying with the imagination. I was once called to a home to pray for a seriously ill baby girl. Her four-year-old brother was in the room, and so I told him I needed his help to pray for his baby sister. He was delighted, and so was I since I know that children can often pray with unusual effectiveness. He climbed up into the chair beside me. 'Let's play a little game,' I said. 'Since we know that Jesus is always with us, let's imagine that he is sitting over in the chair across from us.

He is waiting patiently for us to centre our attention on him. When we see him, we start thinking more about his love than how sick Julie is. He smiles, gets up, and comes over to us. Then, let's both put our hands on Julie, and when we do, Jesus will put his hands on top of ours. We'll watch the light from Jesus flow into your little sister and make her well. Let's watch the healing power of Christ fight with bad germs until they are all gone. Okay?' Seriously, the little one nodded. Together, we prayed in this childlike way and then thanked the Lord that what we had prayed was the way it was going to be. Now, I do not know exactly what happened, nor how it was accomplished, but I do know that the next morning Julie was perfectly well.

Let me insert a word of caution at this point. We are not trying to conjure up something in our imagination that is not so. Nor are we trying to manipulate God and tell him what to do. Quite the opposite. We are asking God to tell us what to do. God is the ground of our beseeching, as Julian of Norwich put it, and we are utterly dependent upon him. Our prayer is to be like a reflex action to God's prior initiative upon the heart. The ideas, the pictures, the words are of no avail unless they proceed from the Holy Spirit who, as you know, is interceding for us 'with sighs too deep for words' (Rom. 8:26).

Children who experience problems in the classroom often respond readily to prayer. A friend of mine who teaches emotionally handicapped children decided God wanted him to pray for them. Of course, he did not tell the children what he was doing; he simply did it. When one of the children would crawl under his desk and assume a foetal position, my teacher friend would take the child in his arms and pray silently that the resurrected Christ would heal the hurt and self-hate within the boy. So as not to embarrass him, the teacher would walk around the room continuing his regular duties while he prayed. After a while the child would relax and was soon back at his desk. Sometimes my friend would ask the boy if he ever remembered what it felt like to win a race. If the boy said yes, he would encourage him to picture himself crossing the finish line with all his friends cheering him on and loving him. In that way the child was able to cooperate in the prayer project as well as reinforce his own self-acceptance. (Is it not ironic that people will be deeply concerned over the issue of prayer in the public schools but will seldom utilise the opportunity to pray for schoolchildren in this way, against which there can be no law!) By the end of the school year, every child but two was able to return to a regular classroom. Coincidence? Perhaps, but as Archbishop William Temple notes, the coincidences occur much more frequently when he prays.

God desires that marriages be healthy, whole, and permanent. You may know of marriages that are in deep trouble and need your help. Perhaps the husband is having an affair with some other woman. Ask God if this is a prayer task for you. If so, consider praying once a day for thirty days for this marriage. Picture the husband meeting the other woman and feeling dismayed and shocked that he had ever thought of getting involved with her. Watch the very thought of an illicit affair become distasteful to him. Imagine him walking into their home and seeing his wife and being overwhelmed with a sense of love for her. Envision them taking walks together and falling in love with each other as they did years ago. See them increasingly able to open up and talk and care. Ask God to build a large brick wall between the husband and the other woman. Construct a home for the husband and wife, not of brick and mortar, but of love and consideration. Fill it with the peace of Christ.

Your pastor and the services of worship need to be bathed in prayer. Paul prayed for his people; he asked his people to pray for him. Charles Spurgeon attributed his success to the prayers of his church. Frank Laubach told his audiences, 'I am very sensitive and know whether you are praying for me. If one of you lets me down, I feel it. When you are praying for me, I feel a strange power. When *every* person in a congregation prays intensely while the pastor is preaching, a miracle happens.'[10] Saturate the services of worship with your prayers. See the Lord high and lifted up filling the sanctuary with his presence.

We can pray for sexual deviations with genuine assurance that a real and lasting change can occur. Sex is like a river – it is a good and wonderful blessing when kept within its proper channel. A river that overflows its banks is a dangerous thing, and so are perverted sexual drives. What are the God-created banks for sex? One man with one woman in marriage for life. When praying for persons with sexual problems, it is a joy to picture a river that has overflowed its banks and invite the Lord to bring it back into its natural channel.

Your own children can and should be changed through your prayers. Pray for them in the daytime with their participation; pray for them at night when they are asleep. One delightful approach is to go into the bedroom and lightly place your hands on the sleeping child. Ask Christ to flow through your hands healing every emotional trauma and hurt feeling your child experienced that day. Fill him or her with the peace and joy of the Lord.

As a priest of Christ, you can perform a wonderful service by taking children into your arms and blessing them. In the Bible parents brought their children to Jesus not so he would play with them or even teach them, but so he would lay his hands on them and bless them (Mark 10:13–16). He has given you the ability to do the same. Blessed is the child who is blessed by adults who know how to bless!

'Flash Prayers' is an excellent idea developed by Frank Laubach in his many books on prayer. He purposed to learn how to live so that 'to *see* anybody will be to pray! To *hear* anybody, as these children talking, that boy crying, may be to pray!'[11] Flashing hard and straight prayers at people is a great thrill and can bring interesting results. I have tried it, inwardly asking the joy of the Lord and a deeper awareness of his presence to rise up within every person I meet. Sometimes people reveal no response, but other times they turn and smile as if addressed.

In a bus or plane we can invite Jesus to walk down the aisles, touching people on the shoulder and saying, 'I love you. My greatest delight would be to forgive you and give you good things. You have beautiful qualities still in the bud that I would unfold if only you will say yes. I'd love to rule your life if you'll let me.' Frank Laubach has suggested that if thousands of us would experiment with 'swishing prayers' at everyone we meet and would share the results, we could learn a great deal about how to pray for others. We could change the whole atmosphere of a nation if thousands of us would constantly throw a cloak of prayer around everyone in our circle of nearness. 'Units of prayer combined, like drops of water, make an ocean which defies resistance.'[12]

We must learn to pray against evil. The old writers urged us to wage spiritual warfare against 'the world, the flesh, and the devil.' We must never forget that the enemy of our souls prowls about like a 'roaring lion' seeking whom he may devour (1 Pet. 5:8). We in prayer fight against the principalities and powers. And we need to pray prayers of protection; surrounding ourselves with the life of Christ, covering ourselves with the blood of Christ, and sealing ourselves with the cross of Christ.

We must never wait until we *feel* like praying before we pray for others. Prayer is like any other work; we may not feel like working, but once we have been at it for a bit, we begin to feel like working. We may not feel like practising the piano, but once we play for a while, we feel like doing it. In the same way, our prayer muscles need to be limbered up a bit and once the blood-flow of intercession begins, we will find that we feel like praying.

We need not worry that this work will take up too much of our time, for 'It takes no time, but it occupies all our time.'[13] It is not prayer in addition to work but prayer simultaneous with work. We precede, enfold, and follow all our work with prayer. Prayer and action become wedded. Thomas Kelly witnesses: 'There is a way of ordering our mental life on more than one level at once. On one level we may be thinking, discussing, seeing, calculating, meeting all the demands of external affairs. But deep within, behind the scenes, at a profounder level, we may also be in prayer and adoration, song and worship, and a gentle receptiveness to divine breathings.'[14]

We have so much to learn, so far to go. Certainly the yearning of our hearts is summed up by Archbishop Tait when he says, 'I want a life of greater, deeper, truer prayer.'[15]

FOR STUDY

As I travel I find several common misconceptions that defeat the work of prayer.

The first misconception is the notion that prayer mainly involves asking things from God. Answers to prayer are wonderful, but they are only secondary to the main function of prayer, which is a growing perpetual communion. To sink down into the light of Christ and become comfortable in that posture, to sing 'He walks with me and He talks with me' and know it as a radiant reality, to discover God in all of the moments of our days and to be pleased rather than perturbed at the discovery – this is the stuff of prayer. It is out of this refreshing life of communion that answered prayer comes as a happy by-product.

The second misconception is to view prayer as always a struggle, 'getting under the burden of prayer', as we say. I certainly would not want to deny those times of intensity and difficulty, but I have not found that to be the most common experience. Nor would I want to minimise the sense of awe and even terror which we feel in the presence of the Sovereign of the universe. And yet, the most frequent experience is one of lightness, joy, comfort, serenity. Even laughter comes at times, though it is richer and less pretentious (should I say more holy) than ordinary laughing. There is a feeling of companionship, though again it is of a different quality from the ordinary human variety. Perhaps it is that we are becoming the friend of God.

A third misconception is that we live in a closed universe, that everything is fixed. We think, 'Since everything is set and God knows the end from the beginning, why pray?' The question is a good one. Perhaps you have had the frustrating experience of talking with an employer about some company policy being considered for adoption. Your employer may invite you to share your concerns and seems to listen intently. Then later you discover that the decision had already been made long before you ever entered the room. Many folk feel that way about prayer. But if the apostle Paul is right that 'we are God's fellow workers' (1 Cor. 3:9), then ours is indeed an open universe. We are working with God to determine the outcome of things. It needs to be said reverently, but it does need to be said – we are co-creators with God in advancing His kingdom upon the earth.

A fourth misconception is the fear that our faith will crumble if our prayers are not answered the first time, every time. As one person put it to me, 'If God doesn't answer this prayer, it is all over; I will never be able to believe in prayer again.' It is this fear that causes us to gravitate toward vague prayers – then if nothing happens no one is the wiser. But suppose I walk into my office and turn on the light switch and nothing happens. Would I say, 'Well, I never believed in electricity anyway!' No, I would assume something is wrong, and I would set out to find out what it is: perhaps the bulb is burned out or the connection is faulty. The same is true with prayer, and very often I have found the problem is indeed a faulty connection at our end.

A fifth misconception about prayer is the common teaching, 'Pray once! Any more than that shows a lack of faith.' Now I understand the good intentions of people who teach this way but, very frankly, it flies in the face of a great deal of biblical experience and teaching, especially Jesus' parables of importunity. We are to keep at this work, mainly I think because we are the channel through which God's life and light flows into individuals or situations. And, incidentally, I have found prayer to be the most helpful of the Disciplines in freeing us from the monsters of the past because of the inner healing that comes through the hands of those who pray for us.

May I call you to the adventure of prayer – nothing draws us closer to the heart of God.

Daily Scripture Readings

Sunday	–	The pattern of prayer. Matthew 6:5–15
Monday	–	The prayer of worship. Psalm 103
Tuesday	–	The prayer of repentance. Psalm 51
Wednesday	–	The prayer of thanksgiving. Psalm 150
Thursday	–	The prayer of guidance. Matthew 26:36–46
Friday	–	The prayer of faith. James 5:13–18
Saturday	–	The prayer of command. Mark 9:14–29

Study Questions

1 Why do I say, 'To pray is to change?' Have you ever experienced that in your own life?
2 How can we keep from being discouraged by the example of the 'giants of the faith'?
3 What difference would it make in our praying to believe that we live in an 'open universe' or a 'closed universe'?
4 Why is it important to view prayer as a learning process?
5 Distinguish between the prayer of faith and the prayer of guidance.
6 Frank Laubach said, 'I want to learn how to live so that to see someone is to pray for them.' Take up that experiment for one whole day and record what you learn from the experience.
7 What is your response to the idea of using the imagination in the work of prayer?
8 *Look* at someone today and imagine what they could be if they received a double portion of the light of Christ. By

faith give it to them and record what you learn from the experience.

9 What should we do when we don't feel like praying?

10 What experience have you had of the Thomas Kelly statement on pages 54–55?

Suggestions for Further Reading

Ávila, Theresa of, *The Interior Castle*, ed. Halcyon Backhouse, London: Hodder & Stoughton, 1988. Written by a sixteenth century Spanish Carmelite, this book describes seven inward dwelling places into which the soul enters through the gateway of prayer, and in the seventh, which is in the centre, God dwells in the greatest splendour.

Gardiner, Ken, *Standing in the Gap*, Kingsway: 1985. An interesting study of intercession.

Hallesby, Ole, *Prayer*, Leicester: InterVarsity Press, 1961. Written by one of Norway's leading devotional writers, this book is aimed at helping the average Christian develop a more meaningful life of prayer.

Leech, Kenneth, *True Prayer*, London: Sheldon Press, 1980. Henri Nouwen said it well, '*True Prayer* not only speaks about prayer, but it creates the space in the reader where prayer can grow and mature.'

Murray, Andrew, *The Prayer Life*, Basingstoke: Marshall Pickering, 1989 (March). A study of the prayer life, and the importance of surrender and obedience to God, by a great preacher and pray-er of the last century.

Murray, Andrew, *With Christ in the School of Prayer*, Basingstoke: Marshall Pickering, 1983. A grand classic dealing with the ministry of intercession.

Sanders, J. Oswald, *Prayer Power Unlimited*, Crowborough: Highland Books, 1985. A practical guide to personal prayer with useful discussion questions at the end of each chapter.

4

The Discipline of Fasting

Some have exalted religious fasting beyond all Scripture and reason; and others have utterly disregarded it.

— John Wesley

In a culture where the landscape is dotted with shrines to the Golden Arches and an assortment of Pizza Temples, fasting seems out of place, out of step with the times. In fact, fasting has been in general disrepute both in and outside the Church for many years. For example, in my research I could not find a single book published on the subject of Christian fasting from 1861 to 1954, a period of nearly one hundred years. More recently a renewed interest in fasting has developed, but we have far to go to recover a biblical balance.

What would account for this almost total disregard of a subject so frequently mentioned in Scripture and so ardently practised by Christians through the centuries? Two things. First, fasting has developed a bad reputation as a result of the excessive ascetic practices of the Middle Ages. With the decline of the inward reality of the Christian faith, an increasing tendency to stress the only thing left, the outward form, developed. And whenever there is a form devoid of spiritual power, law will take over because law always carries with it a sense of security and manipulative power. Hence, fasting was subjected to the most rigid regulations and practised with extreme self-mortification and flagellation. Modern culture reacts strongly to these excesses and tends to confuse fasting with mortification.

Second, the constant propaganda fed us today convinces us that if we do not have three large meals each day, with several snacks in between, we are on the verge of starvation. This, coupled with the popular belief that it is a positive virtue to satisfy every human appetite, has made fasting seem obsolete. Anyone who seriously attempts to fast is bombarded with objections. 'I understand that fasting is injurious to your health.' 'It will sap your strength so you can't work.' 'Won't it destroy healthy body tissue?' All of this, of course, is utter nonsense based upon prejudice. While the human body can survive only a short time without air or water, it can go for many days before starvation begins. Without needing to subscribe to the inflated claims of some groups, it is not an exaggeration to say that, when done correctly, fasting can have beneficial physical effects.

Scripture has so much to say about fasting that we would do well to look once again at this ancient Discipline. The list of biblical personages who fasted reads like a 'Who's Who' of Scripture: Moses the lawgiver, David the king, Elijah the prophet, Esther the Queen, Daniel the seer, Anna the prophetess, Paul the apostle, Jesus Christ the incarnate Son. Many of the great Christians throughout church history fasted and witnessed to its value; among them were Martin Luther, John Calvin, John Knox, John Wesley, Jonathan Edwards, David Brainerd, Charles Finney, and Pastor Hsi of China.

Fasting, of course, is not an exclusively Christian Discipline; all the major religions of the world recognise its merit. Zoroaster practised fasting as did Confucius and the Yogis of India. Plato, Socrates, and Aristotle all fasted. Even Hippocrates, the father of modern medicine, believed in fasting. Now the fact that all these persons, in and out of Scripture, held fasting in high regard does not make it right or even desirable, but it should make us pause long enough to be willing to reevaluate the popular assumptions of our day concerning the Discipline of fasting.

FASTING IN THE BIBLE

Throughout Scripture fasting refers to abstaining from food for spiritual purposes. It stands in distinction to the hunger strike, the purpose of which is to gain political power or attract attention to a good cause. It is also distinct from health dieting which stresses abstinence from food for physical, not spiritual, purposes. Because of the secularisation of modern society, 'fasting' (if it is done at all) is usually motivated either by vanity or by the desire for power. That is not to say that these forms of 'fasting' are wrong necessarily, but their objective is different from the fasting described in Scripture. Biblical fasting always centres on spiritual purposes.

In Scripture the normal means of fasting involves abstaining from all food, solid or liquid, but not from water. In the forty-day fast of Jesus, we are told that 'he ate nothing' and that toward the end of the fast 'he was hungry' and Satan tempted him to eat, indicating that the abstaining was from food but not from water (Luke 4:2). From a physical standpoint, this is what is usually involved in a fast.

Sometimes what could be considered a partial fast is described; that is, there is a restriction of diet but not total abstention. Although the normal fast seemed to be the custom of the prophet Daniel, there was a three-week period in which he declares, 'I ate no delicacies, no meat or wine entered my mouth, nor did I anoint myself at all' (Dan. 10:3). We are not told the reason for this departure from his normal practice of fasting; perhaps his governmental tasks precluded it.

There are also several examples in Scripture of what has been called an 'absolute fast,' or abstaining from both food and water. It appears to be a desperate measure to meet a dire emergency. Upon learning that execution awaited herself and her people,

Esther instructed Mordecai, 'Go, gather all the Jews . . . and hold a fast on my behalf, and neither eat nor drink for three days, night or day. I and my maids will also fast as you do' (Esther 4:16). Paul engaged in a three-day absolute fast following his encounter with the living Christ (Acts 9:9). Since the human body cannot go without water much more than three days, both Moses and Elijah engaged in what must be considered supernatural absolute fasts of forty days (Deut. 9:9; 1 Kings 19:8). It must be underscored that the absolute fast is the exception and should never be engaged in unless one has a very clear command from God, and then for no more than three days.

In most cases fasting is a private matter between the individual and God. There are, however, occasional times of corporate or public fasts. The only annual public fast required in the Mosaic law was on the day of atonement (Lev. 23:27). It was to be *the day* in the Jewish calendar when the people were to be in sorrow and affliction as atonement for their sins. (Gradually, other fast days were added until today there are over twenty!) Also, fasts were called in times of group or national emergency: 'Blow the trumpet in Zion; sanctify a fast; call a solemn assembly; gather the people' (Joel 2:15). When Judah was invaded, King Jehoshaphat called the nation to fast (2 Chron. 20:1–4). In response to the preaching of Jonah, the entire city of Nineveh including the animals – involuntarily, no doubt – fasted. Before the trip back to Jerusalem, Ezra had the exiles fast and pray for safety while travelling on the bandit-infested road (Ezra 8:21–23).

The group fast can be a wonderful and powerful experience provided there is a prepared people who are of one mind in these matters. Serious problems in churches or other groups can be dealt with and relationships healed through unified group prayer and fasting. When a sufficient number of people rightly understand what is involved, national calls to prayer and fasting can also have beneficial results. The King of Britain called for a day of solemn prayer and fasting because of a threatened invasion by the French in 1756. On February 6 John Wesley recorded in his Journal, 'The fast day was a glorious day, such as London has scarce seen since the Restoration. Every church in the city was more than full, and a solemn seriousness sat on every face. Surely God heareth prayer, and there will yet be a lengthening of our tranquillity.' In a footnote he wrote, 'Humility was turned into national rejoicing for the threatened invasion by the French was averted.'[1]

Throughout history what could be called regular fasts also developed. By the time of Zechariah four regular fasts were held (Zech. 8:19). The boast of the Pharisee in Jesus' parable evidently described a common practice of the day, 'I fast twice a week' (Luke 18:12).* The Didache prescribed two fast days a week: Wednesday and Friday. Regular fasting was made obligatory at the Second Council of Orleans in the sixth century. John Wesley sought to revive the teaching of the Didache and urged early Methodists to fast on Wednesdays and Fridays. He felt so strongly about this matter, in fact, that he refused to ordain anyone to the Methodist ministry who did not fast on those two days.

Regular or weekly fasting has had such a profound effect in the lives of some that they have sought to find a biblical command for it so that it may be urged upon all Christians. The search is in vain. There simply are no biblical laws that command regular fasting. Our freedom in the gospel, however, does not mean licence; it means opportunity. Since there are no laws to bind us, we are free to fast on any day. Freedom for the apostle Paul meant that he was engaged in 'fastings often' (2 Cor. 11:27, KJV). We should always bear in mind the apostolic counsel, 'Do not use your freedom as an opportunity for the flesh' (Gal. 5:13).

There is a 'discipline' that has gained a certain popularity today that is akin, but not identical, to fasting. It is called 'watchings' and stems from Paul's use of the term in connection

---

* A frequent practice of the Pharisees was to fast on Mondays and Thursdays because those were market days and so there would be bigger audiences to see and admire their piety.

with his sufferings for Christ (2 Cor. 6:5, 11:27, KJV). It refers to abstaining from sleep in order to attend to prayer or other spiritual duties. There is no indication that this has any essential connection to fasting, otherwise we would be confined to very short fasts indeed! While 'watchings' may have value and God at times may call us to go without sleep for specific needs, we must take care not to elevate things that have only the slightest biblical precedent into major obligations. Paul's warning should always be kept before us for, in any discussion of the Disciplines, we will discover many things that '. . . have indeed an appearance of wisdom in promoting rigour of devotion and self-abasement and severity to the body, but they are of no value in checking the indulgence of the flesh' (Col. 2:23).

IS FASTING A COMMANDMENT?

One issue that understandably concerns many people is whether or not Scripture makes fasting obligatory upon all Christians. Numerous attempts have been made to answer this question, resulting in a variety of conclusions. One of the finest defences of an affirmative answer was penned in 1580 by Thomas Cartwright in a book, something of a classic in the field, entitled *The Holy Exercise of a True Fast*.

Although many passages of Scripture deal with this subject, two stand out in importance. The first is Jesus' startling teaching about fasting in the Sermon on the Mount.* Two factors bear directly on the issue at hand. His teaching on fasting is directly in the context of his teaching on giving and praying. It is as if there is an almost unconscious assumption that giving, praying,

---

* No attempt is made here to refute the heresy in Dispensationalism that the Sermon on the Mount applies to a future age rather than today. For a discussion of this issue, see 'The Hermeneutics of Dispensationalism' by Daniel P. Fuller (doctoral thesis, North-western Baptist Seminary, Chicago).

and fasting are all part of Christian devotion. We have no more reason to exclude fasting from the teaching than we do giving or praying. Second, Jesus states, 'When you fast . . .' (Matt. 6:16). He seems to make the assumption that people will fast, and is giving instruction on how to do it properly. Martin Luther said, 'It was not Christ's intention to reject or despise fasting . . . it was His intention to restore proper fasting.'[2]

Having said this, however, we must realise that these words of Jesus do not constitute a command. Jesus was giving instruction on the proper exercise of a common practice of his day. He did not speak a word about whether it was a right practice or if it should be continued. So, although Jesus does not say 'If you fast,' neither does he say 'You *must* fast.' His word is, very simply, 'When you fast.'

The second crucial statement of Jesus about fasting comes in response to a question by the disciples of John the Baptist. Perplexed over the fact that both they and the Pharisees fasted but Jesus' disciples did not, they asked 'Why?' Jesus replied, 'Can the wedding guests mourn as long as the bridegroom is with them? The days will come, when the bridegroom is taken away from them, and then they will fast' (Matt. 9:15). That is perhaps the most important statement in the New Testament on whether or not Christians should fast today.

In the coming of Jesus, a new day had dawned. The kingdom of God had come among them in present power. The Bridegroom was in their midst; it was a time for feasting, not fasting. There would, however, come a time for his disciples to fast although not in the legalism of the old order.

The most natural interpretation of the days when Jesus' disciples will fast is the present Church age, especially in light of its intricate connection with Jesus' statement on the new wine-skins of the kingdom of God which follows immediately (Matt. 9:16, 17). Arthur Wallis argues that Jesus is referring to the present Church age rather than just the three-day period between his death and resurrection. He concludes his argument, 'We are therefore compelled to refer the days of His absence to the period of this age, from the time He ascended to the Father until He shall return from heaven. This is evidently how His apostles understood Him, for it was not until after His ascension to the Father that we read of them fasting (Acts 13:2, 3) . . . It is this age of the Church to which our Master referred when He said, "Then they will fast." The time is now!'[3]

There is no way to escape the force of Jesus' words in this passage. He made it clear that he expected his disciples to fast after he was gone. Although the words are not couched in the form of a command, that is only a semantic technicality. It is clear from this passage that Christ both upheld the Discipline of fasting and anticipated that his followers would do it.

Perhaps it is best to avoid the term 'command' since in the strictest sense Jesus did not command fasting. But it is obvious that he proceeded on the principle that the children of the kingdom of God would fast. For the person longing for a more intimate walk with God, these statements of Jesus are drawing words.

Where are the people today who will respond to the call of Christ? Have we become so accustomed to 'cheap grace' that we instinctively shy away from more demanding calls to obedience? 'Cheap grace is grace without discipleship, grace without the cross.'[4] Why has the giving of money, for example, been unquestionably recognised as an element in Christian devotion and fasting so disputed? Certainly we have as much, if not more, evidence from the Bible for fasting as we have for giving. Perhaps in our affluent society fasting involves a far larger sacrifice than the giving of money.

THE PURPOSE OF FASTING

It is sobering to realise that the very first statement Jesus made about fasting dealt with the question of motive (Matt. 6:16–18). To use good things to our own ends is always the sign of false religion. How easy it is to take something like fasting and try to use it to get God to do what we want. At times there is such stress upon the blessings and benefits of fasting that we would be tempted to believe that with a little fast we could have the world, including God, eating out of our hands.

Fasting must forever centre on God. It must be God-initiated and God-ordained. Like the prophetess Anna, we need to be 'worshipping with fasting' (Luke 2:37). Every other purpose must be subservient to God. Like that apostolic band at Antioch, 'fasting' and 'worshipping the Lord' must be said in the same breath (Acts 13:2). Charles Spurgeon writes, 'Our seasons of fasting and prayer at the Tabernacle have been high days indeed; never has Heaven's gate stood wider; never have our hearts been nearer the central Glory.'[5]

God questioned the people in Zechariah's day, 'When ye fasted . . . did ye at all fast unto me, even to me?' (Zech. 7:5, KJV). If our fasting is not unto God, we have failed. Physical benefits, success in prayer, the enduing with power, spiritual insights – these must never replace God as the centre of our fasting. John Wesley declares, 'First, let it [fasting] be done unto the Lord with our eye singly fixed on Him. Let our intention herein be this, and this alone, to glorify our Father which is in heaven . . .'[6] That is the only way we will be saved from loving the blessing more than the Blesser.

Once the primary purpose of fasting is firmly fixed in our hearts, we are at liberty to understand that there are also secondary purposes in fasting. More than any other Discipline, fasting reveals the things that control us. This is a wonderful benefit to the true disciple who longs to be transformed into the image of Jesus Christ. We cover up what is inside us with food and other good things, but in fasting these things surface. If pride controls us, it will be revealed almost immediately. David writes, 'I humbled my soul with fasting' (Ps. 69:10). Anger, bitterness, jealousy, strife, fear – if they are within us, they will surface during fasting. At first we will rationalise that our anger is due to our hunger; then we will realise that we are angry because the spirit of anger is within us. We can rejoice in this knowledge because we know that healing is available through the power of Christ.

Fasting reminds us that we are sustained: 'by every word that proceeds from the mouth of God' (Matt. 4:4). Food does not sustain us; God sustains us. In Christ, 'All things hold together' (Col. 1:17). Therefore, in experiences of fasting we are not so much abstaining from food as we are feasting on the word of God. Fasting is feasting! When the disciples brought lunch to Jesus, assuming that he would be starving, he declared, 'I have food to eat of which you do not know . . . My food is to do the will of him who sent me, and to accomplish his work' (John 4:32, 34). This was not a clever metaphor, but a genuine reality. Jesus was, in fact, being nourished and sustained by the power of God. That is the reason for his counsel on fasting in Matthew 6. We are told not to act miserable when fasting because, in point of fact, we are not miserable. We are feeding on God and, just like the Israelites who were sustained in the wilderness by the miraculous manna from heaven, so we are sustained by the word of God.

Fasting helps us keep our balance in life. How easily we begin to allow nonessentials to take precedence in our lives. How quickly we crave things we do not need until we are enslaved by them. Paul writes, ' "All things are lawful for me," but I will not be enslaved by anything' (1 Cor. 6:12). Our human cravings and desires are like rivers that tend to overflow their banks; fasting helps keep them in their proper channels. 'I pommel my body and subdue it,' says Paul (1 Cor. 9:27). Likewise, David writes, 'I afflicted myself with fasting' (Ps. 35:13). This is not excessive asceticism; it is discipline and discipline brings freedom. In the fourth century Asterius said that fasting ensured that the stomach would not make the body boil like a kettle to the hindering of the soul.[7]

Numerous people have written on the many other values of

fasting such as increased effectiveness in intercessory prayer, guidance in decisions, increased concentration, deliverance for those in bondage, physical well-being, revelations, and so on. In this, as in all matters, we can expect God to reward those who diligently seek him.

THE PRACTICE OF FASTING

Contemporary men and women are largely ignorant of the practical aspects of fasting. Those who desire to fast need to acquaint themselves with this basic information.

As with all the Disciplines, a progression should be observed; it is wise to learn to walk well before we try to run. Begin with a partial fast of twenty-four hours' duration; many have found lunch to lunch to be the best time. This means that you would not eat two meals. Fresh fruit juices are excellent to drink during the fast. Attempt this once a week for several weeks. In the beginning you will be fascinated with the physical aspects of your experience, but the most important thing to monitor is the inner attitude of the heart. Outwardly you will be performing the regular duties of your day, but inwardly you will be in prayer and adoration, song, and worship. In a new way, cause every task of the day to be a sacred ministry to the Lord. However mundane your duties, for you they are a sacrament. Cultivate a 'gentle receptiveness to divine breathings.'[8] Break your fast with a light meal of fresh fruits and vegetables and a good deal of inner rejoicing.

After two or three weeks you are prepared to attempt a normal fast of twenty-four hours. Drink only water but use healthy amounts of it. Many feel distilled water is best. If the taste of water bothers you, add one teaspoon of lemon juice. You will probably feel some hunger pangs or discomfort before the time is up. That is not real hunger; your stomach has been trained through years of conditioning to give signals of hunger at certain hours. In many ways the stomach is like a spoiled child, and a spoiled child does not need indulgence, but needs discipline. Martin Luther says '. . . the flesh was wont to grumble dreadfully.'⁹ You must not give in to this 'grumbling.' Ignore the signals, or even tell your 'spoiled child' to calm down, and in a brief time the hunger pangs will pass. If not, sip another glass of water and the stomach will be satisfied. You are to be the master of your stomach, not its slave. If family obligations permit it, devote the time you would normally use eating to meditation and prayer.

It should go without saying that you should follow Jesus' counsel to refrain from calling attention to what you are doing. The only ones who should know you are fasting are those who have to know. If you call attention to your fasting, people will be impressed and, as Jesus said, that will be your reward. You, however, are fasting for far greater and deeper rewards. The following was written by an individual who, as an experiment, had committed himself to fast once a week for two years. Notice the progression from the superficial aspects of fasting toward the deeper rewards.

'1. I felt it a great accomplishment to go a whole day without food. Congratulated myself on the fact that I found it so easy . . .

2. Began to see that the above was hardly the goal of fasting. Was helped in this by beginning to feel hunger . . .

3. Began to relate the food fast to other areas of my life where I was more compulsive . . . I did not have to have a seat on the bus to be contented, or to be cool in the summer and warm when it was cold.

4. . . . Reflected more on Christ's suffering and the suffering of those who are hungry and have hungry babies . . .

5. Six months after beginning the fast discipline, I began to see why a two-year period has been suggested. The experience changes along the way. Hunger on fast days became acute, and the temptation to eat stronger. For the first time I was

using the day to find God's will for my life. Began to think about what it meant to *surrender* one's life.

6. I now know that prayer and fasting must be intricately bound together. There is no other way, and yet that way is not yet combined in me.'[10]

After having achieved several fasts with a degree of spiritual success, move on to a thirty-six-hour fast: three meals. With that accomplished, it is time to seek the Lord as to whether he wants you to go on a longer fast. Three to seven days is a good time period and will probably have a substantial impact on the course of your life.

It is wise to know the process your body goes through in the course of a longer fast. The first three days are usually the most difficult in terms of physical discomfort and hunger pains. The body is beginning to rid itself of the toxins that have built up over years of poor eating habits, and it is not a comfortable process. This is the reason for the coating on the tongue and bad breath. Do not be disturbed by these symptoms; rather be grateful for the increased health and well-being that will result. You may experience headaches during this time, especially if you are an avid coffee or tea drinker. Those are mild withdrawal symptoms that will pass though they may be very unpleasant for a time.

By the fourth day the hunger pains are beginning to subside though you will have feelings of weakness and occasional dizziness. The dizziness is only temporary and caused by sudden changes in position. Move more slowly and you will have no difficulty. The weakness can come to the point where the simplest task takes great effort. Rest is the best remedy. Many find this the most difficult period of the fast.

By the sixth or seventh day you will begin to feel stronger and more alert. Hunger pains will continue to diminish until by the ninth or tenth day they are only a minor irritation. The body will have eliminated the bulk of toxins and you will feel good. Your sense of concentration will be sharpened and you will feel as if you could continue fasting indefinitely. Physically this is the most enjoyable part of the fast.

Anywhere between twenty-one and forty days or longer, depending on the individual, hunger pains will return. This is the first stage of starvation and the pains signal that the body has used up its reserves and is beginning to draw on the living tissue. The fast should be broken at this time.

The amount of weight lost during a fast varies greatly with the individual. In the beginning a loss of two pounds a day, decreasing to one pound a day as the fast progresses, is normal. During fasting you will feel the cold more, simply because the body metabolism is not producing the usual amount of heat. If care is observed to keep warm, this is no difficulty. It should be obvious to all that there are some people who for physical reasons should not fast: diabetics, expectant mothers, heart patients, and others. If you have any question about your fitness to fast, seek medical advice.

Before commencing an extended fast, some are tempted to eat a good deal to 'stock up.' That is most unwise; in fact, slightly lighter than normal meals are best for the day or two before a fast. You would also be well advised to abstain from coffee or tea three days before beginning a longer fast. If the last meal in the stomach is fresh fruits and vegetables, you should have no difficulty with constipation.

An extended fast should be broken with fruit or vegetable juice, with small amounts taken at first. Remember that the stomach has shrunk considerably and the entire digestive system has gone into a kind of hibernation. By the second day you should be able to eat fruit and then milk or yogurt. Next you can eat fresh salads and cooked vegetables. Avoid all salad dressing, grease, and starch. Extreme care should be taken not to overeat. It is good during this to consider future diet and eating habits to see if you need to be more disciplined and in control of your appetite.

Although the physical aspects of fasting intrigue us, we must never forget that the major work of scriptural fasting is in the realm of the spirit. What goes on spiritually is much more important than what is happening bodily. You will be engaging in spiritual warfare that will necessitate using all the weapons of Ephesians 6. One of the most critical periods spiritually is at the end of the fast when we have a natural tendency to relax. But I do not want to leave the impression that all fasting is a heavy spiritual struggle – I have not found it so. It is also '. . . righteousness and peace and joy in the Holy Spirit' (Rom. 14:17).

Fasting can bring breakthroughs in the spiritual realm that will never happen in any other way. It is a means of God's grace and blessing that should not be neglected any longer. Wesley declares, '. . . it was not merely by the light of reason . . . that the people of God have been, in all ages, directed to use fasting as a means: . . . but they have been . . . taught it of God Himself, by clear and open revelations of His Will . . . Now, whatever reasons there were to quicken those of old, in the zealous and constant discharge of this duty, they are of equal force still to quicken us.'[11]

Now is the time for all who hear the voice of Christ to obey it.

FOR STUDY

The central ideal in fasting is the voluntary denial of an otherwise normal function for the sake of intense spiritual activity. There is nothing wrong with these normal functions in life; it is simply that there are times when we set them aside in order to concentrate. When we view fasting from this perspective we can see its reasonableness as well as its broader dimensions. The Bible deals with fasting in regard to food, but allow me to take the central principle and apply it to other aspects of contemporary culture.*

First, there is a need today to learn to fast from people. We have a tendency to just devour people, and we usually get severe heartburn from it! I suggest that we learn to fast from people not because we are antisocial but precisely because we love people intensely and when we are with them, we want to be able to do them good and not harm. The Discipline of solitude and the Discipline of community go hand in hand. Until we have learned to be alone we cannot be with people in a way that will help them, for we will bring to that relationship our own scatteredness. Conversely, until we have learned to be with people, being alone will be a dangerous thing, for it will cut us off from hurting, bleeding humanity.

Second, let's learn times to fast from the media. It has always amazed me that many people seem incapable (or at least unwilling) to go through an entire day concentrating on a single thing. Their train of thought is constantly broken up by this demand and that – the newspaper, the radio, the television, the magazines. No wonder we feel fractured and fragmented. Obviously, there is a time for the media, but there is also a time to be without the media. We send our children to summer camp and they come back thrilled because 'God spoke to me!' What happened at camp was simple: they merely got rid of enough distractions for a long enough period of time to concentrate. We can do that through the course of our ordinary days.

Third, I would suggest times of fasting from the telephone. The telephone is a wonderful invention, but it must not control us. I have known people who stop praying in order to answer the telephone! I want to let you in on a secret: you are under no obligation to answer that gadget every time it rings. In our home, when we are eating or when I am reading stories to the children,

---

* Some of the following ideas have appeared in a somewhat different form in another book of mine, *Freedom of Simplicity,* London: Triangle/ SPCK, 1981.

we do not answer the telephone because I want my boys to know they are more important than any phone call. And it is terribly offensive to interrupt an important conversation just to answer a machine.

Fourth, I would like to suggest the Discipline of fasting from billboards. I still remember the day I was driving on the Los Angeles freeway system when all of a sudden I realised that for one solid hour my mind had been dominated by the billboards. Now when I suggest that we fast from billboards, I do not mean that we should refrain from looking at them, but that the billboard should be a signal to us of another reality. When the ad man shouts out to us his four-letter obscenities, 'More, more, more', let it remind us of another four-letter word, a rich, full-bodied word, 'Less, less, less'. When we are bombarded with bigger than life pictures of foxy ladies and well-fed babies, perhaps that can trigger in our minds another world, a world in which four hundred and sixty million people are the victims of acute hunger (ten thousand of them will be dead by this time tomorrow), a world in which a million pigs in Indiana have superior housing to a billion people on this planet.

That leads me to my fifth and final suggestion, which is that we discover times to fast from our gluttonous consumer culture that we find so comfortable. For our souls' sake, we need times when we go among Christ's favourites – the broken, the bruised, the dispossessed – not to preach to them but to learn from them. For the sake of our balance, for the sake of our sanity, we need times when we are among those who, in the words of Mahatma Gandhi, live an 'eternal compulsory fast'.

Fasting is a Spiritual Discipline ordained by God for the good of the Christian fellowship. May God find within us hearts that are open to appropriate this means of His grace.

Daily Scripture Readings

Sunday   – The example of Christ. Luke 4:1–13
Monday   – God's chosen fast. Isaiah 58:1–7
Tuesday   – A partial fast. Daniel 10:1–14
Wednesday – A normal fast. Nehemiah 1:4–11
Thursday   – An absolute fast. Esther 4:12–17
Friday   – The inauguration of the Gentile mission. Acts 13:1–3
Saturday   – The appointment of elders in the Churches. Acts 14:19–23

Study Questions

1 Check your first reaction to the thought of fasting?
   _____ ugh
   _____ hmmm
   _____ wow!
   _____ ok
   _____ freedom
   _____ you must be joking
2 How does Christian fasting differ from the hunger strike and health fasting?
3 Define 'a normal fast', 'a partial fast', and 'an absolute fast'.
4 What is the primary purpose of fasting?
5 How can fasting show what controls your life?
6 What is the most difficult thing about fasting for you?
7 Fast for two meals (twenty-four hours) and give the time saved to God. Record anything you learn from the experience.
8 Try fasting from the media for one week and see what you learn about yourself.
9 Discuss the question of whether fasting is only a cultural expression of Christian faith or whether it is for all cultures at all times.

10 In his day John Wesley required that every minister ordained in the Methodist Church regularly fast two days a week. Discuss the implications of such a requirement in our day.

Suggestions for Further Reading

Smith, David R., *Fasting*, London: Rushworth Literature Enterprise, 1969. An excellent study.

5

The Discipline of Study

He that studies only men, will get the body of knowledge without the soul; and he that studies only books, the soul without the body. He that to what he sees, adds observation, and to what he reads, reflection, is in the right road to knowledge, provided that in scrutinising the hearts of others, he neglects not his own.

— CALEB COLTON

The purpose of the Spiritual Disciplines is the total transformation of the person. They aim at replacing old destructive habits of thought with new life-giving habits. Nowhere is this purpose more clearly seen than in the Discipline of study. The apostle Paul tells us that we are transformed through the renewal of the mind (Rom. 12:2). The mind is renewed by applying it to those things that will transform it. 'Finally, brethren, whatever is true, whatever is honourable, whatever is just, whatever is pure, whatever is lovely, whatever is gracious, if there is any excellence, if there is anything worthy of praise, *think* about these things' (Phil. 4:8, [italics added]). The Discipline of study is the primary vehicle to bring us to '*think* about these things.' Therefore, we should rejoice that we are not left to our own devices but have been given this means of God's grace for the changing of our inner spirit.

Many Christians remain in bondage to fears and anxieties

simply because they do not avail themselves of the Discipline of study. They may be faithful in church attendance and earnest in fulfilling their religious duties, and still they are not changed. I am not here speaking only of those who are going through mere religious forms, but of those who are genuinely seeking to worship and obey Jesus Christ as Lord and Master. They may sing with gusto, pray in the Spirit, live as obediently as they know, even receive divine visions and revelations, and yet the tenor of their lives remains unchanged. Why? Because they have never taken up one of the central ways God uses to change us: study. Jesus made it unmistakably clear that the knowledge of the truth will set us free. 'You will know the truth, and the truth will make you free' (John 8:32). Good feelings will not free us. Ecstatic experiences will not free us. Getting 'high on Jesus' will not free us. Without a knowledge of the truth, we will not be free.

This principle is true in every area of human endeavour. It is true in biology and mathematics. It is true in marriages and other human relationships. But it is especially true in reference to the spiritual life. Many are hampered and confused in the spiritual walk by a simple ignorance of the truth. Worse yet, many have been brought into the most cruel bondage by false teaching. 'You traverse sea and land to make a single proselyte, and when he becomes a proselyte, you make him twice as much a child of hell as yourselves' (Matt. 23:15).

Let us therefore apply ourselves to learning what constitutes the Spiritual Discipline of study, to identify its pitfalls, to practise it with joy, and to experience the liberation it brings.

WHAT IS STUDY?

Study is a specific kind of experience in which through careful attention to reality the mind is enabled to move in a certain direction. Remember, the mind will always take on an order conforming to the order upon which it concentrates. Perhaps we observe a tree or read a book. We see it, feel it, understand it, draw conclusions from it. And as we do, our thought processes take on an order conforming to the order in the tree or book. When this is done with concentration, perception, and repetition, ingrained habits of thought are formed.

The Old Testament instructs the Israelites to write the Laws on gates and doorposts and bind them to their wrists so that 'they shall be as frontlets between your eyes' (Deut. 11:18). The purpose of this instruction is to direct the mind repeatedly and regularly toward certain modes of thought about God and human relationships. A rosary or a prayer wheel has the same objective. Of course, the New Testament replaces laws written on the doorposts with laws written on the heart and leads us to Jesus, our ever-present and inward Teacher.

We must once again emphasise that the ingrained habits of thought that we formed *will* conform to the order of the thing being studied. *What* we study determines the kind of habits that are formed, which is why Paul urges us to focus on things that are true, honourable, just, pure, lovely, and gracious.

The process that occurs in study should be distinguished from meditation. Meditation is devotional; study is analytical. Meditation will relish a word; study will explicate it. Although meditation and study often overlap, they constitute two distinct experiences. Study provides a certain objective framework within which meditation can successfully function.

In study there are two 'books' to be studied: verbal and nonverbal. Books and lectures, therefore, constitute only half the field of study, perhaps less. The world of nature and, most important, the careful observation of events and actions are the primary nonverbal fields of study.

The principal task of study is a perception into the reality of a given situation, encounter, book, etc. We can go through a major crisis, for example, without any perception of the real nature of the tragic situation. But if we carefully observe and reflect upon what occurred, we can learn a great deal.

FOUR STEPS

Study involves four steps. The first is repetition. Repetition regularly channels the mind in a specific direction, thus ingraining habits of thought. We may smile condescendingly at the old teaching method of recitation, but we must realise that sheer repetition without even understanding what is being repeated does affect the inner mind. Ingrained habits of thought can be formed by repetition alone, thus changing behaviour. This is one reason why so many forms of spirituality emphasise the regular rehearsal of the deeds of God. This is also the central rationale behind psychocybernetics, which trains the individual to repeat certain affirmations regularly (for example, I love myself unconditionally). It is not even important that the person believe what he or she is repeating, only that it be repeated. The inner mind is thus trained and will eventually respond by modifying behaviour to conform to the affirmation. This principle has, of course, been known for centuries but only recently has it received scientific confirmation.

This is why the issue of television programming is so important. With innumerable murders being portrayed each evening on prime time TV, the repetition alone trains the inner mind in destructive thought patterns.

Concentration is the second step in study. If, in addition to bringing the mind repeatedly to the subject matter, the person will concentrate on what is being studied, learning is vastly increased. Concentration centres the mind. It focuses the attention on what is being studied. The human mind has an incredible ability to concentrate. It constantly receives thousands of stimuli, each one of which is stored in its memory banks while it focuses on only a few. This natural ability of the brain is enhanced when, with singleness of purpose, we centre our attention upon a desired object of study.

We live in a culture that does not value concentration. Distraction is the order of the day. Many will, for example, go through all the activities of the day and evening with the radio on. Some will read a book and watch TV at the same time. Most people find it virtually impossible to go through an entire day focusing on a single thing. We are the lesser for this dissipation of our energies.

When we not only repeatedly focus the mind in a particular direction, centring our attention on the subject, but understand what we are studying, we reach a new level. Comprehension then is the third step in the Discipline of study.

Jesus, as you remember, reminds us that it is not just the truth but the *knowledge* of the truth that sets us free (John 8:32). Comprehension focuses on the knowledge of the truth. All of us have had the experience of reading something over and over and then, all of sudden, we understand what it means. This 'eureka' experience of understanding catapults us on to a new level of growth and freedom. It leads to insight and discernment. It provides the basis for a true perception of reality.

One further step is needed: reflection. Although comprehension defines what we are studying, reflection defines the *significance* of what we are studying. To reflect, to ruminate, on the events of our time leads us to the inner reality of those events. Reflection brings us to see things from God's perspective. In reflection we come to understand not only our subject matter, but ourselves. Jesus speaks often of ears that do not hear and eyes that do not see. When we ponder the meaning of what we study, we come to hear and see in a new way.

It soon becomes obvious that study demands humility. Study simply cannot happen until we are willing to be subject to the subject matter. We must submit to the system. We must come as student, not teacher. Not only is study directly dependent upon humility, but it is conducive to it. Arrogance and a teachable spirit are mutually exclusive.

All of us know persons who have taken some course of study or attained some academic degree who parade their information in an offensive manner. We should feel profound sorrow for such people. They do not understand the Spiritual Discipline of study. They have mistaken the accumulation of information for knowledge. They equate the spouting of words with wisdom. How tragic! The apostle John defines eternal life as the knowledge of God. 'And this is eternal life, that they know thee the only true God, and Jesus Christ whom thou hast sent' (John 17:3). Even a touch of this experiential knowledge is sufficient to give us a profound sense of humility.

Now, having laid the basis, let us move on to consider the practical implementation of the Discipline of study.

STUDY OF BOOKS

When we consider study, we most naturally think of books or other writings. Though only half of the field, as I stated earlier, books are the most obvious and clearly important.

Unfortunately, many seem to think that studying a book is a simple task. No doubt this flippant attitude accounts for the poor reading habits of so many people. Studying a book is an extremely complex matter, especially for the novice. As with tennis or typing, when we are first learning it seems that there are a thousand details to master and we wonder how on earth we will keep everything in mind at the same time. Once we reach proficiency, however, the mechanics become second nature, and we are able to concentrate on our tennis game or the material to be typed.

The same is true with studying a book. Study is an exacting art involving a labyrinth of details. To convince people that they must *learn* to study is the major obstacle. Most people assume that because they know how to read words they know how to study. This limited grasp of the nature of study explains why so many people gain so little from reading books.

When we read a book, three intrinsic and three extrinsic

rules govern our study.* The intrinsic rules may, in the beginning, necessitate three separate readings but in time can be done concurrently. The first reading involves *understanding* the book: what is the author saying? The second reading involves *interpreting* the book: what does the author mean? The third reading involves *evaluating* the book: is the author right or wrong? Most of us tend to do the third reading right away and often never do the first and second readings at all. We give a critical analysis of a book before we understand what it says. We judge a book to be right or wrong before we interpret its meaning. The wise writer of Ecclesiastes says that there is a time for every matter under heaven, and the time for critical analysis of a book comes *after* careful understanding and interpretation.

The intrinsic rules of study, however, are in themselves inadequate. To read successfully we need the extrinsic aids of *experience, other books*, and *live discussion*.

Experience is the only way we can interpret and relate to what we read. We read a book on tragedy with different eyes when we have walked through the valley of the shadow ourselves. Experience that has been understood and reflected upon informs and enlightens our study.

Other books can include dictionaries, commentaries, and other interpretative literature, but great books that precede or advance the issue being studied are more significant. Books often have meaning only when they are read in relation to other writings. People will find it exceedingly difficult to understand the New Testament books of Romans or Hebrews, for example, without a grounding in the literature of the Old Testament. It is nearly impossible to read *The Federalist Papers* without first having read the Articles of Confederation and the US Constitution. The great writings that take up the central

---

* These matters are covered in detail in Mortimer J. Adler's *How to Read a Book*, New York: Simon & Schuster, 1940. I am indebted to him for these insights into the Discipline of study.

issues of life interact with one another. They cannot be read in isolation.

Live discussion refers to the ordinary interaction that occurs among human beings as they pursue a particular course of study. Often my students and I will read from Plato or St Augustine and have only a fragmentary grasp of the meaning or significance of what we have read. But when we gather for discussion, debate, and Socratic dialogue insights emerge that would never have come without this exchange. We interact with the author, we interact with each other, and new creative ideas are born.

The first and most important book we are to study is the Bible. The psalmist asks, 'How can a young man keep his way pure?' He then answers his own question, 'By guarding it according to thy word,' and adds, 'I have laid up thy word in my heart, that I might not sin against thee' (Ps. 119:9, 11). Probably the 'word' that the psalmist refers to is the Torah, but Christians throughout the centuries have found this to be true in their study throughout Scripture. 'All scripture is inspired by God and profitable for teaching, for reproof, for correction, and for training in righteousness, that the man of God may be complete, equipped for every good work' (2 Tim. 3:16, 17). Note that the central purpose is not doctrinal purity (though that is no doubt involved) but inner transformation. We come to the Scripture to be changed, not to amass information.

We must understand, however, that a vast difference exists between the study of Scripture and the devotional reading of Scripture. In the study of Scripture a high priority is placed upon interpretation: what it means. In the devotional reading of Scripture a high priority is placed upon application: what it means for me. All too often people rush to the application stage and bypass the interpretation stage: they want to know what it means for them before they know what it means! Also, we are not seeking spiritual ecstasy in study; in fact, ecstasy can be a hindrance. When we study a book of the Bible we are seeking to be controlled by the intent of the author. We are determined to hear what he is saying, not what we want him to say. We want life-transforming truth, not just good feelings. We are willing to pay the price of barren day after barren day until the meaning is clear. This process revolutionises our lives.

The apostle Peter found some things in the epistles of 'our beloved brother Paul' that were 'hard to understand' (2 Pet. 3:15, 16). If Peter found it so, we will as well. We will need to work at it. Daily devotional reading is certainly commendable, but it is not study. Anyone who is after 'a little word from God for today' is not interested in the Discipline of study.

The average adult Sunday School class is far too superficial and devotional to help us study the Bible. (There are exceptions and some churches offer serious courses in the Bible.) Perhaps you live close to a seminary or university where you can attend courses. If so, you are fortunate, especially if you find a teacher who dispenses *life* as well as information. If, however, that is not the case (and even if it is) you can do several things to begin studying the Bible.

Some of my most profitable experiences of study have come through structuring a private retreat of two to three days' duration. No doubt you will object that, given your schedule, you cannot possibly find that kind of time. I want you to know that it is no easier for me to set aside the time than for anyone else. I fight and struggle for every retreat, scheduling it into my diary many weeks in advance. I have suggested this idea to many groups and found that professional people with busy schedules, labourers with rigid schedules, homemakers with multiple schedules, and others can, in fact, find time for a private study retreat. I have discovered that the most difficult problem is not finding time but convincing myself that this is important enough to set aside the time.

Scripture tells us that following the marvellous resurrection of Dorcas, Peter 'tarried many days in Joppa with one Simon a tanner' (Acts 9:43, KJV). It was while tarrying in Joppa that the Holy Spirit got through to Peter (with visual aids no less) about his cultural and ethnic prejudices. What would have happened if, instead of tarrying, Peter had immediately struck out on a speaking tour to tell of the resurrection of Dorcas? Is it possible that he would have failed to come to that shattering insight from the Holy Spirit, 'Truly I perceive that God shows no partiality, but in every nation any one who fears him and does what is right is acceptable to him' (Acts 10:34)? No one knows. But I do know this: God desires various 'tarrying' places for all of us where he can teach us in special ways.

For many people, a weekend is a good time for such an experience. Others can arrange a block of time in the middle of the week. If only one day is possible, a Sunday is often excellent.

The best place is almost anywhere, as long as it is away from home. To leave the house or apartment not only sets us free from the telephone and domestic responsibilities, but it also sets our minds into a learning mode. Motels, as well as cabins, work well. Camping is less desirable since the tasks of living distract us more. Most retreat centres can accommodate private retreatants; Catholic centres in particular have a long tradition of encouraging private retreats and therefore have appropriate facilities.

Organised group retreats almost never take study seriously so you will probably need to structure the retreat yourself. Because you are alone you will need to discipline yourself and use your time carefully. If you are new at it you will not want to overdo and thus burn yourself out. With experience, however, you can put in ten to twelve hours of good study each day.

What should you study? That depends on what you need. I do not know your needs, but I know that one of the great needs among Christians today is simply the reading of large portions of Scripture. Much of our Bible reading is fragmentary and sporadic. I actually have known students who have taken Bible courses and never even read, as a whole, the book being studied. Consider taking a major book of the Bible, like Genesis or Jeremiah, and read it straight through. Notice the structure and flow of the book. Note areas of difficulty and return to them later. Jot down thoughts and impressions. Sometimes it is wise to combine the study of the Bible with the study of some great, devotional classic. Such retreat experiences can transform your life.

Another approach to the study of the Bible is to take a smaller book, like Ephesians or 1 John, and read it through each day for a month. More than any single effort this will put the structure of the book into your mind. Read it without trying to fit it into established categories. Expect to hear new things in new ways. Keep a journal of your findings. In the course of these studies you will obviously want to make use of the best secondary aids available.

In addition to studying the Bible, do not neglect the study of some of the experiential classics in Christian literature. Begin with *The Confessions of St. Augustine*. Next turn to *The Imitation of Christ* by Thomas à Kempis. Don't neglect *The Practice of the Presence of God* by Brother Lawrence. For an added pleasure read *The Little Flowers of St. Francis* by Brother Ugolino. Perhaps you might want something a bit heavier next like the *Pensées* of Blaise Pascal. Enjoy the *Table Talks* of Martin Luther before you wade into Calvin's *Institutes of the Christian Religion*. Consider reading the pacemaker of religious journal writing, *The Journal of George Fox*, or perhaps the better-known *Journal of John Wesley*. Read carefully William Law's *A Serious Call to a Devout and Holy Life*; its words carry a contemporary ring. From the twentieth century read *A Testament of Devotion* by Thomas Kelly, *The Cost of Discipleship* by Dietrich Bonhoeffer, and *Mere Christianity* by C. S. Lewis.

Obviously this is only a sampling. I completely passed over the *Revelations of Divine Love* by Julian of Norwich, *Introduction to the Devout Life* by Francis de Sales, *The Journal of John Woolman*, and many other books. Nor should we forget the great body of literature by men and women from many walks of life. Many of these thinkers have unusual perception into the human predicament. Writers like Lao-tse of China and Zarathustra of Persia,

Shakespeare and Milton, Cervantes and Dante, Tolstoy and Dostoevski, and, in our century, Dag Hammarskjöld.

One word of caution is in order. Do not be overwhelmed or discouraged by all the books you have not read. You will probably not read all those listed here and will undoubtedly read others not noted. These writings have been listed to help you see the excellent amount of literature at our disposal to guide us in the spiritual walk. Many others have travelled the same path and have left markers. Remember that the key to the Discipline of study is not reading many books, but experiencing what we do read.

STUDY OF NONVERBAL 'BOOKS'

We now come to the least recognised but perhaps the most important field of study: the observation of reality in things, events, and actions. The easiest place to begin is with nature. It is not difficult to see that the created order has many things to teach us.

Isaiah tells us that '. . . the mountains and the hills before you shall break forth into singing, and all the trees of the field shall clap their hands' (Isa. 55:12). The handiwork of the Creator can speak to us and teach us if we will listen. Martin Buber tells the story of the rabbi who went to a pond every day at dawn to learn 'the song with which the frogs praise God.'[1]

We begin the study of nature by paying attention. We *see* flowers or birds. We observe them carefully and prayerfully. André Gide describes the time when he observed a moth being reborn from its chrysalis during a classroom lecture. He was filled with wonder, awe, joy at this metamorphosis, this resurrection. Enthusiastically, he showed it to his professor who replied with a note of disapproval, 'What! Didn't you know that a chrysalis is the envelope of a butterfly? Every butterfly you see has come out of a chrysalis. It's perfectly natural.' Disillusioned, Gide wrote, 'Yes, indeed, I knew my *natural* history as well, perhaps better than he

. . . But because it was natural, could he not see that it was marvellous? Poor creature! From that day, I took a dislike to him and a loathing to his lessons.'[2] Who wouldn't! Gide's professor had only amassed information; he had not studied. And so the first step in the study of nature is reverent observation. A leaf can speak of order and variety, complexity and symmetry. Evelyn Underhill writes, 'Gather yourself up, as the exercises of recollection have taught you to do. Then . . . stretch out by a distinct act of loving will towards one of the myriad manifestations of life that surround you . . . As to the object of contemplation, it matters little. From Alp to insect, anything will do, provided that your attitude be right.'[3]

The next step is to make friends with the flowers and the trees and the little creatures that creep upon the earth. Like the fabled Dr Doolittle, talk with the animals. Of course, you can't really talk to each other . . . or can you? There is certainly a communication that goes beyond words, and often animals seem to respond to our friendship and compassion. I know this because I have experimented with it and so have some first-rate scientists, and we have found it to be true. Perhaps the stories of St Francis taming the wolf of Gubbio and preaching to the birds are not so farfetched. Of this much we can be sure: if we love the creation, we will learn from it, In *The Brothers Karamazov* Dostoevski counsels, 'Love all God's creation, the whole and every grain of sand in it. Love every leaf, every ray of God's light. Love the animals, love the plants, love everything. If you love everything, you will perceive the divine mystery in things. Once you perceive it, you will begin to comprehend it better every day.'[4]

There are, of course, many other 'books' beside nature that we should study. If we will observe the relationships that go on between human beings, we will receive a graduate-level education. Watch, for example, how much of our speech is aimed at justifying our actions. We find it almost impossible to act and allow the act to speak for itself. No, we must explain it, justify it, demonstrate the rightness of it. Why do we feel this compulsion to set the record straight? Because of pride and fear, because our reputations are at stake!

This compulsion is particularly easy to observe among sales-people, writers, ministers, professors – all those who earn their living by being good with words. If, however, we gradually make ourselves one of the principal subjects of study we will be delivered from a haughty spirit. In time we will be unable to pray like the Pharisee, 'God, I thank thee that I am not like other men . . .' (Luke 18:11).

We should become attentive to the ordinary relationships we encounter throughout the day: at home, work, school. We notice the things that control people. Remember, we are not trying to condemn or judge anyone; we are only trying to learn. If we do find a judging spirit emerging within ourselves, we observe that and learn.

As I mentioned earlier, one of the principal objects of our study should be ourselves. We should learn the things that control *us*. We observe our inner feelings and mood swings. What controls our moods? Why do we like certain people and dislike others? What do these things teach us about ourselves?*

In doing all this we are not trying to be amateur psychologists or sociologists. Nor are we obsessed with excessive introspection. We study these matters with a spirit of humility, needing a large dose of grace. We want only to follow the dictum of Socrates: 'Know thyself.' And through the blessed Holy Spirit we are expecting Jesus to be our living and ever-present Teacher.

We would do well to study institutions and cultures and the forces that shape them. Also, we should ponder the events of our

---

* This counsel is for reasonably mature and well-adjusted individuals. It is not for mental depressives or others who are bowed low by the burdens of life. For them these exercises are too depressing and self-defeating. If you find your days too heavy for this kind of study, please do not attempt it. But there is hope and there is something you can do. See the chapters on confession and guidance.

time, noting first, with a spirit of discernment, what things our culture lifts up as 'great events.' Let's look at the values of the culture – not what people say they are, but what they actually are.

Let's learn to ask questions. What are the assets and liabilities of a technological society? What has the fastfood industry done to the tradition of a family gathering for dinner? Why do we find it difficult in our culture to have time to develop relationships? Is Western individualism beneficial or destructive? What in our culture is in harmony with the gospel and what is at odds with it? One of the most important functions of Christian prophets in our day is the ability to perceive the consequences of various forces in our culture and to make value judgments upon them.

Study produces joy. Like any novice, we will find it hard work in the beginning. But the greater our proficiency, the greater our joy. Alexander Pope says, 'There is no study that is not capable of delighting us after a little application to it.'[5] Study is well worth our most serious effort.

FOR STUDY

The mind will always take on an order conforming to the order of whatever it concentrates upon. Once some friends gave us the loan of their beach house on the Oregon coast. It was a secluded spot where virtually the only building in sight was an old lighthouse on the far peninsula, and the only visitors were seagulls. The cabin had no TV and no telephone. There was a radio, but it didn't work. But there was a record player and two old records – the sound track from *Oklahoma* and *Johnny Appleseed*. How nice, I thought, one record for the children and one for the adults. In the course of a week I suppose we played those two records some fifty times. For months afterwards I found myself singing or humming those songs – in the shower, in board meetings, in church. I even sang them in my dreams.

What happened was simple: unconsciously, the functioning of my mind began taking on the order of the music.

This is why the problem of mind pollution is so crucial. Now when I speak of mind pollution I am not thinking only of 'bad' books, films and so on, but of mediocre books and films. You see, unless we set before ourselves a 'habitual vision of greatness' we will surely degenerate. This is why it is ruinous to have so much of our Christian literature of such poor literary quality. The sad fact of the modern world is that, in the main, men do not read at all, and many women are captives to the escapist romance novel which is of such poor quality that it should not even be considered literature. We simply must raise our sights.

Have you ever pondered why people do not read in our day? It is certainly not because we lack the time. In 1981 America spent 75,000 man-years playing video games* and God knows how many more thousands (or millions?) entranced by television. Though I have yet to join the video-game craze (I'm too self-conscious), I certainly don't mind a TV programme now and then, but abject slavery is another thing altogether. This week my son's fifth-grade teacher polled the class on their weekend activities and found the majority of the class watched over fifteen hours of TV and read under one hour. Only one other student besides Joel had watched under two hours of TV and had read around seven hours.

In order to raise our sights and take the Spiritual Discipline of study seriously may I put in a plug for disciplined reading. In my courses at the university I usually require seven or eight books in each class. At first students think they are being sent to the guillotine, but by the end of the term, they are thrilled to discover such a rich world, a world that makes *pac man* or *The Dukes of Hazard* look drab and dull.

Our children are required to read each evening. Both boys go to their room at 8:00 p.m. (Notice, this means that we must say

---

* *Time* magazine, 18 January 1982.

'No' to most evening church meetings and entertainment extravaganzas, though we will make rare exceptions.) Joel, our ten-year-old, is allowed to read for one hour. Nathan, our seven-year-old, reads for fifteen minutes. And with only minimal encouragement from us, they have taken to some substantial literature – Joel is presently devouring *The Lord of the Rings*. We also read together out loud. Recently Nathan has requested *The Chronicles of Narnia* and so (although Joel has read it many times) we all sit together after supper and share in the wonderful adventures of Peter, Susan, Edmund and Lucy in the magical land of Narnia. Next we plan to read aloud *The Pilgrim's Progress*.

Study is of course a much larger Discipline than reading, and many who read never study, but reading is an important element in study and should not be lost. I'm sure you will find God waiting for you as you engage in the ministry of study.

Daily Scripture Readings

Sunday	–	The call to study. Proverbs 1:1–9, 23:12, 23
Monday	–	The source of truth. James 1:5, Hebrews 4:11–13, 2 Timothy 3:16–17
Tuesday	–	What to study. Philippians 4:8–9, Colossians 3:1–17
Wednesday	–	The value of Study. Luke 10:38–42
Thursday	–	Active study. Ezra 7:10, James 1:19–25
Friday	–	Study in the evangelistic enterprise. Acts 17:1–3 & 10–12, 19:8–10
Saturday	–	The study of a non-verbal book. Proverbs 24:30–34

Study Questions

1 Why does study more fully bring about the purpose of the Spiritual Disciplines, which is the transformation of the individual? (I.e. what does it do that other Disciplines do not do?)

2 What is study? (This is an important question because there is a general ignorance among Christians regarding its answer.)

3 Have you ever had any experience with the study of non-verbal books?

4 The four steps into study which I give are repetition, concentration, comprehension and reflection. Which of these four do you feel is the most important in bringing about the goal of the transformation of the individual?

5 Outside of the Bible, which book has had the most profound impact upon your own life? Why?

6 On page 85 I write, 'In study we are not seeking spiritual ecstasy; in fact, ecstasy can be a hindrance.' How could it be a hindrance?

7 List three things which you could do this next week in order to follow the dictum of Socrates, 'Know thyself'.

8 Study a plant or tree for ten minutes and write down what you learn from the experience.

9 Why does study produce joy?

10 Consider the purchase of a serious book on the Spiritual life to read this next week.

Suggestions for Further Reading

MacDonald, Gordon, *Ordering Your Private World*, Crowborough: Highland Books, 1987. This book explains the inner life in practical ways, helping us to reappraise our frantic life-styles and bring order and peace to the chaos of our spirits.

Richards, Lawrence O., *Creative Personal Bible Study*, Basingstoke: Marshall Pickering, 1989. This book shows us how to dismantle the barriers that we erect between the Bible and ourselves and, in a series of exercises, leads us to a fresh and dynamic method of personal study.

Stott, John R. W., *Understanding the Bible*, London: Scripture Union, 1984. An exceedingly helpful resource for personal

Bible study covering issues of interpretation and authority as well as the basic flow of the biblical story.

PART II

The Outward Disciplines

6

The Discipline of Simplicity

When we are truly in this interior simplicity our whole appearance is franker, more natural. This true simplicity . . . makes us conscious of a certain openness, gentleness, innocence, gaiety, and serenity, which is charming when we see it near to and continually, with pure eyes. O, how amiable this simplicity is! Who will give it to me? I leave all for this. It is the Pearl of the Gospel.

– François Fénelon

Simplicity is freedom. Duplicity is bondage. Simplicity brings joy and balance. Duplicity brings anxiety and fear. The preacher of Ecclesiastes observes that 'God made man simple; man's complex problems are of his own devising' (Eccles. 7:29, JB). Because many of us are experiencing the liberation God brings through simplicity we are once again singing an old Shaker hymn:

> 'Tis the gift to be simple,
>   'Tis the gift to be free,
> 'Tis the gift to come down where you ought to be,
>   And when we find ourselves in the place just right,
> 'Twill be in the valley of love and delight.

When true simplicity is gained,

To bow and to bend we shan't be ashamed.
To turn, turn will be our delight
'Till by turning, turning we come round right.

The Christian Discipline of simplicity is an *inward* reality that results in an *outward* life-style. Both the inward and the outward aspects of simplicity are essential. We deceive ourselves if we believe we can possess the inward reality without its having a profound effect on how we live. To attempt to arrange an outward life-style of simplicity without the inward reality leads to deadly legalism.

Simplicity begins in inward focus and unity. It means to live out of what Thomas Kelly calls 'The Divine Centre.' Kierkegaard captured the nucleus of Christian simplicity well in the profound title of his book, *Purity of Heart Is to Will One Thing*.

Experiencing the inward reality liberates us outwardly. Speech becomes truthful and honest. The lust for status and position is gone because we no longer need status and position. We cease from showy extravagance not on the grounds of being unable to afford it, but on the grounds of principle. Our goods become available to others. We join the experience that Richard E. Byrd, after months alone in the barren Arctic, recorded in his journal, 'I am learning . . . that a man can live profoundly without masses of things.'[1]

Contemporary culture lacks both the inward reality and the outward life-style of simplicity. We must live in the modern world, and we are affected by its fractured and fragmented state. We are trapped in a maze of competing attachments. One moment we make decisions on the basis of sound reason and the next moment out of fear of what others will think of us. We have no unity or focus around which our lives are oriented.

Because we lack a divine Centre our need for security has led us into an insane attachment to things. We really must understand that the lust for affluence in contemporary society is psychotic. It is psychotic because it has completely lost touch with reality.

We crave things we neither need nor enjoy. 'We buy things we do not want to impress people we do not like.'[2] Where planned obsolescence leaves off, psychological obsolescence takes over. We are made to feel ashamed to wear clothes or drive cars until they are worn out. The mass media have convinced us that to be out of step with fashion is to be out of step with reality. It is time we awaken to the fact that conformity to a sick society is to be sick. Until we see how unbalanced our culture has become at this point, we will not be able to deal with the mammon spirit within ourselves nor will we desire Christian simplicity.

This psychosis permeates even our mythology. The modern hero is the poor boy who purposefully becomes rich rather than the rich boy who voluntarily becomes poor. (We still find it hard to imagine that a girl could do either!) Covetousness we call ambition. Hoarding we call prudence. Greed we call industry.

Further, it is important to understand that the modern counterculture is hardly an improvement. It is a superficial change in life-style without dealing seriously with the root problems of a consumer society. Because the counterculture has always lacked a positive centre it has inevitably degenerated into trivia. Arthur Gish states, 'Much of the counter culture is a mirror of the worst features of the old sick society. The revolution is not free dope, free sex, and abortions on demand . . . The pseudo-libertarian eroticism, elements of sadomasochism, and sexist advertisements in much of the underground press is part of the perversion of the old order and an expression of death.'[3]

Courageously, we need to articulate new, more human ways to live. We should take exception to the modern psychosis that defines people by how much they can produce or what they earn. We should experiment with bold new alternatives to the present death-giving system. The Spiritual Discipline of simplicity is not a lost dream, but a recurrent vision throughout history. It can be recaptured today. It must be.

THE BIBLE AND SIMPLICITY

Before attempting to forge a Christian view of simplicity it is necessary to destroy the prevailing notion that the Bible is ambiguous about economic issues. Often it is felt that our response to wealth is an individual matter. The Bible's teaching in this area is said to be strictly a matter of private interpretation. We try to believe that Jesus did not address himself to practical economic questions.

No serious reading of Scripture can substantiate such a view. The biblical injunctions against the exploitation of the poor and the accumulation of wealth are clear and straightforward. The Bible challenges nearly every economic value of contemporary society. For example, the Old Testament takes exception to the popular notion of an absolute right to private property. The earth belongs to God, says Scripture, and therefore cannot be held perpetually (Lev. 25:23). The Old Testament legislation of the year of Jubilee stipulated that all land was to revert back to its original owner. In fact, the Bible declares that wealth itself belongs to God, and one purpose of the year of Jubilee was to provide a regular redistribution of wealth. Such a radical view of economics flies in the face of nearly all contemporary belief and practice. Had Israel faithfully observed the Jubilee it would have dealt a death blow to the perennial problem of the rich becoming richer and the poor becoming poorer.

Constantly the Bible deals decisively with the inner spirit of slavery that an idolatrous attachment to wealth brings. 'If riches increase, set not your heart on them,' counsels the psalmist (Ps. 62:10). The tenth commandment is against covetousness, the inner lust to have, which leads to stealing and oppression. The wise sage understood that 'He who trusts in his riches will wither' (Prov. 11:28).

Jesus declared war on the materialism of his day. (And I would suggest that he declares war on the materialism of our day as well.) The Aramaic term for wealth is 'mammon' and Jesus condemns it as a rival God: 'No servant can serve two masters; for either he will hate the one and love the other, or he will be devoted to the one and despise the other. You cannot serve God and mammon' (Luke 16:13). He speaks frequently and unambiguously to economic issues. He says, 'Blessed are you poor, for yours is the kingdom of God' and 'Woe to you that are rich, for you have received your consolation' (Luke 6:20, 24). He graphically depicts the difficulty of the wealthy entering the kingdom of God to be like a camel walking through the eye of a needle. With God, of course, all things are possible, but Jesus clearly understood the difficulty. He saw the grip that wealth can have on a person. He knew that 'where your treasure is, there will your heart be also,' which is precisely why he commanded his followers: 'Do not lay up for yourselves treasures on earth' (Matt. 6:21, 19). He is not saying that the heart should or should not be where the treasure is. He is stating the plain fact that wherever you find the treasure, you *will* find the heart.

He exhorted the rich young ruler not just to have an inner attitude of detachment from his possessions, but literally to get rid of his possessions if he wanted the kingdom of God (Matt. 19:16–22). He says, 'Take heed, and beware of all covetousness; for a man's life does not consist in the abundance of his possessions' (Luke 12:15). He counselled people who came seeking God, 'Sell your possessions, and give alms; provide yourselves with purses that do not grow old, with a treasure in the heavens that does not fail . . .' (Luke 12:33). He told the parable of the rich farmer whose life centred in hoarding – we would call him prudent; Jesus called him a fool (Luke 12:16–21). He states that if we really want the kingdom of God we must, like a merchant in search of fine pearls, be willing to sell everything we have to get it (Matt. 13:45, 46). He calls all who would follow him to a joyful life of carefree unconcern for possessions: 'Give to every one who begs from you; and of him who takes away your goods do not ask them again' (Luke 6:30).

Jesus speaks to the question of economics more than any

other single social issue. If, in a comparatively simple society, our Lord lays such strong emphasis upon the spiritual dangers of wealth, how much more should we who live in a highly affluent culture take seriously the economic question.

The Epistles reflect the same concern. Paul says, 'Those who desire to be rich fall into temptation, into a snare, into many senseless and hurtful desires that plunge men into ruin and destruction' (1 Tim. 6:9). A bishop is not to be a 'lover of money' (1 Tim. 3:3). A deacon is not to be 'greedy for gain' (1 Tim. 3:8). The writer to the Hebrews counsels, 'Keep your life free from love of money, and be content with what you have; for he has said, "I will never fail you nor forsake you"' (Heb. 13:5). James blames killings and wars on the lust for possessions: 'You desire and do not have; so you kill. And you covet and cannot obtain; so you fight and wage war' (James 4:1, 2). Paul calls covetousness idolatry and commands stern discipline against anyone guilty of greed (Eph. 5:5; 1 Cor. 5:11). He lists greed alongside adultery and thievery and declares that those who live in such things will not inherit the kingdom of God. Paul counsels the wealthy not to trust in their wealth, but in God, and to share generously with others (1 Tim. 6:17–19).

Having said all this, I must hasten to add that God intends that we should have adequate material provision. There is misery today from a simple lack of provision just as there is misery when people try to make a life out of provision. Forced poverty is evil and should be renounced. Nor does the Bible condone an extreme asceticism. Scripture declares consistently and forcefully that the creation is good and to be enjoyed. Asceticism makes an unbiblical division between a good spiritual world and an evil material world and so finds salvation in paying as little attention as possible to the physical realm of existence.

Asceticism and simplicity are mutually incompatible. Occasional superficial similarities in practice must never obscure the radical difference between the two. Asceticism renounces possessions. Simplicity sets possessions in proper perspective.

Asceticism finds no place for a 'land flowing with milk and honey.' Simplicity rejoices in this gracious provision from the hand of God. Asceticism finds contentment only when it is abased. Simplicity knows contentment in both abasement and abounding (Phil. 4:12).

Simplicity is the only thing that sufficiently reorients our lives so that possessions can be genuinely enjoyed without destroying us. Without simplicity we will either capitulate to the 'mammon' spirit of this present evil age, or we will fall into an un-Christian legalistic asceticism. Both lead to idolatry. Both are spiritually lethal.

Descriptions of the abundant material provision God gives his people abound in Scripture. 'For the Lord your God is bringing you into a good land . . . a land . . . in which you will lack nothing' (Deut. 8:7–9). Warnings about the danger of provisions that are not kept in proper perspective also abound. 'Beware lest you say in your heart, "My power and the might of my hand have gotten me this wealth" ' (Deut. 8:17).

The Spiritual Discipline of simplicity provides the needed perspective. Simplicity sets us free to receive the provision of God as a gift that is not ours to keep and can be freely shared with others. Once we recognise that the Bible denounces the materialist and the ascetic with equal vigour, we are prepared to turn our attention to the framing of a Christian understanding of simplicity.

A PLACE TO STAND

Archimedes once declared, 'Give me a place to stand and I will move the earth.' Such a focal point is important in every Discipline but is acutely so with simplicity. Of all the Disciplines simplicity is the most visible and therefore the most open to corruption. The majority of Christians have never seriously wrestled with the problem of simplicity, conveniently ignoring Jesus' many words on the subject. The reason is simple: this

Discipline directly challenges our vested interests in an affluent life-style. But those who take the biblical teaching on simplicity seriously are faced with severe temptations towards legalism. In the earnest attempt to give concrete expression to Jesus' economic teaching, it is easy to mistake our particular expression of the teaching for the teaching itself. We wear this attire or buy that kind of house and canonise our choices as the simple life. This danger gives special importance to finding and clearly articulating an Archimedian focal point for simplicity.

We have such a focal point in the words of Jesus: 'Therefore I tell you, do not be anxious about your life, what you shall eat or what you shall drink, nor about your body, what you shall put on. Is not life more than food, and the body more than clothing? Look at the birds of the air: they neither sow nor reap nor gather into barns, and yet your heavenly Father feeds them. Are you not of more value than they? And which of you by being anxious can add one cubit to his span of life? And why are you anxious about clothing? Consider the lilies of the field, how they grow; they neither toil nor spin; yet I tell you, even Solomon in all his glory was not arrayed like one of these. But if God so clothes the grass of the field, which today is alive and tomorrow is thrown into the oven, will he not much more clothe you, O men of little faith? Therefore do not be anxious, saying, "What shall we eat?" or "What shall we drink?" or "What shall we wear?" For the Gentiles seek all these things; and your heavenly Father knows that you need them all. *But seek first his kingdom and his righteousness, and all these things shall be yours as well*' (Matt. 6:25–33, [italics added]).

The central point for the Discipline of simplicity is to seek the kingdom of God and the righteousness of his kingdom *first* and then everything necessary will come in its proper order. It is impossible to overestimate the importance of Jesus' insight at this point. Everything hinges upon maintaining the 'first' things as first. Nothing must come before the kingdom of God, including the desire for a simple life-style.

Simplicity itself becomes idolatry when it takes precedence over seeking the kingdom. In a particularly penetrating comment on this passage of Scripture, Søren Kierkegaard considers what sort of effort could be made to pursue the kingdom of God. Should a person get a suitable job in order to exert a virtuous influence? His answer: no, we must *first* seek God's kingdom. Then should we give away all our money to feed the poor? Again the answer: no, we must *first* seek God's kingdom. Well, then perhaps we are to go and preach this truth to the world that people are to seek first God's kingdom? Once again the answer is a resounding: no, we are *first* to seek the kingdom of God. Kierkegaard concludes, 'Then in a certain sense it is nothing I shall do. Yes, certainly, in a certain sense it is nothing, become nothing before God, learn to keep silent; in this silence is the beginning, which is, *first* to seek God's Kingdom.'[4]

Focus upon the kingdom produces the inward reality, and without the inward reality we will degenerate into legalistic trivia. Nothing else can be central. The desire to get out of the rat race cannot be central, the redistribution of the world's wealth cannot be central, the concern for ecology cannot be central. Seeking *first* God's kingdom and the righteousness, both personal and social, of that kingdom is the only thing that can be central in the Spiritual Discipline of simplicity.

The person who does not seek the kingdom first does not seek it at all. Worthy as all other concerns may be, the moment *they* become the focus of our efforts they become idolatry. To centre on them will inevitably draw us into declaring that our particular activity *is* Christian simplicity. And, in fact, when the kingdom of God is genuinely placed first, ecological concerns, the poor, the equitable distribution of wealth, and many other things will be given their proper attention.

As Jesus made clear in our central passage, freedom from anxiety is one of the inward evidences of seeking first the kingdom of God. The inward reality of simplicity involves a life of joyful unconcern for possessions. Neither the greedy nor the miserly know this liberty. It has nothing to do with abundance of possessions or their lack. It is an inward spirit of trust. The sheer fact that a person is living without things is no guarantee that he or she is living in simplicity. Paul taught us that the love of money is the root of all evil, and I have discovered that often those who have it the least love it the most. It is possible for a person to be developing an outward life-style of simplicity and to be filled with anxiety. Conversely, wealth does not bring freedom from anxiety. Kierkegaard writes, '. . . riches and abundance come hypocritically clad in sheep's clothing pretending to be security against anxieties and they become then the object of anxiety . . . they secure a man against anxieties just about as well as the wolf which is put to tending the sheep secures them . . . against the wolf.'[5]

Freedom from anxiety is characterised by three inner attitudes. If what we have we receive as a gift, and if what we have is to be cared for by God, and if what we have is available to others, then we will possess freedom from anxiety. *This is the inward reality of simplicity*. However, if what we have we believe we have got, and if what we have we believe we must hold on to, and if what we have is not available to others, then we will live in anxiety. Such persons will never know simplicity regardless of the outward contortions they may put themselves through in order to live 'the simple life.'

To receive what we have as a gift from God is the first inner attitude of simplicity. We work but we know that it is not our work that gives us what we have. We live by grace even when it comes to 'daily bread.' We are dependent upon God for the simplest elements of life: air, water, sun. What we have is not the result of our labour, but of the gracious care of God. When we are tempted to think that what we own is the result of our personal efforts, it takes only a little drought or a small accident to show us once again how utterly dependent we are for everything.

To know that it is God's business, and not ours, to care for what we have is the second inner attitude of simplicity. God is able to protect what we possess. We can trust him. Does that mean that we should never take the keys out of the car or lock the door? Of course not. But we know that the lock on the door is not what protects the house. It is only common sense to take normal precautions, but if we believe that precaution itself protects us and our goods, we will be riddled with anxiety. There simply is no such thing as 'burglar proof' precaution. Obviously, these matters are not restricted to possessions but include such things as our reputation and our employment. Simplicity means the freedom to trust God for these (and all) things.

To have our goods available to others marks the third inner attitude of simplicity. If our goods are not available to the community when it is clearly right and good, then they are stolen goods. The reason we find such an idea so difficult is our fear of the future. We cling to our possessions rather than sharing them because we are anxious about tomorrow. But if we truly believe that God is who Jesus says he is, then we do not need to be afraid. When we come to see God as the almighty Creator *and* our loving Father, we can share because we know that he will care for us. If someone is in need, we are free to help them. Again, ordinary common sense will define the parameters of our sharing and save us from foolishness.

When we are seeking first the kingdom of God, these three attitudes will characterise our lives. Taken together they define what Jesus means by 'do not be anxious.' They comprise the inner reality of Christian simplicity. And we can be certain that when we live this way the 'all these things' that are necessary to carry on human life adequately will be ours as well.

THE OUTWARD EXPRESSION OF SIMPLICITY

To describe simplicity only as an inner reality is to say something false. The inner reality is not a reality until there is an outward expression. To experience the liberating spirit of simplicity *will* affect how we live. As I have warned earlier, every attempt to give specific application to simplicity runs the risk of a deterioration into legalism. It is a risk, however, that we must take, for to refuse to discuss specifics would banish the Discipline to the theoretical. After all, the writers of Scripture constantly took that risk.* And so I follow their lead and suggest ten controlling principles for the outward expression of simplicity. They should never be viewed as laws but as only one attempt to flesh out the meaning of simplicity for today.

First, buy things for their usefulness rather than their status. Cars should be bought for their utility, not their prestige. Consider riding a bicycle. When you are considering an apartment, a condominium, or a house, thought should be given to livability rather than how much it will impress others. Don't have more living space than is reasonable. After all, who needs seven rooms for two people?

Consider your clothes. Most people have no need for more clothes. They buy more not because they need clothes, but because they want to keep up with the fashions. Hang the fashions! Buy what you need. Wear your clothes until they are worn out. Stop trying to impress people with your clothes and impress them with your life. If it is practical in your situation, learn the joy of making clothes. And for God's sake (and I mean that quite literally) have clothes that are practical rather than ornamental. John Wesley writes, 'As . . . for apparel, I buy the most lasting and, in general, the plainest I can. I buy no furniture but what is necessary and cheap.'[6]

---

* It is sad to realise that often the attempt of Scripture to apply the principle of simplicity to a given culture has been universalised by succeeding generations and turned into soul-killing laws. Witness, for example, the laws against Christians braiding their hair or wearing rings because Peter had said to the people of his day. 'Let not yours be the outward adorning with braiding of hair, decoration of gold, and wearing of robes' (1 Pet. 3:3).

Second, reject anything that is producing an addiction in you. Learn to distinguish between a real psychological need, like cheerful surroundings, and an addiction. Eliminate or cut down on the use of addictive, nonnutritional drinks: alcohol, coffee, tea, Coca-Cola, and so on. Chocolate has become a serious addiction for many people. If you have become addicted to television, by all means sell your set or give it away. Any of the media that you find you cannot do without, get rid of: radios, stereos, magazines, videos, newspapers, books. If money has a grip on your heart, give some away and feel the inner release. Simplicity is freedom, not slavery. Refuse to be a slave to anything but God.

Remember, an addiction, by its very nature, is something that is beyond your control. Resolves of the will alone are useless in defeating a true addiction. You cannot just decide to be free of it. But you can decide to open this corner of your life to the forgiving grace and healing power of God. You can decide to allow loving friends who know the ways of prayer to stand with you. You can decide to live simply one day at a time in quiet dependence upon God's intervention.

How do you discern an addiction? Very simply, you watch for undisciplined compulsions. A student friend told me about one morning when he went out to get his newspaper and found it missing. He panicked, wondering how he could possibly start the day without the newspaper. Then he noticed a morning paper in his neighbour's yard, and he began to plot how he could sneak over and steal it. Immediately he realised that he was dealing with a genuine addiction. He rushed inside and called the newspaper office to cancel his subscription. The receptionist, obviously filling out a form, asked courteously, 'Why are you cancelling your subscription to the newspaper?' My friend blurted out, 'Because I'm addicted!' Undaunted, the receptionist replied, 'Would you like to cancel your entire subscription or would you like to keep the Sunday edition?' to which he exclaimed, 'No, I'm going cold turkey!' Now, obviously not everyone should cancel their subscription to the newspaper, but for this young man it was an important act.

Third, develop a habit of giving things away. If you find that you are becoming attached to some possession, consider giving it to someone who needs it. I still remember the Christmas I decided that rather than buying or even making an item, I would give away something that meant a lot to me. My motive was selfish: I wanted to know the liberation that comes from even this simple act of voluntary poverty. The gift was a ten-speed bike. As I went to the person's home to deliver the present, I remember singing with new meaning the worship chorus, 'Freely, freely you have received; freely, freely give.' When my son Nathan was six years old he heard of a classmate who needed a lunch box and asked me if he could give him his own lunch box. Hallelujah!

De-accumulate! Masses of things that are not needed complicate life. They must be sorted and stored and dusted and re-sorted and re-stored *ad nauseam*. Most of us could get rid of half our possessions without any serious sacrifice. We would do well to follow the counsel of Thoreau: 'Simplify, simplify.'

Fourth, refuse to be propagandised by the custodians of modern gadgetry. Timesaving devices almost never save time. Beware of the promise. 'It will pay for itself in six months.' Most gadgets are built to break down and wear out and so complicate our lives rather than enhance them. This problem is a plague in the toy industry. Children do not need to be entertained by dolls that cry, eat, wet, sweat, and spit. An old rag doll can be more enjoyable and more lasting. Often children find more joy in playing with old pots and pans than with the latest space set. Look for toys that are educational and durable. Make some yourself.

Usually gadgets are an unnecessary drain on the energy resources of the world. The United States has less than six percent of the world's population, but consumes about thirty-three percent of the world's energy. Air conditioners in the United

States alone use the same amount of energy as does the entire country of China.[7] Environmental responsibility alone should keep us from buying the majority of the gadgets produced today.

Propagandists try to convince us that because the newest model of this or that has a new feature (trinket?), we must sell the old one and buy the new one. Sewing machines have new stitches, stereos have new buttons, cars have new designs. Such media dogma needs to be carefully scrutinised. Often 'new' features seduce us into buying what we do not need. Probably that refrigerator will serve us quite well for the rest of our lives even without the automatic ice maker and the fancy exterior.

Fifth, learn to enjoy things without owning them. Owning things is an obsession in our culture. If we own it, we feel we can control it; and if we can control it, we feel it will give us more pleasure. The idea is an illusion. Many things in life can be enjoyed without possessing or controlling them. Share things. Enjoy the beach without feeling you have to buy a piece of it. Enjoy public parks and libraries.

Sixth, develop a deeper appreciation for the creation. Get close to the earth. Walk whenever you can. Listen to the birds. Enjoy the texture of grass and leaves. Smell the flowers. Marvel in the rich colours everywhere. Simplicity means to discover once again that 'the earth is the LORD's and the fullness thereof' (Ps. 24:1).

Seventh, look with a healthy scepticism at all 'buy now, pay later' schemes. They are a trap and only deepen your bondage. Both Old and New Testaments condemn usury for good reasons. ('Usury' in the Bible is not used in the modern sense of exorbitant interest; it referred to any kind of interest at all.) Charging interest was viewed as an unbrotherly exploitation of another's misfortune, hence a denial of community. Jesus denounced usury as a sign of the old life and admonished his disciples to 'lend, expecting nothing in return' (Luke 6:35).

These words of Scripture should not be elevated into some

kind of universal law obligatory upon all cultures at all times. But neither should they be thought of as totally irrelevant to modern society. Behind these biblical injunctions stand centuries of accumulated wisdom (and perhaps some bitter experiences!). Certainly prudence, as well as simplicity, demands that we use extreme caution before incurring debt.

Eighth, obey Jesus' instructions about plain, honest speech. 'Let what you say be simply "Yes" or "No"; anything more than this comes from evil' (Matt. 5:37). If you consent to do a task, do it. Avoid flattery and half-truths. Make honesty and integrity the distinguishing characteristics of your speech. Reject jargon and abstract speculation whose purpose is to obscure and impress rather than to illuminate and inform.

Plain speech is difficult because we so seldom live out of the divine Centre, so seldom respond only to heavenly promptings. Often fear of what others may think or a hundred other motives determine our 'yes' or 'no' rather than obedience to divine urgings. Then if a more attractive opportunity arises we quickly reverse our decision. But if our speech comes out of obedience to the divine Centre, we will find no reason to turn our 'yes' into 'no' and our 'no' into 'yes.' We will be living in simplicity of speech because our words will have only one Source. Søren Kierkegaard writes: 'If thou art absolutely obedient to God, then there is no ambiguity in thee and . . . thou art mere simplicity before God . . . One thing there is which all Satan's cunning and all the snares of temptation cannot take by surprise, and that is simplicity.'[8]

Ninth, reject anything that breeds the oppression of others. Perhaps no person has more fully embodied this principle than the eighteenth-century Quaker tailor John Woolman. His famous *Journal* is abundant with tender references to his desire to live so as not to oppress others. 'Here I was led into a close and laborious inquiry whether I . . . kept clear from all things which tended to stir up or were connected with wars: . . . my heart was deeply concerned that in [the] future I might in all things keep steadily to the pure truth, and live and walk in the plainness and simplicity of a sincere follower of Christ . . . And here luxury and covetousness, with the numerous oppressions and other evils attending them, appeared very afflicting to me . . .'[9] This is one of the most difficult and sensitive issues for us to face, but face it we must. Do we sip our coffee and eat our bananas at the expense of exploiting Latin American peasants? In a world of limited resources, does our lust for wealth mean the poverty of others? Should we buy products that are made by forcing people into dull assembly-line jobs? Do we enjoy hierarchical relationships in the company or factory that keep others under us? Do we oppress our children or spouse because we feel certain tasks are beneath us?

Often our oppression is tinged with racism, sexism, and nationalism. The colour of the skin still affects one's position in the company. The sex of a job applicant still affects the salary. The national origin of a person still affects the way he or she is perceived. May God give us prophets today who, like John Woolman, will call us 'from the desire of wealth' so that we may be able to 'break the yoke of oppression.'[10]

Tenth, shun anything that distracts you from seeking first the kingdom of God. It is so easy to lose focus in the pursuit of legitimate, even good things. Job, position, status, family, friends, security – these and many more can all too quickly become the centre of attention. George Fox warns, '. . . there is the danger and the temptation to you, of drawing your minds into your business, and clogging them with it; so that ye can hardly do anything to the service of God . . . and your minds will go into the things, and not over the things . . . And then, if the Lord God cross you, and stop you by sea and land, and take [your] goods and customs from you, that your minds should not be cumbered, then that mind that is cumbered, will fret, being out of the power of God.'[11]

May God give you – and me – the courage, the wisdom, the

strength always to hold the kingdom of God as the number-one priority of our lives. To do so is to live in simplicity.*

FOR STUDY

Simplicity is openness, unself-consciousness, naturalness. It is the opposite of subtlety, cunning, duplicity.

Where simplicity abounds words can be taken at face value: there is no hidden agenda. And yet, simplicity is not synonymous with 'easy to understand'. Jesus was not easy to understand, nor was Paul, but both were characterised by simplicity of speech. Their intent was not to confuse or deceive but to clarify and illuminate.

Simplicity frees us from the tyranny of the self, the tyranny of things and the tyranny of people.**

The self clamours for attention, self-recognition, applause. Through artful deception it appears to be younger, wiser, richer, saintlier than is actually the case. It will go to extravagant lengths to seem to belong to the intelligentsia. In meetings it will quote authors it has never read or maintain a discreet silence in supposed superiority over so uneducated a group.

Confront and challenge the tyranny of the self with the following questions:

Am I pretending to be an expert where I am only an amateur?
Do I really read the books I quote?
Do I use rhetoric as a curtain to conceal my true intentions?
Do I give the impression of being more godly (or more profane, whichever will give more status in the group) than I truly am?
Do I try to impress people with my degrees, titles, or honours?

---

* For those looking for a fuller discussion of Christian simplicity see my book, *Freedom of Simplicity*, London: Triangle/SPCK, 1981.
** These brief words are adopted from material in Albert Day's book *Discipline and Discovery*.

Simplicity also prevails against the tyranny of things. Out of fear that others might discover who we are, we create an artificial world of ostentatious display, extravagant ornamentation and pretentious style. We call upon the beautician, the tailor and the dressmaker to create an impression of perpetual youth. We buy clothes, cars and houses beyond our means in a frantic attempt to appear successful.

Rebuke the tyranny of things with the following questions:

Am I living contentedly within my income?
Do I act my age?
Am I a compulsive buyer?
Do I try to impress people with gadgets?
Do I buy what I can afford and what my responsibility to the poor suggests?

Finally, there is the tyranny of people. What horrendous gymnastics we will put ourselves through just to ensure that others will have a good opinion of us! How desperately and sincerely we labour to create the right impression. Instead of becoming good we resort to all sorts of devices to make people think we are good.

Joyfully attack the tyranny of people with the following questions:

Can I allow an unfavourable comment about myself to stand, without any need to straighten out the matter?
In recounting events do I shift the story ever so slightly to make myself appear in a more favourable light?
Must I always make excuses for my behaviour?
Do I aim at excellence in my work without regard for what people may say or think?
Can I accept compliments freely without any need to shrug them off in self-conscious modesty?

Only the simple are free. All others are tyrannised by the ambitious self, the demand for recognition through things, and a preoccupation with the opinions of others. François Fénelon declared, 'Simplicity is an uprightness of soul which prevents self-consciousness. Verily such simplicity is a great treasure!'

Daily Scripture Readings

Sunday   –   Simplicity as singleness of heart. Matthew 6:19–24
Monday   –   Simplicity as trust. Matthew 6:25–34
Tuesday   –   Simplicity as obedience. Genesis 15
Wednesday –   The generosity of simplicity. Leviticus 25:8–12
Thursday   –   Simplicity in speech. Matthew 5:33–37, James 5:12
Friday   –   Simplicity and justice. Amos 5:11–15, 24, Luke 4:16–21
Saturday   –   The freedom from covetousness. Luke 12:13–34

Study Questions

1 What are the two aspects of simplicity and why are *both* essential?
2 In one paragraph, attempt to set forth the biblical teaching on possessions.
3 What would the concept of the year of Jubilee look like in modern society (Lev. 25:8–12)?
4 What do I set forth as the focal point for an understanding of Christian simplicity?
5 What are the three inward attitudes of simplicity? Of the three, which do you find the most difficult for you personally?
6 What is the great danger in setting forth an outward expression to Christian simplicity? Why *must* we take the risk?
7 Which of the ten controlling principles for outward

simplicity is the most helpful to you? Are there any you feel are unrealistic?

8 What is producing an addiction in you?

9 Wrestle with the implications of the ninth principle. (Reject anything that will breed the oppression of others.)

10 List one thing which you could do this next week to simplify your life. Do it.

Suggestions for Further Reading

Foster, Richard, *Freedom of Simplicity*, London: Triangle/SPCK, 1981. Attempts to place simplicity within the context of the whole of Christian devotion and to bring together the various emphases upon inner and outer simplicity.

Hengel, Martin, *Property and Riches in the Early Church*, Philadelphia, USA: Fortress Press, 1974. A scholarly study of the Christian approach to property and riches from the time of Christ – there is also a brief discussion of Old Testament views – up to about the fourth century. Extensive attention is given to the Ante-Nicene Fathers.

Sider, Ronald J., *Rich Christians in an Age of Hunger*, London: Hodder & Stoughton, 1978. Extremely valuable biblical and practical study of the question of justice in modern society. 'Must' reading.

Sugden, Christopher, *Radical Discipleship*, Basingstoke: Marshall Pickering, 1981. A challenging and biblical analysis of the calling to a truly Christian lifestyle.

7

The Discipline of Solitude

Settle yourself in solitude and you will come upon Him in yourself.
— Teresa of Ávila

Jesus calls us from loneliness to solitude. The fear of being left alone petrifies people. A new child in the neighbourhood sobs to her mother, 'No one ever plays with me.' A college freshman yearns for his high school days when he was the centre of attention: 'Now, I'm a nobody.' A business executive sits dejected in her office, powerful, yet alone. An old woman lies in a nursing home waiting to go 'Home.'

Our fear of being alone drives us to noise and crowds. We keep up a constant stream of words even if they are inane. We buy radios that strap to our wrists or fit over our ears so that, if no one else is around, at least we are not condemned to silence. T. S. Eliot analyses our culture well when he writes, 'Where shall the world be found, where will the word resound? Not here, there is not enough silence.'[1]

But loneliness or clatter are not our only alternatives. We can cultivate an inner solitude and silence that sets us free from loneliness and fear. Loneliness is inner emptiness. Solitude is inner fulfilment.

Solitude is more a state of mind and heart than it is a place. There is a solitude of the heart that can be maintained at all times. Crowds, or the lack of them, have little to do with this inward attentiveness. It is quite possible to be a desert hermit and never experience solitude. But if we possess inward solitude we do not fear being alone, for we know that we are not alone. Neither do we fear being with others, for they do not control us. In the midst of noise and confusion we are settled into a deep inner silence. Whether alone or among people, we always carry with us a portable sanctuary of the heart.

Inward solitude has outward manifestations. There is the freedom to be alone, not in order to be away from people but in order to hear the divine Whisper better. Jesus lived in inward 'heart solitude.' He also frequently experienced outward solitude. He inaugurated his ministry by spending forty days alone in the desert (Matt. 4:1–11). Before he chose the twelve he spent the entire night alone in the desert hills (Luke 6:12). When he received the news of John the Baptist's death, he 'withdrew from there in a boat to a lonely place apart' (Matt. 14:13). After the miraculous feeding of the five thousand Jesus 'went up into the hills by himself . . .' (Matt. 14:23). Following a long night of work, 'in the morning, a great while before day, he rose and went out to a lonely place . . .' (Mark 1:35). When the twelve returned from a preaching and healing mission, Jesus instructed them, 'Come away by yourselves to a lonely place' (Mark 6:31). Following the healing of a leper Jesus 'withdrew to the wilderness and prayed' (Luke 5:16). With three disciples he sought out the silence of a lonely mountain as the stage for the transfiguration (Matt. 17:1–9). As he prepared for his highest and most holy work, Jesus sought the solitude of the garden of Gethsemane (Matt. 26:36–46). I could go on, but perhaps this is sufficient to show that the seeking out of solitary places was a regular practice for Jesus. So it should be for us.

Dietrich Bonhoeffer in *Life Together* titled one of his chapters 'The Day Together' and the following chapter 'The Day Alone.' Both are essential for spiritual success. He writes, 'Let him who cannot be alone beware of community . . . Let him who is not in community beware of being alone . . . Each by itself has profound pitfalls and perils. One who wants fellowship without solitude plunges into the void of words and feelings, and one who seeks solitude without fellowship perishes in the abyss of vanity, self-infatuation, and despair.'[2]

Therefore, we must seek out the recreating stillness of solitude if we want to be with others meaningfully. We must seek the fellowship and accountability of others if we want to be alone safely. We must cultivate both if we are to live in obedience.

SOLITUDE AND SILENCE

Without silence there is no solitude. Though silence sometimes involves the absence of speech, it always involves the act of listening. Simply to refrain from talking, without a heart listening to God, is not silence. 'A day filled with noise and voices can be a day of silence, if the noises become for us the echo of the presence of God, if the voices are, for us, messages and solicitations of God. When we speak of ourselves and are filled with ourselves, we leave silence behind. When we repeat the intimate words of God that he has left within us, our silence remains intact.'[3]

We must understand the connection between inner solitude and inner silence; they are inseparable. All the masters of the interior life speak of the two in the same breath. For example, *The Imitation of Christ*, which has been the unchallenged master-piece of devotional literature for five hundred years, has a section titled 'On the Love of Solitude and Silence.' Dietrich Bonhoeffer makes the two an inseparable whole in *Life Together* as does Thomas Merton in *Thoughts in Solitude*. In fact, I wrestled for some time trying to decide whether to title this chapter the Discipline of solitude or the Discipline of silence, so closely connected are the two in the great devotional literature. Of necessity, therefore, we must come to understand and experience the transforming power of silence if we are to know solitude.

There is an old proverb to the effect that 'all those who open their mouths, close their eyes!' The purpose of silence and solitude is to be able to see and hear. Control rather than no noise is the key to silence. James saw clearly that the person who could control his tongue is perfect (James 3:1–12). Under the Discipline of silence and solitude we learn when to speak and when to refrain from speaking. The person who views the Disciplines as laws will always turn silence into an absurdity: 'I'll not speak for the next forty days!' This is always a severe temptation to any true disciple who wants to live under silence and solitude. Thomas à Kempis writes, 'It is easier to be silent altogether than to speak with moderation.'4 The wise preacher of Ecclesiastes says that there is 'a time to keep silence and a time to speak' (Eccles. 3:7). Control is the key.

James' analogies of the rudder and the bridle suggest to us that the tongue guides as well as controls. The tongue guides our course in many ways. If we tell a lie, we are led to telling more lies to cover up the first lie. Soon we are forced to behave in a certain way in order to give credence to the lie. No wonder James declares that 'the tongue is a fire' (James 3:6).

The disciplined person is the person who can do what needs to be done when it needs to be done. The mark of a championship basketball team is a team that can score points when they are needed. Most of us can get the ball into the hoop eventually, but we can't do it when it is needed. Likewise, a person who is under the Discipline of silence is a person who can say what needs to be said when it needs to be said. 'A word fitly spoken is like apples of gold in a setting of silver' (Prov. 25:11). If we are silent when we should speak, we are not living in the Discipline of silence. If we speak when we should be silent, we again miss the mark.

THE SACRIFICE OF FOOLS

In Ecclesiastes we read, 'To draw near to listen is better than to offer the sacrifice of fools' (Eccles. 5:1). The sacrifice of fools is humanly initiated religious talk. The preacher continues, 'Be not rash with your mouth, nor let your heart be hasty to utter a word before God, for God is in heaven, and you upon earth; therefore let your words be few' (Eccles. 5:2).

When Jesus took Peter, James, and John up to the mountain and was transfigured before them, Moses and Elijah appeared and carried on a conversation with Jesus. The Greek text goes on to say, 'And *answering*, Peter said to them . . . if you will I will make here three shelters . . .' (Matt. 17:4, [italics added]). That is so telling. No one was even speaking to Peter. He was offering the sacrifice of fools.

John Woolman's *Journal* contains a moving and tender account of learning control over the tongue. His words are so graphic that they are best quoted in full:

'I went to meetings in an awful frame of mind, and endeavoured to be inwardly acquainted with the language of the true Shepherd. One day, being under a strong exercise of spirit, I stood up and said some words in a meeting; but not keeping close to the Divine opening, I said more than was required of me. Being soon sensible of my error, I was afflicted in mind some weeks, without any light or comfort, even to that degree that I could not take satisfaction in anything. I remembered God, and was troubled, and in the depth of my distress he had pity upon me, and sent the Comforter. I then felt forgiveness for my offence; my mind became calm and quiet, and I was truly thankful to my gracious Redeemer for his mercies. About six weeks after this, feeling the spring of Divine love opened, and a concern to speak, I said a few words in a meeting, in which I found peace. Being thus humbled and disciplined under the cross, my understanding became more strengthened to distinguish the pure spirit which inwardly moves upon the heart, and which taught me to wait in silence sometimes many weeks together, until I felt that rise which prepares the creature to stand like a trumpet, through which the Lord speaks to his flock.'[5]

What a description of the learning process one goes through in the Discipline of silence! Of particular significance was Woolman's increased ability from this experience to 'distinguish the pure spirit which inwardly moves upon the heart.'

One reason we can hardly bear to remain silent is that it makes us feel so helpless. We are so accustomed to relying upon words to manage and control others. If we are silent, who will take control? God will take control, but we will never let him take control until we trust him. Silence is intimately related to trust.

The tongue is our most powerful weapon of manipulation. A frantic stream of words flows from us because we are in a constant process of adjusting our public image. We fear so deeply what we think other people see in us that we talk in order to straighten out their understanding. If I have done some wrong thing (or even some right thing that I think you may misunderstand) and discover that you know about it, I will be very tempted to help you understand my action! Silence is one of the deepest Disciplines of the Spirit simply because it puts the stopper on all self-justification.

One of the fruits of silence is the freedom to let God be our justifier. We don't need to straighten others out. There is a story of a medieval monk who was being unjustly accused of certain offences. One day he looked out his window and saw a dog biting and tearing on a rug that had been hung out to dry. As he watched, the Lord spoke to him saying, 'That is what is happening to your reputation. But if you will trust me, I will care for you – reputation and all.' Perhaps more than anything else, silence brings us to believe that God can care for us – 'reputation and all.'

George Fox often speaks of 'the spirit of bondage' and how the world lays in that spirit. Frequently he identifies the spirit of bondage with the spirit of subservience to other human beings. In his *Journal* he speaks of 'bringing people off of men,' away from that spirit of bondage to law through other human beings. And silence is one way of bringing us into this liberation.

The tongue is a thermometer; it gives us our spiritual temperature. It is also a thermostat; it regulates our spiritual temperature. Control of the tongue can mean everything. Have we been set free so that we can hold our tongue? Bonhoeffer writes, 'Real silence, real stillness, really holding one's tongue comes only as the sober consequence of spiritual stillness.'[6] St Dominic is reported to have visited St Francis, and throughout the entire meeting neither spoke a single word. Only when we learn to be truly silent are we able to speak the word that is needed *when* it is needed.

Catherine de Haeck Doherty writes, 'All in me is silent and . . . I am immersed in the silence of God.'[7] It is in solitude that we come to experience the 'silence of God' and so receive the inner silence that is the craving of our hearts.

THE DARK NIGHT OF THE SOUL

To take seriously the Discipline of solitude will mean that at some point or points along the pilgrimage we will enter what St John of the Cross vividly describes as 'the dark night of the soul.' The 'dark night' to which he calls us is not something bad or destructive. On the contrary, it is an experience to be welcomed much as a sick person might welcome a surgery that promises health and well-being. The purpose of the darkness is not to punish or to afflict us. It is to set us free. It is a divine appointment, a privileged opportunity to draw close to the divine Centre. St John calls it 'sheer grace,' adding:

> O guiding night!
> O night more lovely than the dawn!
> O night that has united

The Lover with His beloved,
Transforming the beloved in her Lover.[8]

What does the dark night of the soul involve? We may have a sense of dryness, aloneness, even lostness. Any overdependence on the emotional life is stripped away. The notion, often heard today, that such experiences should be avoided and that we always should live in peace and comfort, joy, and celebration only betrays the fact that much contemporary experience is surface slush. The dark night is one of the ways God brings us into a hush, a stillness so that he may work an inner transformation upon the soul.

How is this dark night expressed in daily life? When solitude is seriously pursued, there is usually a flush of initial success and then an inevitable letdown – and with it a desire to abandon the pursuit altogether. Feelings leave and there is the sense that we are not getting through to God. St John of the Cross describes it this way, '. . . the darkness of the soul mentioned here . . . puts the sensory and spiritual appetites to sleep . . . It binds the imagination and impedes it from doing any good discursive work. It makes the memory cease, the intellect become dark and unable to understand anything, and hence it causes the will also to become arid and constrained, and all the faculties empty and useless. And over all this hangs a dense and burdensome cloud which afflicts the soul and keeps it withdrawn from God.'[9]

Twice in his poem 'Canciones del Alma' St John of the Cross uses the phrase, 'My house being now all stilled.'[10] In this graphic line he indicates the importance of allowing all the physical, emotional, psychological, even spiritual senses to be silenced. Every distraction of the body, mind, and spirit must be put into a kind of suspended animation before this deep work of God upon the soul can occur. It is like an operation in which the anaesthetic must take effect before the surgery can be performed. There comes inner silence, peace, stillness. During such a time

Bible reading, sermons, intellectual debate – all fail to move or excite us.

When God lovingly draws us into a dark night of the soul, there is often a temptation to seek release from it and to blame everyone and everything for our inner dullness. The preacher is such a bore. The hymn singing is too weak. The worship service is so dull. We may begin to look around for another church or a new experience to give us 'spiritual goose bumps.' This is a serious mistake. Recognise the dark night for what it is. Be grateful that God is lovingly drawing you away from every distraction so that you can see him clearly. Rather than chafing and fighting, become still and wait.

I am not referring here to the dullness to spiritual things that comes as a result of sin or disobedience, but I am speaking of the person who is seeking hard after God and who harbours no known sin in his heart.

> Who among you fears the LORD
>   and obeys the voice of his servant,
> *who walks in darkness*
>   *and has no light,*
> yet trusts in the name of the LORD
>   and relies upon his God? (Isa. 50:10, [italics added])

The point of the biblical passage is that it is quite possible to fear, obey, trust, and rely upon the Lord and still 'walk in darkness and have no light.' We are living in obedience but we have entered a dark night of the soul.

St John of the Cross indicates that during this experience there is a gracious protection from vices and a wonderful advance in the things of the kingdom of God. '. . . a person at the time of these darknesses . . . will see clearly how little the appetites and faculties are distracted with useless and harmful things and how secure he is from vainglory, from pride and presumption, from an empty and false joy, and from many other evils. By walking in darkness the soul . . . advances rapidly, because it thus gains the virtues.'[11]

What should we do during such a time of inward darkness? First, disregard the advice of well-meaning friends to snap out of it. They do not understand what is occurring. Our age is so ignorant of such things that I recommend that you not even talk about these matters. Above all, do not try to explain or justify why you may be 'out of sorts.' God is your justifier; rest your case with him. If you can actually withdraw to a 'desert place' for a season, do so. If not, go about your daily tasks. But whether in the 'desert' or at home, hold in your heart a deep, inner, listening silence and there be still until the work of solitude is done.

Perhaps St John of the Cross has been leading us into deeper waters than we care to go. Certainly he is talking about a realm that most of us see only 'through a glass darkly.' Yet we do not need to censure ourselves for our timidity to scale these snowy peaks of the soul. These matters are best approached cautiously. But perhaps he has stirred within us a drawing towards higher and deeper experiences, no matter how slight the tug. It is like opening the door of our lives ever so slightly to this realm. That is all God asks, and all he needs.

To conclude our journey into the dark night of the soul, let us ponder these powerful words of our spiritual mentor: 'Oh, then, spiritual soul, when you see your appetites darkened, your inclinations dry and constrained, your faculties incapacitated for any interior exercise, do not be afflicted; think of this as a grace, since God is freeing you from yourself and taking from you your own activity.'[12]

STEPS INTO SOLITUDE

The Spiritual Disciplines are things that we do. We must never lose sight of this fact. It is one thing to talk piously about 'the solitude of the heart,' but if that does not somehow work its way into our experience, then we have missed the point of the Disciplines. We are dealing with actions, not merely states of mind. It is not enough to say, 'Well, I am most certainly in possession of inner solitude and silence; there is nothing that I need to do.' All those who have come into the living silences have done certain things, have ordered their lives in a particular way so as to receive this 'peace that passes all understanding.' If we are to succeed, we must pass beyond the theoretical into life situations.

What are some steps into solitude? The first thing we can do is to take advantage of the 'little solitudes' that fill our day. Consider the solitude of those early morning moments in bed before the family awakens. Think of the solitude of a morning cup of coffee before beginning the work of the day. There is the solitude of bumper-to-bumper traffic during the rush hour. There can be little moments of rest and refreshment when we turn a corner and see a flower or a tree. Instead of vocal prayer before a meal consider inviting everyone to join into a few moments of gathered silence. Once while driving a car-load of chattering children and adults, I exclaimed, 'Let's play a game and see if everyone can be absolutely quiet until we reach the airport' (about five minutes away). It worked, blessedly so. Find new joy and meaning in the little walk from the subway to your apartment. Slip outside just before bed and taste the silent night.

These tiny snatches of time are often lost to us. What a pity! They can and should be redeemed. They are times for inner quiet, for reorienting our lives like a compass needle. They are little moments that help us to be genuinely present where we are.

What else can we do? We can find or develop a 'quiet place' designed for silence and solitude. Homes are being built constantly. Why not insist that a little inner sanctuary be put into the plans, a small place where any family member could go to be alone and silent? What's to stop us? The money? We build elaborate playrooms and family rooms and think it well worth the expense. Those who already own a home could consider enclosing a little section of the garage or patio. Those who live in an apartment could be creative and find other ways to allow for solitude. I know of one family that has a special chair; whenever anyone sits in it he or she is saying, 'Please don't bother me, I want to be alone.'

Let's find places outside the home: a spot in a park, a church sanctuary that is kept unlocked, even a storage closet somewhere. A retreat centre near us has built a lovely one-person cabin specifically for private meditation and solitude. It is called 'The Quiet Place.' Churches invest millions of dollars in buildings. How about constructing one place where an individual can come to be alone for several days? Catherine de Hueck Doherty has pioneered in developing 'Poustinias' (a Russian word meaning 'desert') in North America. These are places specifically designed for solitude and silence.*

In the chapter on study we considered the importance of observing ourselves to see how often our speech is a frantic attempt to explain and justify our actions. Having seen this in ourselves, let's experiment with doing deeds without any words of explanation whatever. We note our sense of fear that people will misunderstand why we have done what we have done. We seek to allow God to be our justifier.

Let's discipline ourselves so that our words are few and full. Let's become known as people who have something to say when we speak. Let's maintain plain speech: do what we say we will do. 'It is better that you should not vow than that you should vow and not pay' (Eccles. 5:5). When our tongue is under our authority the words of Bonhoeffer become true of us: 'Much that is unnecessary remains unsaid. But the essential and the helpful thing can be said in a few words.'[13]

_____

* The story of the development of these centres is described in her book, *Poustinia: Christian Spirituality of the East for Western Man*, London: Fount, 1977.

Go another step. Try to live one entire day without words at all. Do it not as a law, but as an experiment. Note your feelings of helplessness and excessive dependence upon words to communicate. Try to find new ways to relate to others that are not dependent upon words. Enjoy, savour the day. Learn from it.

Four times a year withdraw for three to four hours for the purpose of reorienting your life goals. This can easily be done in one evening. Stay late at your office or do it at home or find a quiet corner in a public library. Reevaluate your goals and objectives in life. What do you want to have accomplished one year from now? Ten years from now? Our tendency is to overestimate what we can accomplish in one year and underestimate what we can accomplish in ten years. Set realistic goals but be willing to dream, to stretch. (This book was a dream in my mind for several years before it became a reality.) In the quiet of those brief hours, listen to the thunder of God's silence. Keep a journal record of what comes to you.

Reorientation and goal setting do not need to be cold and calculating as some suppose. Goals are discovered, not made. God delights in showing us exciting new alternatives for the future. Perhaps as you enter into a listening silence the joyful impression to learn how to weave or how to make pottery emerges. Does that sound too earthy, too unspiritual a goal? God is intently interested in such matters. Are you? Maybe you will want to learn and experience more about the spiritual gifts of miracles, healing, and tongues. Or you may do as one of my friends: spend large periods of time experiencing the gift of helps, learning to be a servant. Perhaps this next year you would like to read all the writings of C. S. Lewis or D. Elton Trueblood. Maybe five years from now you would like to be qualified to work with handicapped children. Does choosing these goals sound like a sales manipulation game? Of course not. It is merely setting a direction for your life. You are going to go somewhere so how much better to have a direction that has been set by communion with the divine Centre.

Under the Discipline of study we explored the idea of study retreats of two or three days' duration. Such experiences are heightened when they are combined with an inner immersion into the silence of God. Like Jesus, we must go away from people so that we can be truly present when we are with people. Take a retreat once a year with no other purpose in mind but solitude.

The fruit of solitude is increased sensitivity and compassion for others. There comes a new freedom to be with people. There is new attentiveness to their needs, new responsiveness to their hurts. Thomas Merton observes, 'It is in deep solitude that I find the gentleness with which I can truly love my brothers. The more solitary I am the more affection I have for them . . . Solitude and silence teach me to love my brothers for what they are, not for what they say.'[14]

Don't you feel a tug, a yearning to sink down into the silence and solitude of God? Don't you long for something more? Doesn't every breath crave a deeper, fuller exposure to his Presence? It is the Discipline of solitude that will open the door. You are welcome to come in and 'listen to God's speech in his wondrous, terrible, gentle, loving, all-embracing silence.'[15]

FOR STUDY

Henri Nouwen has noted that, 'Without solitude it is virtually impossible to live a spiritual life.' Why is this so? Because in solitude we are freed *from* our bondage to people and our inner compulsions, and we are freed *to* love God and know compassion for others.

To enter solitude we must disregard what others think of us. Who will understand this call to aloneness? Even our closest friends will see it as a terrible waste of precious time and as rather selfish and self-centred. But, oh, what liberty is released in our hearts when we let go of the opinions of others! The less we are mesmerised by human voices, the more we are able to hear the divine Voice. The less we are bound by others' expectations, the more we are open to God's expectations.

But in solitude we die not only to others but also ourselves. To be sure, at first we thought solitude was a way to recharge our batteries in order to enter life's many competitions with new vigour and strength. In time, however, we found that solitude did not give us power to win the rat race; on the contrary, it taught us to ignore it altogether. Slowly, we found ourselves letting go of our inner compulsions to win and our frantic efforts to attain. In the stillness our false, busy selves were unmasked and seen for the impostors they truly were.

It is out of our liberation from others and self that our ears become open to hear and our eyes unveiled to see the goodness of God. We can love God because we do not have to love the world. Through our solitude an open inner space has been created through which God finds us. In solitude we experience a second (and third, and fourth, and fifth . . .) conversion. In a deeper more profound way we turn from the idols of the marketplace to the glory of God in the face of Jesus Christ. God takes this useless discipline, this wasted time, to make us His friend.

A happy by-product of becoming the friend of God is an increased compassion for others. Once we have peered into the abyss of our own vanity we can never again look at the struggles of others with condescending superiority. Once we have faced the demons of despair in our own aloneness, we can never again pass off lightly the quiet depression and sad loneliness of those we meet. We become one with all who hurt and are afraid. We are free to give them the greatest gift we possess – the gift of ourselves.

The private retreat is one way to nurture solitude. Earlier I shared several ideas regarding what to do in a private retreat; however, it is of utmost importance that we do not lose sight of our major work on retreat. It can be said in one word – PRAYER. We enter the terrifying silences to listen to God, to experience communion. This purpose needs to be kept before us because, at first, time thus spent will seem so useless, so wasted. We will soon be severely tempted to make 'good use of our time' by reading many books or writing many pages. What we must clearly understand and underscore is that our real task on retreat is to create a space in our lives where God can reach us. Once that space has been created we wait quietly, expectantly, for the work from this point on belongs to God. And I have found Him most eager to usher us into the Holy of Holies and share with us the glories of the Kingdom of God.

In *Fruits of Solitude* William Penn observed that solitude is 'A school few care to learn in, tho' none instructs us better'. May we be among the few that care to learn through this merciful means of God's grace.

Daily Scripture Readings

Sunday	— The freedom to control the tongue. James 3:1–12, Luke 23:6–9
Monday	— Prayer and solitude. Matthew 6:5–6, Luke 5:16
Tuesday	— The insights of solitude. Psalm 8
Wednesday	— The dark night of the soul. Jeremiah 20:7–18
Thursday	— The solitude of the garden. Matthew 26:36–46
Friday	— The solitude of the cross. Matthew 27:32–50
Saturday	— The compassion that comes from solitude. Matthew 9:35–38, 23:37

Study Questions

1 What is the difference between loneliness and solitude? Which do you experience more?
2 Why do we need both solitude and community in order to function with spiritual success?
3 Why do you think that solitude and silence are so closely connected?

4 What is the 'sacrifice of fools'? Have you ever been guilty?
5 Have you ever had any experience akin to Catherine de Hueck Doherty's, 'All in me is silent and . . . I am immersed in the silence of God'? If so you might want to share it with someone, if not you might want to ponder the reason for the lack.
6 Have you ever experienced a 'dark night of the soul'?
7 I mention five possible steps into solitude. Which one would you find most helpful at this point in your life?
8 What keeps you from solitude?
9 What practical reordering of your life could be done in order to create more space for God?
10 What experience in solitude would you like to have, two years from now, that you do not presently possess? Would you be willing this week to plan it into your schedule for some time in the next twenty-four months?

Suggestions for Further Reading

Doherty, Catherine de Hueck, *Poustinia: Christian Spirituality of the East for Western Man*, London: Fount, 1977. A sensitive and highly applicable discussion of how Western culture can find space for the life of solitude.

Dunne, John S., *The Reasons of the Heart*, London: SCM Press, 1978. A journey into solitude and back again, examining the way Christian faith might transform pain and loneliness.

Maloney, George A., S. J., *Alone with the Alone*, Notre Dame, USA: Ave Maria Press, 1982. Helps the individual enter into the experience of God – the Alone – through the format of an eight-day retreat.

Waddell, Helen, trans., *The Desert Fathers*, London: Constable & Co, 1987. Contains many of the wise sayings of the Desert Fathers as well as the stories of their experiences.

8

The Discipline of Submission

A Christian is a perfectly free lord of all, subject to none. A Christian is a perfectly dutiful servant of all, subject to all.

— Martin Luther

Of all the Spiritual Disciplines none has been more abused than the Discipline of submission. Somehow the human species has an extraordinary knack for taking the best teaching and turning it to the worst ends. Nothing can put people into bondage like religion, and nothing in religion has done more to manipulate and destroy people than a deficient teaching on submission. Therefore, we must work our way through this Discipline with great care and discernment in order to ensure that we are the ministers of life, not death.

Every Discipline has its corresponding freedom. If I have schooled myself in the art of rhetoric, I am free to deliver a moving speech when the occasion requires it. Demosthenes was free to be an orator only because he had gone through the discipline of speaking above the ocean roar with pebbles in his mouth. The purpose of the Disciplines is freedom. Our aim is the freedom, not the Discipline. The moment we make the Discipline our central focus, we turn it into law and lose the corresponding freedom.

The Disciplines are for the purpose of realising a greater good. In and of themselves they are of no value whatever. They have value only as a means of setting us before God so that he can give us the liberation we seek. The liberation is the end; the Disciplines are *merely* the means. They are not the answer; they only lead us to the Answer. We must clearly understand this limitation of the Disciplines if we are to avoid bondage. Not only must we understand, but we need to underscore it to ourselves again and again so severe is our temptation to centre on the Disciplines. Let us forever centre on Christ and view the Spiritual Disciplines as a way of drawing us closer to his heart.

THE FREEDOM IN SUBMISSION

I said that every Discipline has its corresponding freedom. What freedom corresponds to submission? It is the ability to lay down the terrible burden of always needing to get our own way. The obsession to demand that things go the way we want them to go is one of the greatest bondages in human society today. People will spend weeks, months, even years in a perpetual stew because some little thing did not go as they wished. They will fuss and fume. They will get mad about it. They will act as if their very life hangs on the issue. They may even get an ulcer over it.

In the Discipline of submission we are released to drop the matter, to forget it. Frankly, most things in life are not nearly as important as we think they are. Our lives will not come to an end if this or that does not happen.

If you will watch these things, you will see, for example, that almost all church fights and splits occur because people do not have the freedom to give in to each other. We insist that a critical issue is at stake; we are fighting for a sacred principle. Perhaps this is the case. Usually it is not. Often we cannot stand to give in simply because it means that we will not get our own way. Only in submission are we enabled to bring this spirit to a place where it no longer controls us. Only submission can free us sufficiently to enable us to distinguish between genuine issues and stubborn self-will.

If we could only come to see that most things in life are not major issues, then we could hold them lightly. We discover that they are no 'big deal.' So often we say, 'Well, I don't care,' when what we really mean (and what we convey to others) is that we care a great deal. It is precisely here that silence fits in so well with all the other Disciplines. Usually the best way to handle most matters of submission is to say nothing. There is the need for an all-encompassing spirit of grace beyond any kind of language or action which sets others and ourselves free.

The biblical teaching on submission focuses primarily on the spirit with which we view other people. Scripture does not attempt to set forth a series of hierarchical relationships but to communicate to us an inner attitude of mutual subordination. Peter, for example, called upon the slaves of his day to live in submission to their masters (1 Pet. 2:18). The counsel seems unnecessary until we realise that it is quite possible for servants to obey their masters without living in a spirit of submission to them. Outwardly we can do what people ask and inwardly be in rebellion against them. This concern for a spirit of consideration towards others pervades the entire New Testament. The old covenant stipulated that we must not murder. Jesus, however, stressed that the real issue was the inner spirit of murder with which we view people. In the matter of submission the same is true; the real issue is the spirit of consideration and respect we have for each other.

In submission we are at last free to value other people. Their dreams and plans become important to us. We have entered into a new, wonderful, glorious freedom – the freedom to give up our own rights for the good of others. For the first time we can love people unconditionally. We have given up the right to demand that they return our love. No longer do we feel that we have to be treated in a certain way. We rejoice in their successes. We feel genuine sorrow in their failures. It is of little consequence that our plans are frustrated if their plans succeed. We discover that it is far better to serve our neighbour than to have our own way.

Do you know the liberation that comes from giving up your rights? It means you are set free from the seething anger and bitterness you feel when someone doesn't act towards you the way you think they should. It means that at last you are able to break that vicious law of commerce that says, 'You scratch my back, I'll scratch your back; you bloody my nose, I'll bloody your nose.' It means you are free to obey Jesus' command, 'Love your enemies and pray for those who persecute you' (Matt. 5:44). It means that for the first time you understand how it is possible to surrender the right to retaliate: 'If any one strikes you on the right cheek, turn to him the other also' (Matt. 5:39).

A TOUCHSTONE

You may have noticed that I have been approaching the matter of submission through the back door. I began by explaining what it does for us before defining what it is. This has been done for a purpose. Most of us have been exposed to such a mutilated form of biblical submission that either we have embraced the deformity or we have rejected the Discipline altogether. To do the former leads to self-hatred; to do the latter leads to self-glorification. Before we become hung on the horns of this dilemma, let's consider a third alternative.

The touchstone for the biblical understanding of submission is Jesus' astonishing statement, 'If any man would come after me, let him deny himself and take up his cross and follow me' (Mark 8:34). Almost instinctively we draw back from these words. We are much more comfortable with words like 'self-fulfilment' and 'self-actualisation' than we are with the thought of 'self-denial.' (In reality, Jesus' teaching on self-denial is the only thing that will bring genuine self-fulfilment and self-actualisation.) Self-denial conjures up in our minds all sorts of images of grovelling and self-hatred. We imagine that it most certainly means the rejection of our individuality and will probably lead to various forms of self-mortification.

On the contrary, Jesus calls us to self-denial without self-hatred. Self-denial is simply a way of coming to understand that we do not have to have our own way. Our happiness is not dependent upon getting what we want.

Self-denial does not mean the loss of our identity as some suppose. Without our identity we could not even be subject to each other. Did Jesus lose his identity when he set his face towards Golgotha? Did Peter lose his identity when he responded to Jesus' cross-bearing command, 'Follow me' (John 21:19)? Did Paul lose his identity when he committed himself to the One who had said, 'I will show him how much he must suffer for the sake of my name' (Acts 9:16)? Of course not. We know that the opposite was true. They found their identity in the act of self-denial.

Self-denial is not the same thing as self-contempt. Self-contempt claims that we have no worth, and even if we do have worth, we should reject it. Self-denial declares that we are of infinite worth and shows us how to realise it. Self-contempt denies the goodness of the creation; self-denial affirms that it is indeed good. Jesus made the ability to love ourselves the pre-requisite for our reaching out to others (Matt. 22:39). Self-love and self-denial are not in conflict. More than once Jesus made it quite clear that self-denial is the only sure way to love ourselves. 'He who finds his life will lose it, and he who loses his life for my sake will find it' (Matt. 10:39).

Again, we must underscore that self-denial means the freedom to give way to others. It means to hold others' interests above our interests. In this way self-denial releases us from self-pity. When we live outside of self-denial, we demand that things go our way. When they do not, we revert to self-pity – 'Poor me!' Outwardly we may submit but we do so in a spirit of martyrdom. This spirit of self-pity, of martyrdom, is a sure sign that the Discipline of submission has gone to seed. This is why self-denial is the foundation for submission; it saves us from self-indulgence.

Modern men and women find it extremely difficult to read the great devotional masters because they make such lavish use of the language of self-denial. It is hard for us to be open to the words of Thomas à Kempis, 'To have no opinion of ourselves, and to think always well and highly of others, is great wisdom and perfection.'[1] We struggle to listen to the words of Jesus, 'If any man would come after me, let him deny himself and take up his cross and follow me' (Mark 8:34). Our difficulty is due primarily to the fact that we have failed to understand Jesus' teaching that the way to self-fulfilment is through self-denial. To save the life is to lose it; to lose it for Christ's sake is to save it (Mark 8:35). George Matheson set into the hymnody of the Church this wonderful paradox of fulfilment through self-denial:

> Make me a captive, Lord,
>   And then I shall be free;
> Force me to render up my sword,
>   And I shall conqueror be.
> I sink in life's alarms
>   When by myself I stand;
> Imprison me within Thine arms,
>   And strong shall be my hand.[2]

Perhaps the air has been sufficiently cleared so that we can look upon self-denial as the liberation that it really is. We must be convinced of this for, as has been stated, self-denial is the touchstone for the Discipline of submission.

REVOLUTIONARY SUBORDINATION AS TAUGHT BY JESUS*

The most radical social teaching of Jesus was his total reversal of the contemporary notion of greatness. Leadership is found in becoming the servant of all. Power is discovered in submission. The foremost symbol of this radical servanthood is the cross. 'He [Jesus] humbled himself and became obedient unto death, even death on a cross' (Phil. 2:8). But note this: Christ not only died a 'cross–death,' he lived a 'cross–life.' The way of the cross, the way of a suffering servant was essential to his Ministry. Jesus lived the cross-life in submission to all human beings. He was the servant of all. He flatly rejected the cultural 'givens' of position and power when he said, 'You are not to be called rabbi . . . Neither be called masters . . .' (Matt. 23:8–10). Jesus shattered the customs of his day when he lived out the cross-life by taking women seriously and by being willing to meet with children. He lived the cross-life when he took a towel and washed the feet of his disciples. This Jesus who easily could have called down a legion of angels to his aid chose instead the cross-death of Calvary. Jesus' life was the cross-life of submission and service. Jesus' death was the cross–death of conquest by suffering.

It is impossible to overstate the revolutionary character of Jesus' life and teaching at this point. It did away with all the claims to privileged position and status. It called into being a whole new order of leadership. The cross-life of Jesus undermined all social orders based on power and self-interest.**

---

* I am indebted to John Howard Yoder for this term and for several of the ideas listed under it. His book, *The Politics of Jesus*, Grand Rapids, Ml: Eerdmans, 1972, contains an excellent chapter on Revolutionary Subordination.

** The Church today has failed to understand or, if it understands, has failed to obey the implications of the cross-life for human society. Guy Hershberger courageously explores some of these implications in his book, *The Way of the Cross in Human Relations*, Scottsdale, PA: Herald Press, 1958. He discusses how the way of servanthood should affect such issues as war, capitalism, trade unions, labour unions, materialism, employer–employer relations, race relations, and others. I am indebted to Hershberger for the term 'cross-life.'

As I noted earlier, Jesus called his followers to live the cross-life. 'If any man would come after me, let him deny himself and take up his cross and follow me' (Mark 8:34). He flatly told his disciples, 'If any one would be first, he must be last of all and servant of all' (Mark 9:35). When Jesus immortalised the principle of the cross-life by washing the disciples' feet, he added, 'I have given you an example, that you also should do as I have done to you' (John 13:15). The cross-life is the life of voluntary submission. The cross-life is the life of freely accepted servanthood.

REVOLUTIONARY SUBORDINATION AS TAUGHT IN THE EPISTLES

Jesus' example and call to follow the way of the cross in all human relationships form the basis for the teaching of the Epistles on submission. The apostle Paul grounds the imperative to the Church to 'count others better than yourselves' in the submission and self-denial of the Lord for our salvation. 'He . . . emptied himself, taking the form of a servant' (Phil. 2:4–7). The apostle Peter, in the middle of his instructions on submission, directly appeals to the example of Jesus as the reason for submission. 'For to this you have been called, because Christ also suffered for you, leaving you an example, that you should follow in his steps . . . When he was reviled, he did not revile in return; when he suffered, he did not threaten; but he trusted to him who judges justly' (1 Pet. 2:21–23). As a preface to the Ephesian *Haustafel** we read, 'Be subject to one another *out of reverence for Christ*' (Eph. 5:21, [italics added]). The call for

---

* A term coined by Martin Luther meaning literally 'house-table,' hence a table of rules for the Christian household. The *Haustafel* has come to be recognised as a particular literary form and can be found in Ephesians 5:21–6:9, Colossians 3:18–4:1, Titus 2:4–10, and 1 Peter 2:18–3:7.

Christians to live the cross-life is rooted in the cross-life of Jesus himself.

The Discipline of submission has been terribly misconstrued and abused from failure to see this wider context. Submission is an ethical theme that runs the gamut of the New Testament. It is a posture obligatory upon *all* Christians: men as well as women, fathers as well as children, masters as well as slaves. We are commanded to live a life of submission because Jesus lived a life of submission, not because we are in a particular place or station in life. Self-denial is a posture fitting for all those who follow the crucified Lord. Everywhere in the *Haustafel* the one and only compelling reason for submission is the example of Jesus.

This singular rationale for submission is staggering when we compare it to other first-century writings. In them there was a constant appeal to submission because that was the way the gods had created things; it was one's station in life. Not a single New Testament writer appeals to submission on that basis. The teaching is revolutionary. They completely ignored all the contemporary customs of superordinate and subordinate and called everyone to 'count others better than yourselves' (Phil. 2:3).

The Epistles first call to subordination those who, by virtue of the given culture, are already subordinate. 'Wives, be subject to your husbands . . . Children, obey your parents . . . Slaves, obey in everything those who are your earthly masters . . .' (Col. 3:18–22 and parallels). The revolutionary thing about this teaching is that these people, to whom first-century culture afforded no choice at all, are addressed as free moral agents. Paul gave personal moral responsibility to those who had no legal or moral status in their culture. He made decision-makers of people who were forbidden to make decisions.

It is astonishing that Paul called them to subordination since they were already subordinate by virtue of their place in first-century culture. The only meaningful reason for such a command was the fact that by virtue of the gospel message they had come to see themselves as free from a subordinate status in society. The gospel had challenged all second-class citizenships, and they knew it. Paul urged voluntary subordination not because it was their station in life, but because it was 'fitting in the Lord' (Col. 3:18).

This feature of addressing moral teaching to the cultural subordinates is also a radical contrast to the contemporary literature of the day. The Stoics, for example, addressed *only* the person on the top side of the social order, encouraging him to do a good job in the superordinate position he already saw as his place. But Paul spoke first to the people that his culture said should not even be addressed and called them to the cross-life of Jesus.

Next, the Epistles turned to the culturally dominant partner in the relationship and also called him to the cross-life of Jesus. The imperative to subordination is reciprocal. 'Husbands, love your wives . . . Fathers, do not provoke your children . . . Masters, treat your slaves justly and fairly . . .' (Col. 3:19–4:1 and parallels). Some most certainly will object that the command to the dominant partner does not use the language of submission. What we fail to see is how much submission those commands demanded of the dominant partner in his cultural setting. For a first-century husband, father, or master to obey Paul's injunction would make a dramatic difference in his behaviour. The first-century wife, child, or slave would not need to change one whit to follow Paul's command. If anything, the sting of the teaching falls upon the dominant partner.[3]

Further, we need to see that these imperatives to husbands, fathers, and masters constitute another form of self-denial. They are just another set of words to convey the same truth, namely, that we can be set free from the need to have things our own way. If a husband loves his wife, he will live in consideration of her needs. He will be willing to give in to her. He will be free to regard her as more important than his own needs. He will be able to regard his children as more important than his own needs (Phil. 2:3).

In Ephesians Paul exhorts slaves to live in a spirit of joyful, voluntary, willing service to their earthly masters. Then he exhorts masters, 'Do the same to them' (Eph. 6:9). Such a thought was incredible in first-century society. Slaves were chattels, not human beings. Yet Paul with divine authority counsels masters to give way to the needs of their slaves.

Perhaps the most perfect illustration of revolutionary subordination is found in Paul's tiny letter to Philemon. Onesimus, Philemon's runaway slave, had become a Christian. He was returning voluntarily to Philemon as part of what it meant for him to be a disciple of Christ. Paul urges Philemon to welcome Onesimus 'no longer as a slave but more than a slave, as a beloved brother . . .' (Philem. 16). John Yoder remarks, This amounts to Paul's instructing Philemon, in the kind of non-coercive instruction which is fitting for a Christian brother, . . . that Onesimus is to be set free.'[4] Onesimus was to be subordinate to Philemon by returning. Philemon was to be subordinate to Onesimus by setting him free. Both were to be mutually subordinate out of reverence for Christ (Eph. 5:21).

The Epistles did not consecrate the existing hierarchical social structure. By making the command to subordination universal they relativised and undercut it. They called for Christians to live as citizens of a new order, and the most fundamental feature of this new order is universal subordination.

THE LIMITS OF SUBMISSION

The limits of the Discipline of submission are at the points at which it becomes destructive. It then becomes a denial of the law of love as taught by Jesus and is an affront to genuine biblical submission (Matt. 5, 6, and 7 and especially 22:37–39).

Peter calls Christians to radical submission to the State when he writes, 'Be subject for the Lord's sake to every human institution, whether it be the emperor as supreme, or to governors . . .' (1 Pet. 2:13, 14). Yet when the properly authorised government of his day commanded the infant Church to stop proclaiming Christ, it was Peter who answered, 'Whether it is right in the sight of God to listen to you rather than to God, you must judge; for we cannot but speak of what we have seen and heard' (Acts 4:19, 20). Upon a similar occasion Peter stated simply, 'We must obey God rather than men' (Acts 5:29).

Understanding the cross-life of Jesus, Paul says, 'Let every person be subject to the governing authorities' (Rom. 13:1). When Paul, however, saw that the State was failing to fulfil its God-ordained function of providing justice for all, he called it to account and insisted that the wrong be righted (Acts 16:37).

Were these men in opposition to their own principle of self-denial and submission? No. They simply understood that submission reaches the end of its tether when it becomes destructive. In fact, they illustrated revolutionary subordination by meekly refusing a destructive command and being willing to suffer the consequences. The German thinker Johannes Hamel says that subordination includes 'the possibility of a spirit-driven resistance, of an appropriate disavowal and a refusal ready to accept suffering at this or that particular point.'[5]

Sometimes the limits of submission are easy to determine. A wife is asked to punish her child unreasonably. A child is asked to aid an adult in an unlawful practice. A citizen is asked to violate the dictates of Scripture and conscience for the sake of the State. In each case the disciple refuses, not arrogantly, but in a spirit of meekness and submission.

Often the limits of submission are extremely hard to define. What about the marriage partner who feels stifled and kept from personal fulfilment because of the spouse's professional career? Is this a legitimate form of self-denial or is it destructive? What about the teacher who unjustly grades a student? Does the student submit or resist? What about the employer who promotes his employees on the basis of favouritism and vested interests? What does the deprived employee do, especially if the raise is needed for the good of his or her family?

These are extremely complicated questions simply because human relationships are complicated. They are questions that do not yield to simplistic answers. There is no such thing as a law of submission that will cover every situation. We must become highly sceptical of all laws that purport to handle every circumstance. Casuistic ethics always fail.

It is not an evasion of the issue to say that in defining the limits of submission we are catapulted into a deep dependence upon the Holy Spirit. After all, if we had a book of rules to cover every circumstance in life, we would not need dependence. The Spirit is an accurate discerner of the thoughts and intents of the heart, both yours and mine. He will be to us a present Teacher and Prophet, instructing us in what to do in every situation.

THE ACTS OF SUBMISSION

Submission and service function concurrently. Hence, much of the practical outflow of submission will come in the next chapter. There are, however, seven acts of submission that I would like to mention briefly.

The first act of submission is to the Triune God. At the beginning of the day we wait, in the words of the hymn writer, 'yielded and still' before Father, Son, and Holy Spirit. The first words of our day form the prayer of Thomas à Kempis, 'As thou wilt; what thou wilt; when thou wilt.'[6] We yield our body, mind, and spirit for his purposes. Likewise, the day is lived in deeds of submission interspersed with constant ejaculations of inward surrender. As the first words of the morning are of submission, so are the last words of the night. We surrender our body, mind, and spirit into the hands of God to do with us as he pleases through the long darkness.

The second act of submission is to the Scripture. As we submit ourselves to the Word of God living (Jesus), so we submit ourselves to the Word of God written (Scripture). We yield ourselves first to hear the Word, second to receive the Word, and third to obey the Word. We look to the Spirit who inspired the Scriptures to interpret and apply them to our condition. The word of Scripture, animated by the Holy Spirit, lives with us throughout the day.

The third act of submission is to our family. The dictum for the household should be 'Let each of you look not only to his own interests, but also to the interests of others' (Phil. 2:4). Freely and graciously the members of the family make allowance for each other. The primary deed of submission is a commitment to listen to the other family members. Its corollary is a willingness to share, which is itself a work of submission.

The fourth act of submission is to our neighbours and those we meet in the course of our daily lives. The life of simple goodness is lived before them. If they are in need, we help them. We perform small acts of kindness and ordinary neighbourliness: sharing our food, baby-sitting their children, mowing their lawn, visiting over important and unimportant matters, sharing our tools. No task is too small, too trifling, for each one is an opportunity to live in submission.

The fifth act of submission is to the believing community, the body of Christ. If there are jobs to be done and tasks to be accomplished, we look at them closely to see if they are God's invitation to the cross-life. We cannot do everything, but we can do some things. Sometimes these are matters of an organisational nature, but most frequently they are spontaneous opportunities for little tasks of service. At times calls to serve the Church universal may come, and if the ministry is confirmed in our hearts, we can submit to it with assurance and reverence.

The sixth act of submission is to the broken and despised. In every culture there are the 'widows and orphans'; that is, the helpless, the undefended (James 1:27). Our first responsibility is to be among them. Like St Francis in the thirteenth century and Kagawa in the twentieth, we must discover ways to identify genuinely with the downtrodden, the rejected. There we must live the cross-life.

The seventh act of submission is to the world. We live in an interdependent, international community. We cannot live in isolation. Our environmental responsibility, or the lack of it, affects not only the people around the world but generations yet to be born. Starving peoples affect us. Our act of submission is a determination to live as a responsible member of an increasingly irresponsible world.

A FINAL NOTE

In our day there has arisen a special problem about submission as it relates to authority. The phenomenon that I am about to describe is something I have observed repeatedly. When people begin to move into the spiritual realm, they see that Jesus is teaching a concept of authority that runs completely counter to the thinking of the systems of this world. They come to perceive that authority does not reside in positions or degrees or titles or tenure or *any* outward symbol. The way of Christ is in another direction altogether – the way of spiritual authority. Spiritual authority is God-ordained and God-sustained. Human institutions may acknowledge this authority or they may not; it makes no difference. The person with spiritual authority may have an outward position of authority or may not; again, it makes no difference. Spiritual authority is marked by both compassion and power. Those who walk in the Spirit can identify it immediately. They know without question that submission is due to the word that has been given in spiritual authority.

But, and here is the difficulty, what about people who are in 'positions of authority' but who do not possess spiritual authority? Since Jesus made it clear that the position does not give the authority, should this person be obeyed? Can we not rather disregard all humanly ordained authority and only look for and submit to spiritual authority? These are the kinds of questions raised by persons who sincerely want to walk in the way of the Spirit. The questions are legitimate and deserve a careful answer.

The answer is not simple, but neither is it impossible. *Revolutionary subordination commands us to live in submission to human authority until it becomes destructive.** Both Peter and Paul called for obedience to the pagan State because they understood the great good that resulted from this human institution. I have found that human 'authorities' often have a great deal of wisdom that we neglect only at our own peril.

To this I shall add another reason of my own why we should submit to persons in positions of authority who do not know spiritual authority. We should do so out of common courtesy and out of compassion for the person in that difficult predicament. I have a deep empathy for people in that plight for I have been there myself more than once. To be in a position of authority and to know that your roots are not deep enough into the divine life to command spiritual authority is a frustrating, almost desperate, quagmire. I know the frantic feeling that makes a person strut and puff and devise clever gimmicks to manipulate people into obedience. Some may find it easy to laugh at these people and disregard their 'authority.' I do not. I weep for them because I know the inward pain and suffering that must be endured to live in such a contradiction.

Further, we may pray for such people that they will be filled with new power and authority. We may also become their friend and help in every way we can. If we will live out the cross-life before them, very soon we may discover that they are increasing in spiritual power, and so are we.

FOR STUDY

In submission we recognise the legitimate authority of others over us. It is nothing more than the simple understanding that 'no man is an island'. Life in community is our rightful home: relationships with other human beings are our inheritance. To

---

* See the section on 'The Limits of Submission.'

confess our commitment to community means to confess our commitment to mutual subordination. Peter crystallised this principle in the simple phrase 'honour all men' (1 Peter 2:17), and Paul set forth the idea in what must be considered the most memorable sentence on the subject, 'Be subject to one another out of reverence for Christ' (Eph. 5:21).

Submission is a concept as broad as life itself and a Discipline found throughout Scripture. It raises issues that are deep and difficult: issues of submission to the ways of God, issues of submission to the state, issues of submission to the Christian fellowship, issues of submission in the Christian household and much more. As we hammer out our understanding of these matters we will always want to hold before us the life and death of Christ as the divine paradigm by which all the verbs of Christian submission are to be conjugated.

In regard to the Christian family the New Testament dared to flesh out the meaning of submission in a body of instructions which Martin Luther called the *Haustafeln*, or 'The Table of Instructions for the Christian Household'.* This teaching was a gracious way of setting forth the function of submission within the family in first-century culture. In our day, however, this body of instructions has been terribly garbled and abused. The following distortions of submission reveal in part the knack we moderns have for taking the best teaching and using it for the worst ends.

The Doormat – This is the person who allows others to misuse and abuse him to such an extent that he is treated as a thing rather than a person. In a false and unhealthy submission he allows others to walk over him as one would a doormat. His opinion is neither sought nor desired, and in time he loses the ability even to have an opinion. Such a person soon becomes an object rather than a subject – a housekeeper rather than a wife, a bread-winner rather than a husband. He is defined by what he

---

* Eph. 5:21 ff., Col. 3:18 ff., Titus 2:4 ff., and 1 Pet. 2:1 ff.

can produce rather than by who he is. In the end he has been 'thing-a-fied'.

The Pleaser – This is the person who wants more than anything else to avoid conflict. He sees a fight coming a mile away and will go to any lengths to keep it from occurring. It is comical (and tragic) to find two 'pleasers' married to each other.

'What would you like to do tonight, Honey?'

'Whatever you would like, Dear.'

'Well, I just want to make you happy.'

'And that is exactly what I want to do for you. I'll do anything that will make you happy.'

'If it would please you, I would be glad to go out to dinner.'

'I'd love to if it would make you happy.'

'Fine, what kind of food do you like?'

'Whatever you would enjoy, Dear!'

. . . and on it goes *ad nauseam*.

The Dependant – This is the person who fears making decisions like the plague. Rather than own up to the maturing process of choice, he finds refuge in a pseudo-submission which allows others to make all his decisions. Fear is at the root of such submission – fear of leading others in the wrong way, fear of making an ill-timed decision, fear of blame if programmes fail. And so he never causes waves, he never offends, and he never accomplishes anything of lasting value.

The Manipulator – This is the person who follows all of the outward rules of submission, but employs every subtle trick to get his own way. Acts of mercy are done to put us into his debt. Words of kindness are given to win us to his side. While fully agreeing with our decision, little hints of doubt are sown through a look or a gesture or perhaps a slight quavering of the voice. Often the practice is so ingrained that the individual himself does not realise that he has taken control of every situation.

The distortions that I have shared are, for the most part, religiously approved means to dehumanising and destructive ends. But Jesus Christ calls us to a more excellent way – a way of love and compassion, a way of submission and service.

Daily Scripture Readings

Sunday	– The call to submission. Mark 8:34, John 12:24–26
Monday	– The example of Christ. Philippians 2:1–11
Tuesday	– The example of Abraham. Genesis 22:1–19
Wednesday	– The example of Paul. Galatians 2:19–21
Thursday	– Submission in the marketplace. Matthew 5:38–48
Friday	– Submission in the family. Ephesians 5:21–6:9, 1 Peter 3:1–9
Saturday	– Submission with reference to the State. Romans 13:1–10, Acts 4:13–20, 5:27–29, 16:35–39

Study Questions

1 How have you seen the Discipline of submission abused?
2 What is the freedom in submission? Have you entered into any experience of this?
3 I write, 'In submission we are at last free to value other people.' What is it about submission that allows this to happen?
4 Why did I begin the chapter by discussing what submission does before I define what it is?
5 What images come to your mind when you think of the word 'self-denial'?
6 Why was Jesus' teaching on submission so revolutionary?
7 In one brief paragraph attempt to summarise what you feel is the teaching of the epistles on submission.
8 What are the limits of submission and why is that important?
9 Of the seven acts of submission, which one do you feel you need to work on most?

10 What do you think it would mean to be in submission to the ways of God? (Ponder this question carefully because it does not yield to pat answers.)

Suggestions for Further Reading

The lack of books below does not reflect my unawareness of contemporary writings but my unwillingness to commend them. The idea of submission pervaded the world view of the old writers (think of à Kempis' *Imitation*) but it is a strange mutation to modern writers. For the most part, contemporary discussions are limited to small corners of the Discipline – the man/woman question and the Shepherding or Discipling concept in certain charismatic circles. To my knowledge, no one has provided us with a full-blown intelligent discussion of this subject.

Murray, Andrew, *Absolute Surrender*, Basingstoke: Marshall Pickering, 1989 (March). A great study encouraging every child of God to yield to the Father in complete surrender.
Schlink, Basilea, *Those Who Love Him*, Basingstoke: Marshall Pickering, 1988. This book shows clearly, practically and with urgency the way of decisive, yielded and unselfish love for Jesus.
Wallis, Jim, *Agenda for Biblical People*, London: Triangle/SPCK, 1986. A definitive call to radical obedience to the Lordship of Jesus Christ in the areas of politics and social concern.

9

The Discipline of Service

Learn the lesson that, if you are to do the work of a prophet, what you need is not a sceptre but a hoe.

— Bernard of Clairvaux

As the cross is the sign of submission, so the towel is the sign of service. When Jesus gathered his disciples for the Last Supper they were having trouble deciding who was the greatest. This was no new issue for them. 'And an argument arose among them as to which of them was the greatest' (Luke 9:46). Whenever there is trouble over who is the greatest, there is trouble over who is the least. That is the crux of the matter for us, isn't it? Most of us know we will never be the greatest; just don't let us be the least.

Gathered at the Passover feast, the disciples were keenly aware that someone needed to wash the others' feet. The problem was that the only people who washed feet were the least. So there they sat, feet caked with dirt. It was such a sore point that they were not even going to talk about it. No one wanted to be considered the least. Then Jesus took a towel and a basin and redefined greatness.

Having lived out servanthood before them, he called them to the way of service: 'If I then, your Lord and Teacher, have washed your feet, you also ought to wash one another's feet. For I have given you an example, that you also should do as I have done to you' (John 13:14, 15). In some ways we would prefer to hear Jesus' call to deny father and mother, houses and land for the sake of the gospel than his word to wash feet. Radical self-denial gives the feel of adventure. If we forsake all, we even have the chance of glorious martyrdom. But in service we must experience the many little deaths of going beyond ourselves. Service banishes us to the mundane, the ordinary, the trivial.

In the Discipline of service there is also great liberty. Service enables us to say 'no!' to the world's games of promotion and authority. It abolishes our need (and desire) for a 'pecking order.' That phrase is so telling, so revealing. How like chickens we are! In the chicken pen there is no peace until it is clear who is the greatest and who is the least and who is at which rung everywhere in between. A group of people cannot be together for very long until the 'pecking order' is clearly established. We can see it so easily in such things as where people sit, how they walk in relation to each other, who always gives way when two people are talking at the same time, who stands back and who steps forward when a job needs to be done. (Depending on the job, it may be a sign of mastery or a sign of servitude.) These things are written across the face of human society.

The point is not that we are to do away with all sense of leadership or authority. Any sociologist would quickly demonstrate the impossibility of such a task. Even among Jesus and the disciples, leadership and authority are seen easily. The point is that Jesus completely redefined leadership and rearranged the lines of authority.

Jesus never taught that everyone had equal authority. In fact, he had a great deal to say about genuine spiritual authority and taught that many did not possess it. But the authority of which Jesus spoke is not the authority of a pecking order. We must clearly understand the radical nature of Jesus' teaching on this matter. He was not just reversing the 'pecking order' as many suppose. He was abolishing it. The authority of which he spoke was not an authority to manipulate and control. It was an authority of function, not of status.

Jesus declares, 'You know that the rulers of the Gentiles lord it over them, and their great men exercise authority over them. *It shall not be so among you* [italics added].' He totally and completely rejected the pecking-order systems of his day. How then was it to be among them? 'Whoever would be great among you must be your servant . . . even as the Son of man came not to be served but to serve' (Matt. 20:25–28). Therefore the spiritual authority of Jesus is an authority not found in a position or a title, but in a towel.

SELF-RIGHTEOUS SERVICE VERSUS TRUE SERVICE

If true service is to be understood and practised, it must be distinguished clearly from 'self-righteous service.'

Self-righteous service comes through human effort. It expends immense amounts of energy calculating and scheming how to render the service. Sociological charts and surveys are devised so we can 'help those people.' True service comes from a relationship with the divine Other deep inside. We serve out of whispered promptings, divine urgings. Energy is expended but it is not the frantic energy of the flesh. Thomas Kelly writes, 'I find He never guides us into an intolerable scramble of panting feverishness.'[1]

Self-righteous service is impressed with the 'big deal.' It is concerned to make impressive gains on ecclesiastical scoreboards. It enjoys serving, especially when the service is titanic. True service finds it almost impossible to distinguish the small from the large service. Where a difference is noted, the true servant is often drawn to the small service, not out of false modesty, but because he genuinely sees it as the more important task. He indiscriminately welcomes all opportunities to serve.

Self-righteous service requires external rewards. It needs to know that people see and appreciate the effort. It seeks human applause – with proper religious modesty of course. True service rests contented in hiddenness. It does not fear the lights and blare of attention, but it does not seek them either. Since it is living out of a new Centre of reference, the divine nod of approval is completely sufficient.

Self-righteous service is highly concerned about results. It eagerly waits to see if the person served will reciprocate in kind. It becomes bitter when the results fall below expectations. True service is free of the need to calculate results. It delights only in the service. It can serve enemies as freely as friends.

Self-righteous service picks and chooses whom to serve. Sometimes the high and powerful are served because that will ensure a certain advantage. Sometimes the low and defenceless are served because that will ensure a humble image. True service is indiscriminate in its ministry. It has heard the command of Jesus to be the 'servant of all' (Mark 9:35). Brother Francis of Assisi notes in a letter, 'Being the servant of all, I am bound to serve all and to administer the balm-bearing words of my lord.'[2]

Self-righteous service is affected by moods and whims. It can serve only when there is a 'feeling' to serve ('moved by the Spirit' as we say). Ill health or inadequate sleep controls the desire to serve. True service ministers simply and faithfully because there is a need. It knows that the 'feeling to serve' can often be a hindrance to true service. The service disciplines the feelings rather than allowing the feeling to control the service.

Self-righteous service is temporary. It functions only while the specific acts of service are being performed. Having served, it can rest easy. True service is a life-style. It acts from ingrained patterns of living. It springs spontaneously to meet human need.

Self-righteous service is insensitive. It insists on meeting the need even when to do so would be destructive. It demands the opportunity to help. True service can withhold the service as freely as perform it. It can listen with tenderness and patience before acting. It can serve by waiting in silence. 'They also serve who only stand and wait.'[3]

Self-righteous service fractures community. In the final analysis, once all the religious trappings are removed, it centres in the glorification of the individual. Therefore it puts others into its debt and becomes one of the most subtle and destructive forms of manipulation known. True service builds community. It quietly and unpretentiously goes about caring for the needs of others. It draws, binds, heals, builds.

SERVICE AND HUMILITY

More than any other single way, the grace of humility is worked into our lives through the Discipline of service. Humility, as we all know, is one of those virtues that is never gained by seeking it. The more we pursue it the more distant it becomes. To think we have it is sure evidence that we don't. Therefore, most of us assume there is nothing we can do to gain this prized Christian virtue, and so we do nothing.

But there *is* something we can do. We do not need to go through life faintly hoping that some day humility may fall upon our heads. Of all the classical Spiritual Disciplines, service is the most conducive to the growth of humility. When we set out on a consciously chosen course of action that accents the good of others and is, for the most part, a hidden work, a deep change occurs in our spirits.

Nothing *disciplines* the inordinate desires of the flesh like service, and nothing *transforms* the desires of the flesh like serving in hiddenness. The flesh whines against service but screams against hidden service. It strains and pulls for honour and recognition. It will devise subtle, religiously acceptable means to call attention to the service rendered. If we stoutly refuse to give in to this lust of the flesh, we crucify it. Every time we crucify the flesh, we crucify our pride and arrogance.

The apostle John writes, 'For all that is in the world, the lust of the flesh and the lust of the eyes and the pride of life, is not of the Father but is of the world' (1 John 2:16). We fail to understand the force of this passage because of our tendency to relegate it all to sexual sin. The 'lust of the flesh' refers to the failure to discipline the natural human passions. C. H. Dodd says that the 'lust of the eyes' refers to 'the tendency to be captivated by outward show.' He defines the 'pride of life' as 'pretentious egoism.'[4] In each case the same thing is seen: infatuation with natural human powers and abilities without any dependence upon God. That is the flesh in operation, and the flesh is the deadly enemy of humility.

The strictest daily discipline is necessary to hold these passions in check. The flesh must learn the painful lesson that it has no rights of its own. It is the work of hidden service that will accomplish this self-abasement.

William Law made a lasting impact upon eighteenth-century England with his book, *A Serious Call to a Devout and Holy Life*. In it Law urges that every day should be viewed as a day of humility. And how does he suggest that we do this? By learning to serve others. Law understood that it is the Discipline of service that brings humility into the life. If we want humility, he counsels us to '. . . condescend to all the weaknesses and infirmities of your fellow-creatures, cover their frailties, love their excellencies, encourage their virtues, relieve their wants, rejoice in their prosperities, compassionate their distress, receive their friendship, overlook their unkindness, forgive their malice, be a servant of servants, and condescend to do the lowest offices to the lowest of mankind.'[5]

The result, then, of this daily discipline of the flesh will be the rise of the grace of humility. It will slip in upon us unawares. Though we do not sense its presence, we are aware of a fresh zest and exhilaration with living. We wonder at the new sense of confidence that marks our activities. Although the demands of life are as great as ever, we live in a new sense of unhurried peace. People whom we once only envied we now view with compassion, for we see not only their position but their pain. People whom we would have passed over before we now 'see' and find to be delightful individuals. Somehow – we cannot exactly explain how – we feel a new spirit of identification with the outcasts, the 'offscourings' of the earth (1 Cor. 4:13).

Even more than the transformation that is occurring within us, we are aware of a deeper love and joy in God. Our days are punctuated with spontaneous breathings of praise and adoration. Joyous hidden service to others is an acted prayer of thanksgiving. We seem to be directed by a new control Centre – and so we are.

YES . . . BUT

A natural and understandable hesitancy accompanies any serious discussion of service. The hesitancy is prudent since it is wise to count the cost before plunging headlong into any Discipline. We experience a fear that comes out something like this: 'If I do that, people will take advantage of me; they will walk all over me.'

Right here we must see the difference between choosing to serve and choosing to be a servant. When we choose to serve, we are still in charge. We decide whom we will serve and when we will serve. And if we are in charge, we will worry a great deal about anyone stepping on us, that is, taking charge over us.

But when we choose to be a servant, we give up the right to be in charge. There is great freedom in this. If we voluntarily choose to be taken advantage of, then we cannot be manipulated. When we choose to be a servant, we surrender the right to decide who and when we will serve. We become available and vulnerable.

Consider the perspective of a slave. A slave sees all of life from the viewpoint of slavery. He does not see himself as possessing the same rights as free men and women. Please understand me,

when this slavery is involuntary it is cruel and dehumanising.*
When the slavery is freely chosen, however, everything is
changed. Voluntary servitude is a great joy.

The imagery of slavery may be difficult for us, but it was not
hard for the apostle Paul. He frequently boasted of his slavery to
Christ, making lavish use of the first-century concept of the
'love slave' (that is, the slave who, out of love, has freely chosen
to remain a slave). We do our best to soften Paul's language by
translating the word 'slave' as 'servant.' But whatever word we
decide to use, let us be certain that we understand that Paul
meant he had freely given up his rights.

Therefore, the fear that we will be taken advantage of and
stepped on is justified. That is exactly what may happen. But
who can hurt someone who has freely chosen to be stepped on?
Thomas à Kempis instructs us to be 'so subject . . . that all men
may go over thee and tread upon thee as upon mire of the
street.'[6]

In *The Little Flowers of St. Francis* a delightful story is told
about how Francis taught Brother Leo the meaning of perfect
joy. As the two walked together in the rain and bitter cold, Francis
reminded Leo of all the things that the world – including the
religious world – believed would bring joy, adding each time
'Perfect joy is not in that.' Finally, in exasperation Brother Leo
asked, 'I beg you in God's name to tell me where perfect joy is,'
whereupon Francis began enumerating the most humiliating,
self-abasing things he could imagine, adding each time 'Oh,
Brother Leo, write that perfect joy is there.' To explain and
conclude the matter he told Brother Leo, 'Above all the graces
and gifts of the Holy Spirit which Christ gives to His friends is
that of conquering oneself and willingly enduring sufferings,
insults, humiliations, and hardships for the love of Christ.'[7]

---

* A good part of my doctoral study was on slavery in America. I am
keenly aware of the horribly demonic nature of involuntary servitude.

We find those words hard to deal with today. (You must understand that I, too, struggle even to listen to the devotional masters on this point.) We fear that such an attitude will lead irrevocably down the path of excessive asceticism and self-mortification. In the Church we are only now emerging from a 'worm theology' that terribly devalued human ability and potential. Does service lead back to that? No, certainly not. No doubt it is a danger we must always guard against. But we must also watch for the enemy in the opposite direction. As Bonhoeffer says, 'If there is no element of asceticism in our lives, if we give free rein to the desires of the flesh . . . we shall find it hard to train for the service of Christ.'[8]

SERVICE IN THE MARKETPLACE

Service is not a list of things that we do, though in it we discover things to do. It is not a code of ethics, but a way of living. To do specific acts of service is not the same thing as living in the Discipline of service. Just as there is more to the game of basketball than the rule book, there is more to service than specific acts of serving. It is one thing to *act* like a servant; it is quite another to *be* a servant. As in all the Disciplines, it is possible to master the mechanics of service without experiencing the Discipline.

To stress the inward nature of service, however, is not enough. Service to be service must take form and shape in the world in which we live. Therefore, we must seek to perceive what service looks like in the marketplace of our daily lives.

At the outset there is the service of hiddenness. Even public leaders can cultivate tasks of service that remain generally unknown. If all of our serving is before others, we will be shallow people indeed. Listen to the spiritual direction of Jeremy Taylor: 'Love to be concealed, and little esteemed: be content to want [lack] praise, never be troubled when thou art slighted or undervalued . . .'[9] Hiddenness is a rebuke to the flesh and can deal a fatal blow to pride.

At first thought it would seem that hidden service is only for the sake of the person served. Such is not the case. Hidden, anonymous ministries affect even people who know nothing of them. They sense a deeper love and compassion among people though they cannot account for the feeling. If a secret service is done on their behalf, they are inspired to deeper devotion, for they know that the well of service is far deeper than they can see. It is a ministry that can be engaged in frequently by all people. It sends ripples of joy and celebration through any community of people.

There is the service of small things. Like Dorcas, we find ways to make 'coats and garments for the widows' (Acts 9:39). The following is a true story. During the frantic final throes of writing my doctoral dissertation I received a phone call from a friend. His wife had taken the car and he wondered if I could take him on a number of errands. Trapped, I consented, inwardly cursing my luck. As I ran out the door, I grabbed Bonhoeffer's *Life Together*, thinking that I might have an opportunity to read in it. Through each errand I inwardly fretted and fumed at the loss of precious time. Finally, at a supermarket, the final stop, I waved my friend on, saying I would wait in the car. I picked up my book, opened it to the marker, and read these words: 'The second service that one should perform for another in a Christian community is that of active helpfulness. This means, initially, simple assistance in trifling, external matters. There is a multitude of these things wherever people live together. Nobody is too good for the meanest service. One who worries about the loss of time that such petty, outward acts of helpfulness entail is usually taking the importance of his own career too solemnly.'[10]

Francis de Sales says that the great virtues and the small fidelities are like sugar and salt. Sugar may have a more exquisite taste, but its use is less frequent. Salt is found everywhere. The great virtues are a rare occurrence; the ministry of small things is a daily service. Large tasks require great sacrifice for a moment; small things require constant sacrifice. 'The small occasions . . . return every moment . . . If we want to be faithful to these small things, nature never has time to breathe, and we must die to all our inclinations. We should a hundred times rather make some great sacrifices to God, however violent and painful, on condition that we be freed with liberty to follow our tastes and habits in every little detail.'[11]

In the realm of the spirit we soon discover that the real issues are found in the tiny, insignificant corners of life. Our infatuation with the 'big deal' has blinded us to this fact. The service of small things will put us at odds with our sloth and idleness. We will come to see small things as the central issues. Fénelon writes, 'It is not elevation of the spirit to feel contempt for small things. It is, on the contrary, because of too narrow points of view that we consider as little what has such far reaching consequences.'[12]

There is the service of guarding the reputation of others or, as Bernard of Clairvaux put it, the service of 'Charity.' How necessary this is if we are to be saved from backbiting and gossip. The apostle Paul taught us to 'speak evil of no one' (Titus 3:2). We may clothe our backbiting in all the religious respectability we want, but it will remain a deadly poison. There is a discipline in holding one's tongue that works wonders within us.

Nor should we be a party to the slanderous talk of others. In one church I served we had a rule on the pastoral team that the members came to appreciate. We refused to allow any person in the congregation to speak disparagingly of one pastor to another pastor. Gently, but firmly, we would ask them to go directly to the offending pastor. Eventually, people understood that we simply would not allow them to talk to us about pastor so-and-so. This rule, held to by the entire team, had beneficial results.

Bernard warns us that the spiteful tongue 'strikes a deadly blow at charity in all who hear him speak and, so far as it can, destroys root and branch, not only in the immediate hearers but also in all others to whom the slander, flying from lip to lip, is afterwards repeated.'[13] Guarding the reputation of others is a deep and lasting service.

There is the service of being served. When Jesus began to wash the feet of those he loved, Peter refused. He would never let his Master stoop to such a menial service on his behalf. It sounds like a statement of humility; in reality it was an act of veiled pride. Jesus' service was an affront to Peter's concept of authority. If Peter had been the master, he would not have washed feet!

It is an act of submission and service to allow others to serve us. It recognises their 'kingdom authority' over us. We graciously receive the service rendered, never feeling we must repay it. Those who, out of pride, refuse to be served are failing to submit to the divinely appointed leadership in the kingdom of God.

There is the service of common courtesy. Such deeds of compassion have fallen on hard times in our day. But we must never despise the rituals of relationship that are in every culture. It is one of the few ways left in modern society to acknowledge the value of one another. We are 'to be gentle, and to show perfect courtesy towards all men' (Titus 3:2).

Missionaries understand the value of courtesy. They would not dare to blunder into some village demanding to be heard without first going through the appropriate rituals of introduction and acquaintanceship. Yet we feel we can violate these rituals in our own culture and still be received and heard. And we wonder why no one will listen.

'But acts of courtesy are so meaningless, so hypocritical,' we complain. That is a myth. They are extremely meaningful and not in the least hypocritical. Once we get over our egocentric arrogance about the fact that people don't really want to know how we are when they say 'How are you?' we can see that it is just an American way of acknowledging our presence. We can wave and acknowledge their presence too without feeling the need to give a prognosis on our latest headache. Words of 'thank you' and 'yes, please,' letters of appreciation and RSVP responses are all services of courtesy. The specific acts will vary from culture to culture, but the purpose is always the same: to acknowledge others and affirm their worth. The service of courtesy is sorely needed in our increasingly computerised and depersonalised society.

There is the service of hospitality. Peter urges us to 'Practise hospitality ungrudgingly to one another' (1 Pet. 4:9). Paul does the same and even makes it one of the requirements for the office of bishop (1 Tim. 3:2; Titus 1:8). There is a desperate need today for Christians who will open their homes to one another. The old idea of the guest house has been made obsolete by the proliferation of modern motels and restaurants, but we may seriously question whether the change is an advance. I have walked through the Spanish missions of California and marvelled at the gracious and adequate provisions that were made for visitors. Perhaps it is the modern, shiny, depersonalised motels that should become obsolete.

I know of a couple who have sought to make the ministry of hospitality a priority in their lives. In any given month they may have as many as seventy people visit their home. It is a service to which they believe God has called them. Perhaps most of us cannot do that much, but we can do something. We can begin somewhere.

Sometimes we limit ourselves because we make hospitality too complicated. I remember an occasion where the hostess was scurrying around, attending to this and that, sincerely wanting to make everyone feel comfortable. My friend startled us all (and put everyone at ease) by saying, 'Helen, I don't want any coffee. I don't want any tea. I don't want any cookies. I don't want a napkin, I just want to visit. Won't you sit down and talk with us!' Just a chance to be together and share – that is the stuff of hospitality.

There is the service of listening. 'The first service that one owes to others in the fellowship consists in listening to them. Just as love for God begins with listening to His Word, so the beginning of love for the brethren is learning to listen to them.'[14] We desperately need the help that can come through listening to one another. We do not need to be trained psychoanalysts to be trained listeners. The most important requirements are compassion and patience.

We do not have to have the correct answers to listen well. In fact, often the correct answers are a hindrance to listening, for we become more anxious to give the answer than to hear. An impatient half-listening is an affront to the person sharing.

To listen to others quiets and disciplines the mind to listen to God. It creates an inward working upon the heart that transforms the affections, even the priorities, of life. When we have grown dull in listening to God, we would do well to listen to others in silence and see if we do not hear God through them. 'Anyone who thinks that his time is too valuable to spend keeping quiet will eventually have no time for God and his brother, but only for himself and for his own follies.'[15]

There is the service of bearing the burdens of each other. 'Bear one another's burdens, and so fulfil the law of Christ' (Gal. 6:2). The 'law of Christ' is the law of love, the 'royal law' as James calls it (James 2:8). Love is most perfectly fulfilled when we bear the hurts and sufferings of each other, weeping with those who weep. And especially when we are with those who are going through the valley of the shadow, weeping is far better than words.

If we care, we will learn to bear one another's sorrows. I say 'learn' because this, too, is a discipline to be mastered. Most of us too easily assume that all we need to do is decide to bear the burdens of others and we can do it. Then we try it for a time, and soon the joy of life has left, and we are heavy with the sorrows of others. It does not need to be so. We can learn to uphold the burdens of others without being destroyed by them. Jesus, who bore the burdens of the whole world, could say, 'My yoke is easy, and my burden is light' (Matt. 11:30). Can we learn to lift the sorrows and pains of others into the strong, tender arms of Jesus so that our burden is lighter? Of course we can. But it takes some practice so, rather than dashing out to bear the burdens of the whole world, let us begin more humbly. We can begin in some small corner somewhere and learn. Jesus will be our Teacher.

Finally, there is the service of sharing the word of Life with one another. The 'Poustinias' that were established by Catherine de Hueck Doherty have a rule: those who go into the deserts of silence and solitude do so for others. They are to bring back any word they receive from God and share it with others. This is a gracious service to be rendered for no individual can hear all that God wants to say. We are dependent upon one another to receive the full counsel of God. The smallest member can bring us a word – we dare not despise the service.

It is, of course, a fearful thing to proclaim these words to each other. The *fact* that God speaks to us does not guarantee that we rightly understand the message. We often mix our word with God's word: 'From the same mouth come blessing and cursing' (James 3:10). Such realities humble us and throw us in deep dependence upon God. But we must not draw back from this service for it is desperately needed today.

The risen Christ beckons us to the ministry of the towel. Such a ministry, flowing out of the inner recesses of the heart, is life and joy and peace. Perhaps you would like to begin by experimenting with a prayer that several of us use. Begin the day by praying, 'Lord Jesus, as it would please you bring me someone today whom I can serve.'

FOR STUDY

In his most famous teaching on service Jesus concluded, 'For the Son of man also came not to be served but to serve, and to give his life as a ransom for many' (Mark 10:45). Our Lord's unique service of redemption through the Cross is unrepeatable. However, we are called to serve through the many little deaths of going beyond self. And as we live out our lives for the good of others, amazingly we find ourselves, we discover our sense of place.

When Paul spoke of the generosity of the believers in Macedonia he noted that 'first they gave themselves' (2 Cor. 8:5). This is the first mark of the Discipline of service. Service cannot be done *in absentia*. It necessitates our personal involvement. Like St Francis of Assisi we must touch the leper, we must reach out to the one in need.

How counter this is to the modern call to watch out for number one. (And may I just add that if you are driven by the need to watch out for number one, God help you, because no one else will!) But in the Kingdom of God we can let go of such drives because we are able to cast all our care upon Him, for He cares for us (1 Peter 5:7).

One reality must be clearly understood in the life of service. The very fact that we are finite means that to say 'yes' to one task of necessity means saying 'no' to other tasks. When I said 'Yes' to the service of writing this study guide, I had to say 'No' to many good and noble tasks. I could not go to special meetings, serve on worthy committees, speak at important gatherings, or even counsel with needy people. To give in to these other quite important ministries would mean failing to serve through writing.

Listen to this heartbreaking story of a young mother who in the beginning thought service meant saying 'Yes' to any and all demands upon her time and energy. 'Someone was *always* dropping in for a visit and staying late, often till two a.m. until we were exhausted. We had *no* time to be together as a family. The routine and discipline of our two small children were disturbed to the point that they were being raised by other people while we had Bible studies and shared with needy folk. The relationship between my husband and me suffered because we were exhausted and had very little time alone. I became the dumping place for preschoolers until I was just about berserk from the responsibility. I became the maker of clothes for many of the women who were working outside the home and simply didn't have time to sew. I became 'the listener' who spent so much time on the phone that there were *many* days that my children's lunches were fixed from things I could reach from the phone and my housework was untouched due to serving others. And on and on it went until I finally cracked, put my foot down and learned to say "No".' This deeply committed woman was having to say 'No' to her children and husband by saying 'Yes' to the demands of other folk.

The point is that we are not omnipresent and we should admit as much. The Discipline of service asks us to serve irrespective of class or status distinctions, but it also recognises our human limitations. Love is a reasoned concern for the wellbeing of all. If I bring people into my home under the supposition that I am serving them, but in the process I destroy my wife and children, I am not living in love. Most likely I am merely gratifying my egocentric need to feel righteous rather than entering into true service. Admittedly the balance is not easy to maintain – significant matters in life seldom are. That is the reason for discipline: remember, the disciplined person is the person who can do what needs to be done when it needs to be done.

Discernment and obedience are the keys. Learning when to say 'No' is important: so is learning when to say 'Yes'. Once we have been burned by a compulsive 'Yes' the temptation will be to say 'No' to everything, or at least those things we find distasteful. But that can be as enslaving as the former state. What we need is to learn the rhythm of the Holy Spirit so that our 'Yes' or 'No' to calls of service will arise out of that harmony.

Daily Scripture Readings

Sunday   – The call to service. Matthew 20:20–28
Monday   – The sign of service. John 13:1–17

Tuesday	– The commitment of service. Exodus 21:2, 5–6, 1 Corinthians 9:19
Wednesday	– The attitude of service. Colossians 3:23–25
Thursday	– Service in the Christian fellowship. Romans 12:9–13
Friday	– The ministry of small things. Matthew 25:31–39
Saturday	– Service exemplified. Luke 10:29–37

Study Questions

1 If the towel is the sign of service, how can that sign be manifested in twenty-first-century culture?
2 Did you find the discussion of self-righteous service as contrasted with true service:
_____ right on
_____ terribly idealistic
_____ naïve
_____ faithful to Scripture but impractical for today
_____ strange?
Discuss your answer with others.
3 Debate the notion that love is a 'reasoned concern for the wellbeing of all', and consider its implications with reference to service.
4 In the book I mention that service works humility into our lives. What in the world do you think humility means? (i.e. what does humility look like?)
5 Have you ever allowed yourself to be taken advantage of and had it turn out to be destructive rather than redemptive?
6 Does the believer have rights that should not be given up for the sake of others?
7 What would the service of hiddenness look like in your life?
8 This next week see if you can find one way each day to exercise the service of common courtesy.
9 When should you say 'No' to the demands people place upon your time and attention?

10 Give this prayer a try some time this month: 'Lord Jesus, I would so appreciate it if you would bring me someone today whom I can serve.'

Suggestions for Further Reading

Bonhoeffer, Dietrich, *Life Together*, trans. by John W. Doberstein, London: SCM Press, 1954. Powerful insights into the life of service, solitude, and confession. Essential reading.

Swindoll, Charles R., *Improving Your Serve*, London: Hodder & Stoughton, 1983. Helpful sermons on the art of unselfish living.

PART III

The Corporate Disciplines

10

The Discipline of Confession

The confession of evil works is the first beginning of good works.
— Augustine of Hippo

At the heart of God is the desire to give and to forgive. Because of this, he set into motion the entire redemptive process that culminated in the cross and was confirmed in the resurrection. The usual notion of what Jesus did on the cross runs something like this: people were so bad and so mean and God was so angry with them that he could not forgive them unless somebody big enough took the rap for the whole lot of them.

Nothing could be further from the truth. Love, not anger, brought Jesus to the cross. Golgotha came as a result of God's great desire to forgive, not his reluctance. Jesus knew that by his vicarious suffering he could actually absorb all the evil of humanity and so heal it, forgive it, redeem it.

This is why Jesus refused the customary painkiller when it was offered him. He wanted to be completely alert for this greatest work of redemption. In a deep and mysterious way he was preparing to take on the collective sin of the human race. Since Jesus lives in the eternal now, this work was not just for those around him, but he took in all the violence, all the fear, all the sin of all the past, all the present, and all the future. This was his highest and most holy work, the work that makes confession and the forgiveness of sins possible.

Some seem to think that when Jesus shouted 'My God, my God, why hast thou forsaken me?' it was a moment of weakness (Mark 15:34). Not at all. *This was his moment of greatest triumph.* Jesus, who had walked in constant communion with the Father, now became so totally identified with humankind that he was the actual embodiment of sin. As Paul writes, 'he made him to be sin who knew no sin' (2 Cor. 5:21). Jesus succeeded in taking into himself all the dark powers of this present evil age and defeated every one of them by the light of his presence. He accomplished such a total identification with the sin of the race that he experienced the abandonment of God. Only in that way could he redeem sin. It was indeed his moment of greatest triumph.

Having accomplished this greatest of all his works, Jesus then took refreshment. 'It is finished,' he announced. That is, this great work of redemption was completed. He could feel the last dregs of the misery of humankind flow through him and into the care of the Father. The last twinges of evil, hostility, anger, and fear drained out of him, and he was able to turn again into the light of God's presence. 'It is finished.' The task is complete. Soon after, he was free to give up his spirit to the Father.

> To shame our sins He blushed in blood;
> He closed His eyes to show us God;
> Let all the world fall down and know
> That none but God such love can show.
>   – Bernard of Clairvaux

This redemptive process is a great mystery hidden in the heart of God. But I know that it is true. I know this not only because the Bible says it is true, but because I have seen its effects in the lives of many people, including myself. It is the ground upon which we can know that confession and forgiveness are realities that transform us. Without the cross the Discipline of confession would be only psychologically therapeutic. But it is so much more. It involves an objective change in our relationship with God and a subjective change in us. It is a means of healing and transforming the inner spirit.

'But I thought that Christ on the cross and redemption deals with salvation,' you may say. It does. But salvation as the Bible speaks of it refers to far more than who comes to faith in Christ or who gets to heaven. The Bible views salvation as both an event and a process. To converted people Paul says, 'Work out your own salvation with fear and trembling' (Phil. 2:12). In a sermon titled 'The Repentance of Believers,' John Wesley spoke of the necessity of Christians coming into more of the forgiving grace of God. The Discipline of confession helps the believer to grow into 'mature manhood, to the measure of the stature of the fullness of Christ' (Eph. 4:13).

'But isn't confession a grace instead of a Discipline?' It is both. Unless God gives the grace, no genuine confession can be made. But it is also a Discipline because there are things we must do. It is a consciously chosen course of action that brings us under the shadow of the Almighty.

'How is it that confession is listed under the Corporate Disciplines? I thought this was a private matter between the individual and God.' Again the answer is not 'either/or,' but 'both/and.' We are grateful for the biblical teaching, underscored in the Reformation, that 'there is one mediator between God and men, the man Christ Jesus' (1 Tim. 2:5). We are also grateful for the biblical teaching, newly appreciated in our day, to 'confess your sins to one another, and pray for one another . . .' (James 5:16). Both are found in Scripture and neither need exclude the other.

Confession is a difficult Discipline for us because we all too often view the believing community as a fellowship of saints before we see it as a fellowship of sinners. We feel that everyone else has advanced so far into holiness that we are isolated and alone in our sin. We cannot bear to reveal our failures and shortcomings to others. We imagine that we are the only ones who have not stepped on to the high road to heaven. Therefore, we hide ourselves from one another and live in veiled lies and hypocrisy.

But if we know that the people of God are first a fellowship of sinners, we are freed to hear the unconditional call of God's love and to confess our needs openly before our brothers and sisters. We know we are not alone in our sin. The fear and pride that cling to us like barnacles cling to others also. We are sinners together. In acts of mutual confession we release the power that heals. Our humanity is no longer denied, but transformed.

AUTHORITY TO FORGIVE

The followers of Jesus Christ have been given the authority to receive the confession of sin and to forgive it in his name. 'If you forgive the sins of any, they are forgiven; if you retain the sins of any, they are retained' (John 20:23). What a wonderful privilege! Why do we shy away from such a life-giving ministry? If we, not out of merit but sheer grace, have been given the authority to set others free, how dare we withhold this great gift! Dietrich Bonhoeffer writes, 'Our brother . . . has been given to us to help us. He hears the confession of our sins in Christ's stead and he forgives our sins in Christ's name. He keeps the secret of our confession as God keeps it. When I go to my brother to confess, I am going to God.'[1]

Such authority in no way threatens the value or efficacy of private confession. It is a wonderful truth that the individual can break through into new life in the cross without the aid of any human mediator. In the days of the Reformation that reality swept into the Church like a breath of fresh air. It became a trumpet call of liberation from the bondage and manipulation that had crept into the ecclesiastical confessional system. But we also need to remember that Luther himself believed in mutual, brotherly confession. In the Large Catechism he writes, 'Therefore when I admonish you to confession I am admonishing you to be a Christian.'[2] Nor should we forget that when the confessional system was first introduced into the Church it sparked a genuine revival of personal piety and holiness.

The person who has known forgiveness and release from persistent, nagging habits of sin through private confession should rejoice greatly in this evidence of God's mercy. But there are others for whom this has not happened. Let me describe what it is like. We have prayed, even begged, for forgiveness, and though we hope we have been forgiven, we sense no release. We doubt our forgiveness and despair at our confession. We fear that perhaps we have made confession only to ourselves and not to God. The haunting sorrows and hurts of the past have not been healed. We try to convince ourselves that God forgives only the sin; he does not heal the memory. But deep within our being we know there must be something more. People have told us to take our forgiveness by faith and not to call God a liar. Not wanting to call God a liar, we do our best to take it by faith. But because misery and bitterness remain in our lives, we again despair. Eventually we begin to believe either that forgiveness is only a ticket to heaven and not meant to affect our lives now, or that we are not worthy of the forgiving grace of God.

Those who in some small way identify with these words can rejoice. We have not exhausted our resources nor God's grace when we have tried private confession. In the Book of Common Prayer, following the call to self-examination and repentance, we read these encouraging words: 'If there be any of you who by this means cannot quiet his own conscience herein but require further comfort or counsel, let him come to me or to some other minister of God's word, and open his grief . . .'[3] God has given us our brothers and sisters to stand in Christ's stead and make God's presence and forgiveness real to us.

The Scripture teaches us that all believers are priests before

God: 'You are a chosen race, a royal priesthood' (1 Pet. 2:9). At the time of the Reformation this was called 'the universal priesthood of all believers.' One of the functions of the Old Testament priest was to bring the forgiveness of sins through the holy sacrifice. The book of Hebrews, of course, makes clear that Jesus Christ is the final and sufficient sacrifice. And Jesus has given to us his priesthood: the ministry of making that sacrifice real in the hearts and lives of other human beings. It is through the voice of our brothers and sisters that the word of forgiveness is heard and takes root in our lives. Bonhoeffer writes: 'A man who confesses his sins in the presence of a brother knows that he is no longer alone with himself; he experiences the presence of God in the reality of the other person. As long as I am by myself in the confession of my sins everything remains in the dark, but in the presence of a brother the sin has to be brought into the light.'[4]

The stylised form of this avenue of help has been called the Confessional or the sacrament of penance. Though many of us, myself included, would feel highly uncomfortable with that form of confession, it does have certain advantages. First, the formalised form of the printed confession does not allow for any excuses or extenuating circumstances. We must confess that we have sinned by our own fault, our own most grievous fault. Our sins cannot be called errors in judgment, nor is there any room to blame them on upbringing or family or mean neighbours. This is a Reality Therapy of the best sort since we are so prone to blame our sins on everybody and everything instead of taking personal responsibility for them.

A second advantage of the Confessional is that the word of forgiveness is expected and given in the absolution. The word of Scripture, or some similar word, is actually spoken out loud. 'If we confess our sins, he is faithful and just, and will forgive our sins and cleanse us from all unrighteousness' (1 John 1:9). The penitent is then told in clear, authoritative words that he is totally forgiven and set free of his sin. The assurance of forgiveness is sealed in the Spirit when it is spoken by our brother or sister in the name of Christ.

There is a third advantage to the institutionalised Confessional, namely, penance. If penance is viewed as a way of earning forgiveness, it is dangerous indeed. But if it is seen as an opportunity to pause a moment to consider the seriousness of our sin, then it has genuine merit. Today we take our offences to the love of God far too lightly. If we had only a tinge of the sense of revulsion that God feels towards sin, we would be moved to holier living. God pleads with us, 'Oh, do not do this abominable thing that I hate!' (Jer. 44:4). The purpose of penance is to help us move into that deeper sense of the sinfulness of sin.

These things, of course, can be accomplished without a formalised Confessional. In fact, when we know what we are about, it is an enormous advance to see the ministry of confession as the common property of the people of God. How can this be done? Perhaps a living example will aid in making these concepts more concrete.

DIARY OF A CONFESSION

Although I had read in the Bible about the ministry of confession in the Christian brotherhood, I had never experienced it until I was pastoring my first church. I did not take the difficult step of laying bare my inner life to another out of any deep burden or sense of sin. I did not feel there was anything wrong in the least – except one thing. I longed for more power to do the work of God. I felt inadequate to deal with many of the desperate needs that confronted me. There had to be more spiritual resources than I was experiencing (and I'd had all the Holy Spirit experiences you're supposed to have; you name them, I'd had them!). 'Lord,' I prayed, 'is there more you want to bring into my life? I want to be conquered and ruled by you. If there is anything blocking the flow of your power, reveal it to me.' He did. Not by an audible voice or even through any human voice, but simply by a growing impression that perhaps something in my past was impeding the flow of his life. So I devised a plan. I divided my life into three periods: childhood, adolescence, adulthood. On the first day I came before God in prayer and meditation, pencil and paper in hand. Inviting him to reveal to me anything during my childhood that needed either forgiveness or healing or both, I waited in absolute silence for some ten minutes. Anything about my childhood that surfaced to my conscious mind, I wrote down. I made no attempt to analyse the items or put any value judgment on them. My assurance was that God would reveal anything that needed his healing touch. Having finished, I put the pencil and paper down for the day. The next day I went through the same exercise for my adolescent years, and the third day for my adult years.

Paper in hand, I then went to a dear brother in Christ. I had made arrangements with him a week ahead so he understood the purpose of our meeting. Slowly, sometimes painfully, I read my sheet, adding only those comments necessary to make the sin clear. When I had finished, I began to return the paper to my briefcase. Wisely, my counsellor/confessor gently stopped my hand and took the sheet of paper. Without a word he took a wastebasket, and, as I watched, he tore the paper into hundreds of tiny pieces and dropped them into it. That powerful, nonverbal expression of forgiveness was followed by a simple absolution. My sins, I knew, were as far away as the east is from the west.

Next, my friend, with the laying on of hands, prayed a prayer of healing for all the sorrows and hurts of the past. The power of that prayer lives with me today.

I cannot say I experienced any dramatic feelings. I did not. In fact, the entire experience was an act of sheer obedience with no compelling feelings in the least. But I am convinced that it set me free in ways I had not known before. It seemed that I was released to explore what were for me new and uncharted regions of the Spirit. Following that event, I began to move into several of the Disciplines described in this book that I had never experienced before. Was there a causal connection? I do not know, and frankly I do not care. It is enough to have obeyed the inner prompting from above.

There was one interesting sidelight. The exposure of my humanity evidently sparked a freedom in my counsellor/friend, for, directly following his prayer for me, he was able to express a deep and troubling sin that he had been unable to confess until then. Freedom begets freedom.

COUNSEL IN THE GIVING OF A CONFESSION

Not only is it true that 'we love, because he first loved us,' but we are enabled to make confession only and especially because he first loved us (1 John 4:19). The evidence of mercy and grace sparks a contrite heart and allows confession to flow. We are drawn to him as Hosea tells us, 'with cords of compassion, with the bands of love' (Hos. 11:4). We come with hopeful hearts, for the One we are coming to waits for us like the father of the prodigal who saw his son when he was still a great way off and in compassion ran and embraced him and welcomed him back (Luke 15:20). His greatest delight is to forgive. He calls his light-filled creatures of heaven into celebration whenever one person makes confession.

What do we do? St Alphonsus Liguori writes, 'For a good confession three things are necessary: an examination of conscience, sorrow, and a determination to avoid sin.'[5]

'An examination of conscience.'* This is a time, as Douglas Steere writes, 'where a soul comes under the gaze of God and

---

* The ancient Christian idea of the examination of conscience as a preparation for confession is light years away from the modern secular idea of 'let your conscience be your guide.' The conscience by itself is depraved and culturally conditioned – a most unreliable guide in matters of ethics and belief.

where in His silent and loving Presence this soul is pierced to the quick and becomes conscious of the things that must be forgiven and put right before it can continue to love One whose care has been so constant.'[6] We are inviting God to move upon the heart and show us areas that need his forgiving and healing touch.

In this experience of opening ourselves to the 'gaze of God' we must be prepared to deal with definite sins. A generalised confession may save us from humiliation and shame, but it will not ignite inner healing. The people who came to Jesus came with obvious, specific sins, and they were forgiven for each one. It is far too easy to avoid our real guilt in a general confession. In our confession we bring concrete sins. By calling them concrete, however, I do not mean only outward sins. I mean definite sins, the sins of the heart – pride, avarice, anger, fear – as well as the sins of the flesh – sloth, gluttony, adultery, murder. We may use the method described earlier. Perhaps we will be drawn to the method Luther used in which he sought to examine himself on the basis of the Ten Commandments. We may be led to another approach altogether.

In our desire to be specific we must not, however, run to the opposite danger of being unduly concerned to rout out every last detail in our lives. With profound common sense Francis de Sales counsels, 'Do not feel worried if you do not remember all your little peccadilloes in confession, for as you often fall imperceptibly, so you are often raised up imperceptibly.'[7]

'Sorrow' is necessary to a good confession. Sorrow as it relates to confession is not primarily an emotion, though emotion may be involved. It is an abhorrence at having committed the sin, a deep regret at having offended the heart of the Father. Sorrow is an issue of the will before it is an issue of the emotions. In fact, being sorrowful in the emotions without a godly sorrow in the will destroys the confession.

Sorrow is a way of taking the confession seriously. It is the opposite of the priest, and undoubtedly the penitent, ridiculed by Chaucer in *The Canterbury Tales*:

Full sweetly heard he confession,
And pleasant was his absolution.[8]

'A determination to avoid sin' is the third essential for a good confession. In the Discipline of confession we ask God to give us a yearning for holy living, a hatred for unholy living. John Wesley once said: 'Give me one hundred preachers who fear nothing but sin and desire nothing but God . . . such alone will shake the gates of hell and set up the kingdom of heaven on earth.'[9] It is the *will* to be delivered from sin that we seek from God as we prepare to make confession. We must desire to be conquered and ruled by God, or if we do not desire it, to desire to desire it. Such a desire is a gracious gift from God. The seeking of this gift is one of the preliminaries for confessing to a brother or sister.

Does all this sound complicated? Do you fear you might miss one of the points and thus render everything ineffectual? It is usually much more complicated in the analysis than in the experience. Remember the heart of the Father; he is like a shepherd who will risk anything to find that one lost sheep. We do not have to make God willing to forgive. In fact, it is God who is working to make us willing to seek his forgiveness.

One further note on the preparation for confession; there must be a definite termination point in the self-examination process. Otherwise, we can easily fall into a permanent habit of self-condemnation. Confession begins in sorrow, but it ends in joy. There is celebration in the forgiveness of sins because it results in a genuinely changed life.

Then there is the practical matter of to whom we should go to confess. It is quite correct theologically to say that every Christian believer can receive the confession of another, but not every Christian believer will have sufficient empathy and under-standing. Though it is unfortunate, it is a fact of life that some people seem unable to keep a confidence. Others are disqualified because they would be horrified at the revealing of certain sins.

Still others, not understanding the nature and value of confession, would shrug it off with a 'That's not so bad.' Fortunately, many people do understand and would be delighted to minister in this way. These people are found by asking God to reveal them to us. They are also found by observing people to see who evidences a lively faith in God's power to forgive and exhibits the joy of the Lord in his or her heart. The key qualifications are spiritual maturity, wisdom, compassion, good common sense, the ability to keep a confidence, and a wholesome sense of humour. Many pastors – though by no means all – can serve in this way. Often ordinary folk who hold no office or title whatever are among the best at receiving a confession.

But what if there is an offence we could never bring ourselves to reveal? What if we lack the courage to open a particular corner of our lives? Then all we need to do is say to our brother or sister: 'I need your help. There is a sin that I cannot bring myself to confess.' Our confessor/friend will 'then adopt an easy means of dragging from its den the wild beast that would devour you. All you will have to do is to answer Yes or No to his interrogations. And behold, both the temporal and the eternal hell have disappeared, the grace of God is recovered, and peace of conscience reigns supreme.'[10]

COUNSEL IN THE RECEIVING OF A CONFESSION

Like any spiritual ministry there is a preparation involved in being able to hear rightly the confession of a brother or sister.

We begin by learning to live under the cross. Bonhoeffer writes, 'Anybody who lives beneath the Cross and who has discerned in the Cross of Jesus the utter wickedness of all men and of his own heart will find there is no sin that can ever be alien to him. Anybody who has once been horrified by the dreadfulness of his own sin that nailed Jesus to the Cross will no longer be horrified by even the rankest sins of a brother.'[11]

This is the one thing that will save us from ever being offended in the confession of another. It forever delivers us from conveying any attitude of superiority. We know the deceptiveness of the human heart, and we know the grace and mercy of God's acceptance. Once we see the awfulness of sin we know that, regardless of what others have done, we ourselves are the chief of sinners.

Therefore, there is nothing that anyone can say that will disturb us. Nothing. By living under the cross we can hear the worst possible things from the best possible people without so much as batting an eyelash. If we live in that reality, we will convey that spirit to others. They know it is safe to come to us. They know we can receive anything they could possibly reveal. They know we will never condescend to them but, instead, understand.

When we live in this spirit, we do not need to tell others that we will keep privileged information privileged. They know we will never betray a confidence. We do not have to tell them. Nor will we ever be tempted to betray it, for we know the godly sorrow that has driven them to this difficult step.

By living under the cross we are delivered from the danger of spiritual domination. We have stood where our brother now stands and so the desire to use his confession against him is gone. Nor do we feel any need to control him or to straighten him out. All we feel is acceptance and understanding.

As we prepare for this sacred ministry it is wise that we regularly pray for an increase of the light of Christ within us so that, as we are with others, we will radiate his life and light into them. We want to learn how to live so that our very presence will speak of the love and forgiving grace of God. Also, we should pray for an increase of the gift of discernment. This is especially important when we minister to them following the confession. We need to be able to perceive the real healing needed in the deep, inner spirit.

It is important that when others are opening their griefs to us we discipline ourselves to be quiet. We will be tempted severely to relieve the tension of the situation by some offhanded comment. This is very distracting and even destructive to the sacredness of the moment. Neither should we try to pry out more details than are necessary. If we feel that out of embarrassment or fear they are holding something back, the best method is to wait silently and prayerfully.

On one occasion a woman was confessing her sorrow to me and to the Lord. When she finished I felt impressed to wait in silence. Presently, she began sharing a deep inward sin that she had never been able to tell anyone. Later she told me that as I waited, she looked at me and 'saw' superimposed upon my eyes the eyes of Another who conveyed to her a love and acceptance that released her to unburden her heart. I had felt nothing nor did I 'see' anything, but I do not doubt her experience for it did result in a wonderful inner healing.

That story illustrates another important factor in receiving a confession. It is often helpful by prayer to set the cross between yourself and the penitent. This protects them from receiving merely human emotion from you and protects you from receiving any harmful influences from them. Everything is filtered through the light of the cross. Your human compassion is heightened and enlivened by divine love. You are praying for them through the power of the cross.

It hardly needs to be said that as they share, you are praying for them. Inwardly and imperceptively (it would be unkind to make a display of your praying) you are sending prayers of love and forgiveness into them. Also, you are praying that they will share the 'key' that will reveal any area needing the healing touch of Christ.

Finally, it is extremely important that you pray for the person and not just counsel with them. Before or during the prayer we should announce to them that the forgiveness that is in Jesus Christ is now real and effective for them. We can say this in words and tones of genuine authority for we have all of heaven behind the absolution (John 20:22, 23).*

The prayer is for the healing of the inner wounds that the sin has caused. It is best to accompany the prayer with the 'laying on of hands' which is an elemental teaching of the Bible and is a means through which God communicates his life-giving power (Heb. 6:2). Invite God to flow into the deep inner mind and heal the sorrows of the past. Picture the healing. Thank him for it. Of this ministry of prayer Agnes Sanford writes, 'One makes a very deep rapport in this kind of prayer. One feels the feelings of the person for whom one prays; so much so that often the tears come from some deep centre of compassion within the soul. Yet, if one weeps, it is not in grief but in joy, knowing that these tears are not one's own but are the tears of the compassionate heart of Christ brooding over this lost one, and the joy of Christ that at last He has been given a channel through which He can reach this person whom He loves.'[12]

The Discipline of confession brings an end to pretence. God is calling into being a Church that can openly confess its frail humanity and know the forgiving and empowering graces of Christ. Honesty leads to confession, and confession leads to change. May God give grace to the Church once again to recover the Discipline of confession.

FOR STUDY

Confession is a corporate Discipline because sin both offends God and creates a wound in the Christian fellowship. In the

---

* In these words of Jesus we have not only the ministry of forgiving sins, but the ministry of retaining sins. 'If you forgive the sins of any, they are forgiven; if you retain the sins of any, they are retained.' The ministry of retaining sins is simply the refusal to try to bring people into something for which they are not ready. Sometimes people are so anxious to get others into the kingdom that they will try to announce their forgiveness before they have sought it or even wanted it. Unfortunately, this malady is characteristic of a great deal of modern evangelism.

early centuries of the Christian era forgiveness and reconciliation involved a lengthy process of healing by which the offender was restored to health through the ministry of the total Christian community. In the early Middle Ages it was turned increasingly into a private sacrament, and following the Reformation Protestants began to view it more and more as a matter exclusively between the individual and God. But in the beginning, confession was not the privatistic event it is today; in fact, in Matthew 18 Jesus expressed its essential communal nature and explained how forgiveness can come into the community without destroying it. It is God who does the forgiving, but often He chooses human beings as the channel of His forgiving grace.

Human beings are such that 'life together' always involves them in hurting one another in some way. And forgiveness is essential in a community of hurt and hurtful persons. In experiencing forgiveness it is important to understand what it is *not*. Four things are often mistaken for forgiveness.

First, some imagine forgiveness means a pretending that it doesn't really matter. 'Oh, that's all right, it really didn't hurt me anyway!' we say. That is not forgiveness; it is lying. And love and lies do not mix well. The truth is that these things matter a great deal, and it does not help to avoid the issue. What we need is not avoidance but reconciliation.

Second, some think that forgiveness means a ceasing to hurt. There is the belief that if we continue to hurt, we must have failed to truly forgive. That is simply not true. Hurting is not evil. We may hurt for a very long time to come. Forgiveness does not mean that we will stop hurting.

Third, many would have us belief that forgiveness means forgetting. 'Forgive and forget,' as we often say. But the truth of the matter is that we cannot forget. We remember; the difference will be that we no longer need or desire to use the memory against others. The memory remains, the vindictiveness leaves. The attempt to force people to forget what cannot be forgotten only puts them in bondage and confuses the meaning of forgiveness.

Fourth, many assume that to forgive means to pretend that the relationship is just the same as before the offence. But this is simply not the case. The relationship will never be the same again. We might just as well make peace with that *fact*. By the grace of God it may be a hundred times better, but it will never be the same.

True confession and forgiveness brings joy to the Christian community and healing to the parties involved. Most wonderful of all it spells reconciliation with God the Father, for as the beloved apostle said so long ago, 'If we confess our sins, he is faithful and just, and will forgive our sins and cleanse us from all unrighteousness' (I John 1:9).

Daily Scripture Readings

Sunday	–	The need for confession and forgiveness. Isaiah 59:1–9, Romans 3:10–18
Monday	–	The promise of forgiveness. Jeremiah 31:34, Matthew 26:28, Ephesians 1:7
Tuesday	–	The assurance of forgiveness. 1 John 1:5–10
Wednesday	–	Jesus Christ our adequate Saviour, Mediator and Advocate. 2 Corinthians 6:21, 1 Timothy 2:5, 1 John 2:1
Thursday	–	A parable of confession. Luke 15:11–24
Friday	–	Authority and forgiveness. Matthew 16:19, 18:18, John 20:23
Saturday	–	The ministry of the Christian fellowship. James 5:13–16

Study Questions

1 In your own words try to describe the theology which lies behind the Discipline of confession.
2 What are the three advantages to formalised confession? Are there disadvantages?
3 I mention three things that are necessary for a good

confession. Which of the three do you find most difficult to experience?

4 What does the idea of living 'under the cross' mean in reference to confession?

5 List two or three dangers that you could imagine would accompany the exercise of the Christian Discipline of confession.

6 Does absolution indicate the forgiveness of sins or does it effect it?

7 When is the Discipline of confession an unhealthy preoccupation with sin and when is it a proper recognition of our need for forgiveness?

8 How would you distinguish between false guilt and genuine guilt?

9 St Augustine calls the sacraments of baptism and communion the *verba visibilia* (visible words) of our forgiveness, and John Stott notes that 'Baptism, being unique and unrepeatable, is the sacrament of our once-for-all justification: Holy Communion, being repeatedly enjoyed, is the sacrament of our daily forgiveness. By them we are assured, audibly and visibly, of our acceptance and forgiveness.' What is your reaction to this idea?

10 Some time this week spend fifteen minutes in silence before God, inviting Him to reveal anything within that needs to be confessed.

Suggestions for Further Reading

Schlink, Basilea, *Repentance: The Joy-Filled Life*, London, Marshall Pickering, 1985. A slender but helpful work by the leader of the Mary Sisterhood, a Lutheran order in Germany.

Tournier, Paul, *Guilt and Grace*, Crowborough: Highland Books, 1987. A perceptive study of guilt, repentance and God's forgiveness and grace.

11

The Discipline of Worship

To worship is to quicken the conscience by the holiness of God, to feed the mind with the truth of God, to purge the imagination by the beauty of God, to open the heart to the love of God, to devote the will to the purpose of God.

— William Temple

To worship is to experience Reality, to touch Life. It is to know, to feel, to experience the resurrected Christ in the midst of the gathered community. It is a breaking into the Shekinah of God, or better yet, being invaded by the Shekinah of God.*

God is actively seeking worshippers. Jesus declares, 'The true worshippers will worship the Father in spirit and truth, for such the Father *seeks* to worship him' (John 4:23, [italics added]). It is God who seeks, draws, persuades. Worship is the human response to the divine initiative. In Genesis God walked in the garden, seeking out Adam and Eve. In the crucifixion Jesus drew men and women to himself (John 12:32). Scripture is replete with examples of God's efforts to initiate, restore, and maintain fellowship with his children. God is like the father of the prodigal

---

* 'Shekinah' means the glory or the radiance of God dwelling in the midst of his people. It denotes the immediate Presence of God as opposed to a God who is abstract or aloof.

who upon seeing his son a long way off, rushed to welcome him home.

Worship is our response to the overtures of love from the heart of the Father. Its central reality is found 'in spirit and truth.' It is kindled within us only when the Spirit of God touches our human spirit. Forms and rituals do not produce worship, nor does the disuse of forms and rituals. We can use all the right techniques and methods, we can have the best possible liturgy, but we have not worshipped the Lord until Spirit touches spirit. The words of the chorus, 'Set my spirit free that I may worship Thee,' reveal the basis of worship. Until God touches and frees our spirit we cannot enter this realm. Singing, praying, praising all may lead to worship, but worship is more than any of them. Our spirit must be ignited by the divine fire.

As a result, we need not be overly concerned with the question of a correct form for worship. The issue of high liturgy or low liturgy, this form or that form is peripheral rather than central. We are encouraged in this perception when we realise that nowhere does the New Testament prescribe a particular form for worship. In fact, what we find is a freedom that is incredible for people with such deep roots in the synagogue liturgical system. They had the reality. When Spirit touches spirit the issue of forms is wholly secondary.

To say that forms are secondary is not to say that they are irrelevant. As long as we are finite human beings we must have forms. We must have 'wineskins' that will embody our experience of worship. But the forms are not the worship; they only lead us into the worship. We are free in Christ to use whatever forms will enhance our worship, and if any form hinders us from experiencing the living Christ – too bad for the form.

THE OBJECT OF OUR WORSHIP

Jesus answers for all time the question of whom we are to worship. 'You shall worship the Lord your God and him only shall you serve' (Matt. 4:10). The one true God is the God of Abraham, Isaac, and Jacob; the God whom Jesus Christ revealed. God made clear his hatred for all idolatries by placing an incisive command at the start of the Decalogue. 'You shall have no other gods before me' (Exod. 20:3). Nor does idolatry consist only in bowing before visible objects of adoration. A. W. Tozer says, 'The essence of idolatry is the entertainment of thoughts about God that are unworthy of Him.'[1] To think rightly about God is, in an important sense, to have everything right. To think wrongly about God is, in an important sense, to have everything wrong.

We desperately need to see who God is: to read about his self-disclosure to his ancient people Israel, to meditate on his attributes, to gaze upon the revelation of his nature in Jesus Christ. When we see the Lord of hosts 'high and lifted up,' ponder his infinite wisdom and knowledge, wonder at his unfathomable mercy and love, we cannot help but move into doxology.

> Glad thine attributes confess,
> Glorious all and numberless.[2]

To see who the Lord is brings us to confession. When Isaiah caught sight of the glory of God he cried, 'Woe is me! For I am lost; for I am a man of unclean lips, and I dwell in the midst of a people of unclean lips; for my eyes have seen the King, the Lord of hosts!' (Isa. 6:5). The pervasive sinfulness of human beings becomes evident when contrasted with the radiant holiness of God. Our fickleness becomes apparent once we see God's faithfulness. To understand his grace is to understand our guilt.

We worship the Lord not only because of who he is, but also because of what he has done. Above all, the God of the Bible is the God who acts. His goodness, faithfulness, justice, mercy all can be seen in his dealings with his people. His gracious actions are not only etched into ancient history, but are engraved into our personal histories. As the apostle Paul says, the only reasonable response is worship (Rom. 12:1). We praise God for who he is, and thank him for what he has done.

THE PRIORITY OF WORSHIP

If the Lord is to be *Lord*, worship must have priority in our lives. The *first* commandment of Jesus is, 'Love the Lord your God with all your heart, and with all your soul, and with all your mind, and with all your strength' (Mark 12:30). The divine priority is worship first, service second. Our lives are to be punctuated with praise, thanksgiving, and adoration. Service flows out of worship. Service as a substitute for worship is idolatry. Activity is the enemy of adoration.

The primary function of the Levitical priests was to 'come near to me to minister to me' (Ezek. 44:15). For the Old Testament priesthood, ministry to God was to precede all other work. And that is no less true of the universal priesthood of the New Testament. One grave temptation we all face is to run around answering calls to service without ministering to the Lord himself.

Today God is calling his Church back to worship. This can be seen in high church circles where there is a renewed interest in intimacy with God. It can be seen in low church circles where there is a renewed interest in liturgy. It can be seen everywhere in between these two. It is as if God is saying, 'I want the hearts of my people back!' And if we long to go where God is going and do what God is doing, we will move into deeper, more authentic worship.

PREPARATION FOR WORSHIP

A striking feature of worship in the Bible is that people gathered in what we could only call a 'holy expectancy.' They believed they would actually hear the *Kol Yahweh*, the voice of God. When Moses went into the Tabernacle, he knew he was entering the presence of God. The same was true of the early Church. It was not surprising to them that the building in which they met shook with the power of God. It had happened before (Acts 2:2, 4:31). When some dropped dead and others were raised from the dead by the word of the Lord, the people knew that God was in their midst (Acts 5:1–11, 9:36–43, 20:7–10). As those early believers gathered they were keenly aware that the veil had been ripped in two, and, like Moses and Aaron, they were entering the Holy of Holies. No intermediaries were needed. They were coming into the awful, glorious, gracious presence of the living God. They gathered with anticipation, knowing that Christ was present among them and would teach them and touch them with his living power.

How do we cultivate this holy expectancy? It begins in us as we enter the Shekinah of the heart. While living out the demands of our day, we are filled with inward worship and adoration. We work and play and eat and sleep, yet we are listening, ever listening, to our Teacher. The writings of Frank Laubach are filled with this sense of living under the shadow of the Almighty. 'Of all today's miracles the greatest is this: to know that I find Thee best when I work listening . . . Thank Thee, too, that the habit of constant conversation grows easier each day. I really do believe *all* thought can be conversations with Thee.'[3]

Brother Lawrence knew the same reality. Because he experienced the presence of God in the kitchen, he knew he would meet God in the Mass as well. He writes, 'I cannot imagine how religious persons can live satisfied without the practice of the Presence of God.'[4] Those who have once tasted the Shekinah of God in daily experience can never again live satisfied without 'the practice of the presence of God.'

Catching the vision from Brother Lawrence and Frank Laubach, I dedicated one whole year to learning how to live with a perpetual openness to Jesus as my present Teacher. I determined to learn his vocabulary: is he addressing me through those singing birds or that sad face? I sought to allow him to move through every action: my fingers while writing, my voice while speaking. My desire was to punctuate each minute with inward whisperings of adoration, praise, and thanksgiving. Often I failed for hours, even days at a time. But each time I came back and tried again. That year did many things for me, but it especially heightened my sense of expectancy in public worship. After all, he had graciously spoken to me in dozens of little ways throughout the week; he will certainly speak to me here as well. In addition, I found it increasingly easier to distinguish his voice from the blare of everyday life.

When more than one or two come into public worship with a holy expectancy, it can change the atmosphere of a room. People who enter harried and distracted are drawn quickly into a sense of the silent Presence. Hearts and minds are lifted upward. The air becomes charged with expectancy.

Here is a practical handle to put on this idea. Live throughout the week as an heir of the kingdom, listening for his voice, obeying his word. Since you have heard his voice throughout the week, you know that you will hear his voice as you gather for public worship. Enter the service ten minutes early. Lift your heart in adoration to the King of glory. Contemplate his majesty, glory, and tenderness as revealed in Jesus Christ. Picture the marvellous vision that Isaiah had of the Lord 'high and lifted up' or the magnificent revelation that John had of Christ with eyes 'like a flame of fire' and voice 'like the sound of many waters' (Isa. 6; Rev. 1). Invite the real Presence to be manifest.

Next, lift into the light of Christ the pastor and other worship leaders. Picture the Shekinah of God's radiance surrounding them. Inwardly release them to speak the truth boldly in the power of the Lord.

When people begin to enter the room, glance around until you see someone who needs your intercessory work. Perhaps their shoulders are drooped, or they seem a bit sad. Lift them into the glorious, refreshing light of his Presence. See the burden tumbling from their shoulders as it did from Pilgrim's in Bunyan's allegory. Hold them as a special intention throughout the service. If only a few in any given congregation will do this, it will deepen the worship experience of all.

Another vital feature of the early Christian community was their sense of being 'gathered' in worship. First, they were gathered in the sense that they actually met as a group, and second, as they met, they were gathered into a unity of spirit that transcended their individualism.

In contrast to the religions of the East, the Christian faith has strongly emphasised corporate worship. Even under highly dangerous circumstances the early community was urged not to forsake the assembling of themselves together (Heb. 10:25). The Epistles speak frequently of the believing community as the 'body of Christ.' As human life is unthinkable without head, arms, and legs, so it was unthinkable for those Christians to live in isolation from one another. Martin Luther witnesses to the fact that 'at home, in my own house, there is no warmth or vigour in me, but in the church when the multitude is gathered together, a fire is kindled in my heart and it breaks its way through.'[5]

In addition, when the people of God meet together, there often comes a sense of being 'gathered' into one mind, becoming of one accord (Phil. 3:15). Thomas Kelly writes: 'A quickening Presence pervades us, breaking down some part of the special privacy and isolation of our individual Lives and blending our spirits within a super-individual Life and Power. An objective, dynamic Presence enfolds us all, nourishes our souls, speaks glad, unutterable comfort with us, and quickens us in depths that had before been slumbering.'[6] When we are truly gathered into worship, things occur that could never occur alone. There is the psychology of the group to be sure, and yet it is so much more; it is divine interpenetration. There is what the biblical writers called *koinonia*, deep inward fellowship in the power of the Spirit.

This experience far transcends *esprit de corps*. It is not in the least dependent upon homogeneous units or even knowing information about one another's lives. There comes a divine melting of our separateness. In the power of the one Spirit we become 'wrapped in a sense of unity and of Presence such as quiets all words and enfolds [us] within an unspeakable calm and interknittedness within a vaster life.'[7] Such fellowship-in-worship makes vicarious worship via the media tasteless and flat.

THE LEADER OF WORSHIP

Genuine worship has only one Leader, Jesus Christ. When I speak of Jesus as the Leader of worship, I mean, first of all, that he is alive and present among his people. His voice can be heard in their hearts and his presence known. We not only read about him in Scripture, we can know him by revelation. He wants to teach us, guide us, rebuke us, comfort us.

Christ is also alive and present in all his offices. In worship we are prone to view Christ only in his priestly office as Saviour and Redeemer. But he is also among us as our Prophet and King. That is, he will teach us about righteousness and give us the power to do what is right. George Fox says, 'Meet together in the Name of Jesus . . . he is your Prophet, your Shepherd, your Bishop, your Priest, in the midst of you, to open to you, and to sanctify you, and to feed you with Life, and to quicken you with Life.'[8]

Further, Christ is alive and present in all his power. He saves us not only from the consequences of sin but from the domination of sin. Whatever he teaches us, he will give us the power to obey. If Jesus is our Leader, miracles should be expected to occur in worship. Healings, both inward and outward, will be the rule, not the exception. The book of Acts will not just be something we read about, but something we are experiencing.

Finally, Christ is the Leader of worship in the sense that he alone decides what human means will be used, if any. Individuals preach or prophesy or sing or pray as they are called forth by their Leader. In this way there is no room for the elevation of private reputations. Jesus alone is honoured. As our living Head calls them forth, any or all of the gifts of the Spirit can be freely exercised and gladly received. Perhaps a word of knowledge is given in which the intent of the heart is revealed and we know that King Jesus is in charge. Perhaps there is a prophecy or an exhortation that puts us on the edge of our seats because we sense that the *Kol Yahweh* has been spoken. Preaching or teaching that comes forth because the living Head has called it forth breathes life into worship. Preaching that is without divine unction falls like a frost on worship. Heart preaching enflames the spirit of worship; head preaching smothers the glowing embers. There is nothing more quickening than Spirit-inspired preaching, nothing more deadening than human-inspired preaching.

With all this lofty talk about Christ as the Leader of worship you might conclude that Human leadership is unimportant. Nothing could be further from the truth. If God does not raise up inspired leaders who can guide people into worship with authority and compassion, then the experience of worship will be nearly impossible. This is the reason for the leadership gifts of the Spirit (Eph. 4:11). Worship leaders who are called out by God must not be shy about their leadership. People need to be led *into* worship: from the Outer Court to the Inner Court and finally into the Holy of Holies. God anoints leaders to bring people through this progression into worship.

AVENUES INTO WORSHIP

One reason worship should be considered a Spiritual Discipline is because it is an ordered way of acting and living that sets us before God so he can transform us. Although we are only responding to the liberating touch of the Holy Spirit, there are divinely appointed avenues into this realm.

The first avenue into worship is to still all humanly initiated activity. The stilling of 'creaturely activity,' as the patriarchs of the inner life called it, is not something to be confined to formal worship services, but is a life-style. It is to permeate the daily fabric of our lives. We are to live in a perpetual, inward, listening silence so that God is the source of our words and actions. If we are accustomed to carrying out the business of our lives in human strength and wisdom, we will do the same in gathered worship. If, however, we have cultivated the habit of allowing every conversation, every business transaction to be divinely prompted, that same sensitivity will flow into public worship. François Fénelon writes, 'Happy the soul which by a sincere self-renunciation, holds itself ceaselessly in the hands of its Creator, ready to do everything which he wishes; which never stops saying to itself a hundred times a day, "Lord, what wouldst thou that I should do?" '[9]

Does that sound impossible? The only reason we believe it to be far beyond us is that we do not understand Jesus as our present Teacher. When we have been under his tutelage for a time, we see how it is possible for every motion of our lives to have its root in God. We wake up in the morning and lie in bed quietly praising and worshipping the Lord. We tell him that we desire to live under his leadership and rule. Driving to work, we ask our Teacher, 'How are we doing?' Immediately our Mentor flashes before our mind that caustic remark we made to our spouse at breakfast, that shrug of disinterest we gave our children on the way out the door. We realise we have been living in the flesh. There is confession, restoration, and a new humility.

We stop at the gas station and sense a divine urging to get acquainted with the attendant, to see her as a person rather than an automaton. We drive on, rejoicing in our new insight into Spirit-initiated activity. And so it goes throughout our day: a prompting here or a drawing there, sometimes a bolting ahead or a lagging behind our Guide. Like a child taking first steps we are learning through success and failure, confident that we have a present Teacher who, through the Holy Spirit, will guide us into all truth. In this way we come to understand what Paul means when he instructs us to 'walk not according to the flesh but according to the Spirit' (Rom. 8:4).

To still the activity of the flesh so that the activity of the Holy Spirit dominates the way we live will affect and inform public worship. Sometimes it will take the form of absolute silence. Certainly it is more fitting to come in reverential silence and awe before the Holy One of eternity than to rush into his Presence with hearts and minds askew and tongues full of words. The scriptural admonition is, 'The LORD is in his holy temple; let all the earth keep silence before him' (Hab. 2:20). The desert Father Ammonas writes: 'Behold, my beloved. I have shown you the power of silence, how thoroughly it heals and how fully pleasing it is to God . . . It is by silence that the saints grew . . . it was because of silence that the power of God dwelt in them, because of silence that the mysteries of God were known to them.'[10]

Praise is another avenue into worship. The Psalms are the literature of worship and their most prominent feature is praise. 'Praise the Lord!' is the shout that reverberates from one end of the Psalter to the other. Singing, shouting, dancing, rejoicing, adoring – all are the language of praise.

Scripture urges us to 'offer the sacrifice of praise to God continually, that is, the fruit of our lips, giving thanks to his name' (Heb. 13:15, KJV). The Old Covenant required the sacrifice of bulls and goats. The New Covenant requires the sacrifice of praise. Peter tells us that as Christ's new royal priesthood we are to offer 'spiritual sacrifices' which means to 'declare the wonderful deeds of him who called you out of darkness into his marvellous light' (1 Pet. 2:5, 9). Peter and John left the Sanhedrin with bleeding backs and praising lips (Acts 5:41). Paul and Silas filled the Philippian jail with their songs of praise (Acts 16:25). In each case they were offering the sacrifice of praise.

The mightiest stirring of praise in the twentieth century has been the charismatic movement. Through it God has breathed new life and vitality into millions. In our day the Church of Jesus Christ is coming into a greater awareness of how central praise is in bringing us into worship.

In praise we see how totally the emotions need to be brought into the act of worship. Worship that is solely cerebral is an aberration. Feelings are a legitimate part of the human personality and should be employed in worship. To make such a statement doesn't mean that our worship should do violence to our rational faculties, but it does mean that our rational faculties alone are inadequate. As Paul counsels, we are to pray with the spirit and pray with the mind, sing with the spirit and sing with the mind (1 Cor. 14:15). That is one reason for the spiritual gift of tongues. It helps us to move beyond mere rational worship into a more inward communion with the Father. Our outward mind may not know what is being said, but our inward spirit understands. Spirit touches spirit.

Singing is meant to move us into praise. It provides a medium for the expression of emotion. Through music we express our joy, our thanksgiving. No less than forty-one psalms command us to 'sing unto the Lord.' If singing can occur in a concentrated manner it serves to focus us. We become centred. Our fragmented minds and spirits flow into a unified whole. We become poised towards God.

God calls for worship that involves our whole being. The body, mind, spirit, and emotions should all be laid on the altar of worship. Often we forget that worship should include the body as well as the mind and the spirit.

The Bible describes worship in physical terms. The root meaning for the Hebrew word we translate as *worship* is 'to prostrate.' The word *bless* literally means 'to kneel.' *Thanksgiving* refers to 'an extension of the hand.' Throughout Scripture we find a variety of physical postures in connection with worship: lying prostrate, standing, kneeling, lifting the hands, clapping the hands, lifting the head, bowing the head, dancing, and wearing sackcloth and ashes. The point is that we are to offer God our bodies as well as all the rest of our being. Worship is appropriately physical.

We are to present our bodies to God in a posture consistent with the inner spirit in worship. Standing, clapping, dancing, lifting the hands, lifting the head are postures consistent with the spirit of praise. To sit still looking dour is simply not appropriate for praise. Kneeling, bowing the head, lying prostrate are postures consistent with the spirit of adoration and humility.

We are quick to object to this line of teaching. 'People have different temperaments,' we argue. 'That may appeal to emotional types, but I'm naturally quiet and reserved. It isn't the kind of worship that will meet my need.' What we must see is that the real question in worship is not, 'What will meet my need?' The real question is, 'What kind of worship does God call for?' It is clear that God calls for wholehearted worship. And it is as reasonable to expect wholehearted worship to be physical as to expect it to be cerebral.

Often our 'reserved temperament' is little more than fear of what others will think of us, or perhaps unwillingness to humble ourselves before God and others. Of course people have different temperaments, but that must never keep us from worshipping with our whole being.

Having said this, I must hasten to add that the physical response to worship is never to be manipulated in any way. We are to give each other freedom to respond to the moving of God upon the heart. In many worship experiences I have seen, at any given moment, people sitting, standing, kneeling, and lying prostrate, and the Spirit of God resting upon them all. Some evidence deep emotion, others show no outward manifestations whatever, but all are under the brooding Spirit of God. 'For freedom Christ has set us free; stand fast therefore, and do not submit again to a yoke of slavery' (Gal. 5:1).

We may, of course, do all the things I have described and never enter into worship, but they can provide avenues through which we place ourselves before God so that our inner spirit can be touched and freed.

STEPS INTO WORSHIP

Worship is something we do. Studying the theology of worship and debating the forms of worship are all good, but by themselves they are inadequate. In the final analysis we learn to worship by worshipping. Let me give a few simple steps that I hope will help in the experience of worship.

First, learn to practise the presence of God daily. Really try to follow Paul's words, 'Pray without ceasing' (1 Thess. 5:17, KJV). Punctuate every moment with inward whisperings of adoration, praise, and thanksgiving. Have personal times of inner worship and confession and Bible study and attentiveness to Christ, your present Teacher. All this will heighten your expectancy in public worship because the gathered experience of worship just becomes a continuation and an intensification of what you have been trying to do all week long.

Second, have many different experiences of worship. Worship God when you are alone. Have home groups not just for Bible study, but for the very experience of worship itself. Gather little groups of two and three and learn to offer up a sacrifice of praise. Many things can happen in smaller gatherings that, just by sheer size, cannot happen in the larger experience. All of these little experiences of worship will empower and impact the larger Sunday gatherings.

Third, find ways to really prepare for the gathered experience of worship. Prepare on Saturday night by going to bed early, by having an inward experience of examination and confession, by going over the hymns and Scripture passages that will be used on Sunday, by gathering early before the actual worship service and filling the room with the presence of God, by letting go of inner distractions so that you can really participate.

Fourth, have a willingness to be gathered in the power of the Lord. That is, as an individual I must learn to let go of my agenda, of my concern, of my being blessed, of my hearing the word of God. The language of the gathered fellowship is not 'I,' but 'we.' There is a submission to the ways of God. There is a submission to one another in the Christian fellowship. There is a desire for God's life to rise up in the group, not just within the individual. If you are praying for a manifestation of the spiritual gifts, it does not have to come upon you but can come upon anybody and upon the group as a whole if that pleases God. Become of one mind, of one accord.

Fifth, cultivate holy dependency. Holy dependency means that you are utterly and completely dependent upon God for anything significant to happen. There is inward travail that the evil will weaken and that the good will rise up. You look forward to God acting and moving and teaching and wooing and winning. The work is God's and not yours.

Sixth, absorb distractions with gratitude. If there is noise or distraction, rather than fussing and fuming about it, learn to take it in and conquer it. If little children are running about, bless them. Thank God that they are alive and that they have energy. Become willing to relax with distractions – they may be a message from the Lord. When I am preaching, I love to have babies and little children in the congregation because sometimes they are the only ones that I can be sure are alive! Learn simply to receive whatever happens in a gathered worship experience, rather than feeling that distractions somehow deter you from worshipping God.

Seventh, learn to offer a sacrifice of worship. Many times you will not 'feel' like worship. Perhaps you have had so many disappointing experiences in the past that you think it is hardly worth it. There is such a low sense of the power of God. Few people are adequately prepared. But you need to go anyway. You need to offer a sacrifice of worship. You need to be with the people of God and say, 'These are my people. As stiff-necked and hard-hearted and sinful as we may be, together we come to God.' Many times I do not feel like worshipping and I have to kneel down and say, 'Lord, I don't feel like worshipping, but I desire to give you this time. It belongs to you. I will waste this time for you.'

Isaac Pennington says that when people are gathered for genuine worship, 'They are like a heap of fresh and burning coals warming one another as a great strength and freshness and vigour of life flows into all.'[11] One log by itself cannot burn for very long, but when many logs are put together, even if they are poor logs, they can make quite a fire. Remember the counsel of Proverbs 27:17 that 'Iron sharpens iron,' and even rather dull lives can help each other if they are willing to try.

So go, even if you don't feel like it. Go, even if worship has been discouraging and dry before. Go, praying. Go, expecting. Go, looking for God to do a new and living work among you.

THE FRUITS OF WORSHIP

Just as worship begins in holy expectancy, it ends in holy obedience. If worship does not propel us into greater obedience, it has not been worship. To stand before the Holy One of eternity is to change. Resentments cannot be held with the same tenacity when we enter his gracious light. As Jesus says, we need to leave our gift at the altar and go set the matter straight (Matt. 5:23, 24). In worship an increased power steals its way into the heart sanctuary, an increased compassion grows in the soul. To worship is to change.

Holy obedience saves worship from becoming an opiate, an escape from the pressing needs of modern life. Worship enables us to hear the call to service clearly so that we respond, 'Here am I! Send me' (Isa. 6:8). Authentic worship will impel us to join in the Lamb's war against demonic powers everywhere – on the personal level, on the social level, on the institutional level. Jesus, the Lamb of God, is our Commander-in-Chief. We receive his orders for service and go '. . . conquering and to conquer . . . with the word of truth . . . returning love for hatred, wrestling with God against the enmity, with prayers and tears night and day, with fasting, mourning and lamentation, in patience, in faithfulness, in truth, in love unfeigned, in long suffering, and in all the fruits of the spirit, that if by any means [we] may overcome evil with good . . .'[12] In all things and in all ways we do exactly what Christ says because we have a holy obedience that has been cultivated over years of experience.

Willard Sperry declares, 'Worship is a deliberate and disciplined adventure in reality.'[13] It is not for the timid or comfortable. It involves an opening of ourselves to the adventurous life of the Spirit. It makes all the religious paraphernalia of temples and priests and rites and ceremonies irrelevant. It involves a willingness to 'Let the word of Christ dwell in you richly, as you teach and admonish one another in all wisdom, and as you sing psalms and hymns and spiritual songs with thankfulness in your hearts to God' (Col. 3:16).

FOR STUDY

On one occasion we are told that St Francis of Assisi 'Rejoiced greatly in Spirit, and he raised his face towards Heaven and stood for a long time with his mind absorbed in God.' He entered worship.

Caught up into God, Julian of Norwich exclaimed, 'I saw Him, and sought Him: and I had Him, I wanted Him . . . he will be seeing and He will be sought: He will be abided and He will be trusted.' She entered worship.

Worship is something that happens. It is experience. When we speak of having a 'worship service' we are usually referring to the various elements of worship – hymns, Scripture readings, preaching, Holy Communion, liturgy. All of these may *lead* us to worship – but worship is much more than any of these expressions. The expressions are important because they are the means of God's grace, but it is quite possible to do them all without worship.

Worship centres in the experience of reality. Whatever ushers us into the Divine Presence should be welcomed. Whatever hinders a genuine encounter with the living Christ should be shunned! The biblical requirements for worship include such matters as confession, adoration, proclamation and so on, but the Bible does not hold us to any universal wineskin or form in which worship must be contained. What we are to be committed to is reality – real worship, real confession, real praise, real adoration. If particular forms at particular times bring us more fully into worship, we are free to use them; if not, too bad for the forms. We are free to use the highest liturgy, no form at all, or anything in between so long as it brings us into real worship. The forms of worship must always be subject to the reality of worship.

Christ alone is the leader of worship, and it is He who decides what is needed and when it is needed. We should recognise and welcome the free exercise of all the Spiritual gifts, as they are used and directed by the Spirit. Christ puts His Word in the mouth of whomever he chooses, and He confirms the same Word in the hearts of the members of His community. If there is any excess He will raise up a prophet to bring the needed correction.

All these lofty words about the priority of reality over forms might make you think that I have little use for worship forms. Nothing could be further from the truth. Worship forms are absolutely essential if we are to enflesh the reality of worship. As long as we are finite we must have forms. And so we bring our bodies, minds, and spirits before God to give Him the glory due His name. We offer the sacrifice of our lips – our singing, our praising, our preaching, our confessing. We offer Him the sacrifice of our bodies – our listening hearts, our Eucharistic celebration, our obedient lives. And it is important to do these things whether we feel like doing them or not. Often I come into a worship experience and must honestly confess, 'Lord, I do not feel like worshipping, I do not feel righteous, I'm tired and distracted in both body and spirit, but I want to give You this time. This hour belongs to You. I love You and to the best of my ability want to give You the glory due Your name. Therefore, I will sing and pray and listen and ask that in Your mercy You will free my spirit to worship You.' And as I do this, often something seems to let go inside: perhaps it is the release of an old fear, or a little bitterness or maybe just a tightfisted determination to come into God. When this happens then the singing of hymns, the reading of Scripture, the confession of sin, the preaching of the Word, the receiving of Communion lead me into praise and adoration, which in turn opens the inner sanctuary of the soul into worship.

In this context may I lift up one form of worship which has a very ancient tradition but has fallen on hard times in our century. It is the use of the dance. For a thousand years Christians did a simple dance movement called the tripudium to many of their hymns. It worked well with any song in 2/2, 3/4, or 4/4 time. As they sang worshippers would take three steps forward, one step back, three steps forward, one step back. In doing this Christians were actually proclaiming a theology with their feet. They were declaring Christ's victory in an evil world, a victory that moves the Church forward but not without setbacks. This simple way to worship with the body can be used in any number of informal worship settings. It can even be done in the sanctuary provided the aisles are wide enough to accommodate three or four abreast, and then worshippers can march around the sanctuary singing the great hymns of the faith.

Above all worship leads us to Christ the Centre, as Bernard of Clairvaux put it so well:

> Jesus, Thou Joy of loving hearts!
> Thou Fount of life! Thou Light of men!
> From the best bliss that earth imparts,
> We turn unfilled to Thee again.

Daily Scripture Readings

Sunday	–	Worship in spirit and truth. John 4:19–24

Sunday – Worship in spirit and truth. John 4:19–24

Monday – Communion: the essence of worship. John 6:52–58, 63

Tuesday – The life of worship. Ephesians 5:18–20, Colossians 3:16–17

Wednesday – The Lord high and lifted up. Isaiah 6:1–8

Thursday – Sing to the Lord. Psalm 96

Friday – Worship of all creation. Psalm 148

Saturday – Worthy is the Lamb. Revelation 5:6–14

Study Questions

1 How can we cultivate 'holy expectancy'?

2 In the book I say that 'God is actively seeking worshippers.' Have you had any sense of God as the 'Hound of Heaven' seeking you out and drawing you into fellowship and communion with Him?

3 The seventeenth-century Quaker theologian, Robert Barclay, spoke of the Quaker worship experience of being 'gathered in the power of the Lord'. He was obviously referring to more than the fact that they had come together in the same room. Discuss what the phrase might mean and once you agree on the meaning, consider what could be done to encourage a fuller sense of that experience in your local church.

4 What forms of worship have you experienced that have been especially meaningful to you? Do you have any sense of why these particular ones have been meaningful as opposed to any other form?

5 Critique my rather bold statement that the Bible does not bind us to any universal form (i.e. wineskin) of worship. Can you think of any worship forms that should be universally binding upon all cultures of Christians at all times?

6 What advantages or disadvantages do you see in the formal-ised liturgy used in churches like the Episcopal Church as opposed to the more informal worship forms used in churches like the Southern Baptist Church?

7 If we truly believe that Christ is alive and present among His people in all His offices, what practical difference would that make in our approach to worship?

8 Do you think experiences of Divine ecstasy are central to worship, peripheral to worship, or destructive of worship?

9 What covenant can you make that will open the door to worship more effectively for you?

10 I write, 'Just as worship begins in Holy Expectancy it ends in Holy Obedience.' What does that mean for you for this next week?

Suggestions for Further Reading

Alexander, Paul, *Creativity in Worship*, Basingstoke: Marshall Pickering, 1987. The author encourages Christians to bring new life and vitality into worship, and shows how artistic disciplines can be employed in services without having to change the basic framework or tradition of worship.

Fellingham, David, *Worship Restored*, Eastbourne: Kingsway, 1987. Scriptural insight and practical guidelines for worship, show-ing the biblical basis for the creativity that is revitalising church life.

Kendrick, Graham, *Worship*, Eastbourne: Kingsway, 1984. A practical book which draws on the author's own experience, designed to help all Christians find a greater depth and meaning in their worship.

12

The Discipline of Guidance

Dwell in the life and love and power and wisdom of God, in unity one with another and with God; and the peace and wisdom of God fill your hearts, that nothing may rule in you but the life, which stands in the Lord God.

– George Fox

In our day heaven and earth are on tiptoe waiting for the emergence of a Spirit-led, Spirit-intoxicated, Spirit-empowered people. All of creation watches expectantly for the springing up of a disciplined, freely gathered, martyr people who know in this life the life and power of the kingdom of God. It has happened before. It can happen again.

Indeed, in movements all over the world we are now beginning to see the breaking forth of the apostolic church of the Spirit. Many are having a deep and profound experience of an Emmanuel of the Spirit – God with us; a knowledge that in the power of the Spirit Jesus has come to guide his people himself; an experience of his leading that is as definite and as immediate as the cloud by day and the pillar of fire by night.

But the knowledge of the direct, active, immediate leading of the Spirit is not sufficient. Individual guidance must yield to corporate guidance. There must also come a knowledge of the direct, active, immediate leading of the Spirit *together*. I do not mean 'corporate guidance' in an organisational sense, but in an organic and functional sense. Church councils and denominational decrees are simply not of this reality.

Much of the teaching on divine guidance in our century has been noticeably deficient on the corporate aspect. We have received excellent instruction on how God leads us through Scripture and through reason and through circumstances and through the promptings of the Spirit upon the individual heart. There has also been teaching – good teaching – on the exceptional means of guidance: angels, visions, dreams, signs, and more. But we have heard little about how God leads through his people, the body of Christ. On that subject there is profound silence.

For this reason I have chosen to list guidance among the Corporate Disciplines and to stress its communal side. God does guide the individual richly and profoundly, but he also guides groups of people and can instruct the individual through the group experience.*

Perhaps the preoccupation with private guidance in Western cultures is the product of their emphasis upon individualism. The people of God have not always been so.

God led the children of Israel out of bondage *as a people*. Everyone saw the cloud and fiery pillar. They were not a gathering of individuals who happened to be going in the same direction; they were a people under the theocratic rule of God. His brooding presence covered them with an amazing immediacy. The people, however, soon found God's unmediated presence too awful, too glorious and begged, 'Let not God speak to us, lest we die' (Exod. 20:19). So Moses became their mediator. Thus began the great ministry of the prophets whose function was to hear God's word and bring it to the people. Although it was a step away from the corporate leading of the Holy Spirit, there remained a sense of being a people together under the

---

* One of the very finest books on the personal side of guidance is *In Search of Guidance* by Dallas Willard, Ventura, CA: Regal Books, 1984.

rule of God. But a day came when Israel rejected even the prophet in favour of a king. From that point on the prophet was the outsider. He was a lonely voice crying in the wilderness; sometimes obeyed, sometimes killed, but almost always on the outside.

Patiently God prepared a people and in the fullness of time Jesus came. And with him dawned a new day. Once again a people were gathered who lived under the immediate, theocratic rule of the Spirit. With quiet persistence Jesus showed them what it meant to live in response to the voice of the Father. He taught them that they, too, could hear the heaven-sent voice and most clearly when together. 'If two of you agree on earth about anything they ask, it will be done for them by my Father in heaven. For where two or three are gathered in my name, there am I in the midst of them' (Matt. 18:19, 20).

In those words Jesus gave his disciples both assurance and authority. There was the assurance that when a people genuinely gathered in his name his will could be discerned. The superintending Spirit would utilise the checks and balances of the different believers to ensure that when their hearts were in unity they were in rhythm with the heartbeat of the Father. Assured that they had heard the voice of the true Shepherd, they were able to pray and act with authority. His will plus their unity equalled authority.

Although Jesus was an outsider to his own people, being crucified beyond the city gates, some people embraced his rulership. And they became a gathered people. 'Now the company of those who believed were of one heart and soul, and no one said that any of the things which he possessed was his own, but they had everything in common. And with great power the apostles gave their testimony to the resurrection' (Acts 4:32, 33). They became a fiery band of witnesses, declaring everywhere that Christ's voice could be heard and his will obeyed.

Perhaps the most astonishing feature of that incendiary fellowship was their sense of corporate guidance. It was beautifully illustrated in the calling forth of Paul and Barnabas to tramp the length and breadth of the Roman empire with the good news of the kingdom of God (Acts 13:1–3). Their call came when a number of people had been together over an extended period of time. It included the use of the Disciplines of prayer, fasting, and worship. Having become a prepared people, the call of God arose out of their corporate worship: 'Set apart for me Barnabas and Saul for the work to which I have called them' (Acts 13:2).

With all our modern methods of missionary recruitment we could profit by giving serious attention to this example of corporate guidance. We would be well advised to encourage groups of people to fast, pray, and worship together until they have discerned the mind of the Lord.

Under corporate guidance the early Church faced and resolved its most explosive issue (Acts 15). Some freelance Christians had gone up to Antioch and had begun preaching the necessity of circumcision for all Christians. The issue was far from trivial. Paul saw at once that it was tantamount to the Jewish cultural captivity of the Church.

Appointed elders and apostles gathered in the power of the Lord not to jockey for position or to play one side against another, but to hear the mind of the Spirit. It was no small task. There was intense debate. Then in a beautiful example of how individual guidance impinges upon corporate guidance, Peter told about his experience with the Italian centurion Cornelius. As he spoke, the ever-brooding Spirit of God did a wonderful work. When Peter finished, the entire assembly fell into silence (Acts 15:12). Finally, the gathered group came into what must be called a glorious, heaven-sent, unified commitment to reject cultural religion and to hold to the everlasting gospel of Jesus Christ. They concluded, 'It has seemed good to the Holy Spirit and to us . . .' (Acts 15:28). They had faced the toughest issue of their day and had discerned the voice from on high. This is the high watermark in the book of Acts.

It was more than a victory regarding an issue; it was a victory of the method used in resolving all issues. As a people they had decided to live under the direct rulership of the Spirit. They had rejected both human totalitarianism and anarchy. They had even rejected democracy, that is, majority rule. They had dared to live on the basis of Spirit-rule; no fifty-one percent vote, no compromises, but Spirit-directed unity. And it worked.

No doubt those experiences in discerning the will of God in community contributed greatly to Paul's understanding of the Church as the body of Christ. He saw that the gifts of the Spirit were given by the Spirit to the body in such a way that interdependence was ensured. No one person possessed everything. Even the most mature needed the help of others. The most insignificant had something to contribute. No one could hear the whole counsel of God in isolation.

Sadly, we must note that by the time John received his great apocalyptic vision the believing community was beginning to cool. By the time of Constantine the church was ready to accept another human king. The vision, however, did not die, and there have been groups throughout the centuries gathered together under the rulership of the Holy Spirit. And today we are beginning to see just such a gathering, and for this we can thank God.

SOME MODELS

The apostolic band did not leap from ground zero to the dizzy heights of Spirit-rulership in a single bound. Neither will we. For the most part they moved into that realm one step at a time, sometimes moving forward a bit, sometimes withdrawing. But by the time Pentecost had come, they were a prepared people.

Having once understood the radical implications of being a people under the direct administration of the Holy Spirit, one of the most destructive things we can do is to say, 'Sounds wonderful. Beginning tomorrow I'll live that way!' Such zealotry only succeeds in making life miserable for ourselves and everyone around us. So, rather than sally off to conquer the world of the Spirit, most of us need to begin with more modest steps. One of the best ways we learn is from models of people who have struggled corporately to hear the voice from on high.

One of the most delightful examples comes from 'the poor little monk of Assisi,' St Francis. Francis, it seems, was in 'great agony of doubt' about whether he should devote himself only to prayer and meditation, which was a common practice in those days, or whether he should also engage in preaching missions. Wisely, Francis sought out counsel. 'As the holy humility that was in him did not allow him to trust in himself or in his own prayers, he humbly turned to others in order to know God's will in this matter.'

He sent messages to two of his most trusted friends, Sister Clare and Brother Silvester, asking them to meet with one of their 'purer and more spiritual companions' and seek the will of God in the matter. Immediately, they gathered to pray and both Sister Clare and Brother Silvester returned with the same answer.

When the messenger returned, St Francis first washed his feet and prepared him a meal. Then, kneeling down before the messenger, St Francis asked him, 'What does my Lord Jesus Christ order me to do?' The messenger replied that Christ had revealed that 'He wants you to go about the world preaching, because God did not call you for yourself alone but also for the salvation of others.' Receiving the message as the undisputed word of Christ, St Francis jumped up saying, 'So let's go – in the name of the Lord,' whereupon he immediately embarked on a preaching mission. That direction gave the early Franciscan movement an unusual combination of mystical contemplation and evangelistic fervour.[1]

In this experience Francis was doing more than seeking out the advice of wise counsellors. He was seeking a way to open the windows of heaven to reveal the mind of Christ, and he took it as such – to the great good of all to whom he ministered.

Another model for corporate guidance can be found in what some call 'meetings for clearness.' Such meetings are called specifically to seek the mind of the Spirit for some individual's question. Once a gifted young man asked my counsel about his future. He had graduated from college and was wrestling with whether or not to go into the pastoral ministry. He had availed himself of all the vocational tests and guidance courses offered and still was undecided. I honestly did not know what was best for him and suggested that he call a meeting for clearness. So he gathered a group of people who knew him well, had spiritual maturity, and were unafraid to be honest and candid with him. There were no earth-shattering visions given to my friend that night, but as this group worshipped and shared they became a supporting community. Over a period of time the gifts and calling of that young man were confirmed, and today he is in the pastoral ministry.

A concept closely akin to this has been pioneered by the Church of the Saviour in Washington, DC. When any member feels that God has led him or her to establish a particular mission group or to venture into a special area of service, they 'sound the call.' This is done at the conclusion of a worship service when the member shares the vision that he or she senses. Afterwards, all who want to are welcome to meet with the person to 'test the call.' Together they probe the issue, praying, questioning, searching. Sometimes there is a sense that the idea was the product of false enthusiasm, and it is abandoned. At other times it is confirmed by the prayers and interaction of the group. Perhaps others in the room are drawn into the call and make it their own. Thus a 'company of the committed' is formed.

Matters of the highest personal importance can be brought to the believing community for discernment. For example, on one occasion two people came before our community stating that they felt the leading of the Lord to be married and desired the confirmation of a Spirit-directed body. Several people who knew the couple well were asked to meet with them. This is their report:

'The special committee appointed to communicate with Mark and Becky regarding their plans to marry is happy to return a most positive report.

We met with Mark and Becky and had a most enjoyable evening of fellowship and prayer. We shared our concern for the sanctity of the family which is the heart of God's plan for human relationships. We were impressed with Mark and Becky's dependence upon the Lord's leading, their anticipation of potential problems, and their mature realisation that successful marriage depends upon continuing commitment to each other and to the Lord.

We are happy to commend Mark and Becky's plans to the [church]. We feel their home will reflect the prayerful and loving influence of their childhood homes and the church community as they unite their love in that relationship ordained by God.

The committee feels a beneficial, special warmth for Mark and Becky which we anticipate will continue in a shepherding relationship. We recommend this precedent to other couples considering marriage.'*

It is possible for business decisions to be made under a sense of the corporate leading of the Holy Spirit. Quakers have done so for years and have demonstrated the feasibility of such an approach. Business meetings should be viewed as worship services. Available facts can be presented and discussed, all with a view to listening to the voice of Christ. Facts are only one

---

* Mark and Becky have given me permission to tell their story.

aspect of the decision-making process and in themselves are not conclusive. The Spirit can lead contrary to or in accord with the available facts. God will implant a spirit of unity when the right path has been chosen and trouble us with restlessness when we have not heard correctly. Unity rather than majority rule is the principle of corporate guidance. Spirit-given unity goes beyond mere agreement. It is the perception that we have heard the *Kol Yahweh*, the voice of God.

A classic and dramatic illustration occurred in 1758. John Woolman and others had pricked the conscience of the Society of Friends over their involvement in the demonic institution of slavery. As Philadelphia Yearly Meeting gathered for its business meetings that year, the slavery issue was a major agenda item. A great deal was at stake and the issue was hotly debated. John Woolman, with head bowed and tears in his eyes, sat through the various sessions in complete silence. Finally, after hours of agonising prayer he rose and spoke. 'My mind is led to consider the purity of the Divine Being and the justice of His judgment, and herein my soul is covered with awfulness . . . Many slaves on this continent are oppressed and their cries have entered into the ears of the Most High . . . It is not a time for delay.' Firmly and tenderly Woolman dealt with the problems of the 'private interests of some persons' and the 'friendships which do not stand upon an immutable foundation.' With prophetic boldness he warned the Yearly Meeting that if it failed to do its 'duty in firmness and constancy' then 'God may by terrible things in righteousness answer us in this matter.'[2]

The entire Yearly Meeting melted into a spirit of unity as a result of this compassionate witness. They responded as one voice to remove slavery from their midst. John Greenleaf Whittier states that those sessions 'must ever be regarded as one of the most important religious convocations in the history of the Christian Church.'[3]

That united decision is particularly impressive when we realise that the Society of Friends was the only body that asked slaveholding members to reimburse their slaves for their time in bondage.* It is also striking to realise that under the prompting of the Spirit, Quakers had voluntarily done something that not one of the antislavery revolutionary leaders – George Washington, Thomas Jefferson, Patrick Henry – was willing to do. So influential was the united decision of 1758 that by the time of the signing of the Declaration of Independence Quakers had completely freed themselves from the institution of slavery.

Many of the Christian communities springing up around the world have discovered the reality and practicality of business decisions through Spirit rule. Such diverse groups as Reba Place Fellowship in Illinois, Society of Brothers in New York, and the Mary Sisterhood in Darmstadt, Germany, all operate on the basis of Spirit-directed unity. Issues are approached with an assurance that the mind of the Spirit can be known. They gather in Christ's name, believing that his will will be fleshed out in their midst. They do not seek compromise, but God-given consensus.

I once attended a business session of some two hundred people in which an issue had been earnestly debated. Though there was a sharp difference of opinion, each of the members sincerely desired to hear and obey the will of God. After a considerable period of time, a united sense of direction began to emerge among all except a few people. Finally, one person stood and said, 'I do not feel right about this course of action, but I hope that the rest of you will love me enough to labour with me until I have the same sense of God's leading as the rest of you or until God opens another way to us.'

As an outside observer, I was touched by how tenderly the group responded to that appeal. All over the auditorium little

---

* There are no accurate figures on the amount that was paid though it was common to pay the yearly wage at that time. In an appeal to the House of Commons to abolish slavery, one Mr F. Buston said that it had cost North Carolina Friends fifty thousand pounds to release their slaves.

groups began gathering to share, to listen, to pray. By the time they had broken through to a united decision, I had received a far greater appreciation for the way in which Christians are to 'maintain the unity of the Spirit in the bond of peace' (Eph. 4:3). Such expressions of the central function of corporate guidance are among the most healthy signs of spiritual vitality today.

THE SPIRITUAL DIRECTOR

In the Middle Ages not even the greatest saints attempted the depths of the inward journey without the help of a spiritual director. Today the concept is hardly understood, let alone practised, except in the Roman Catholic monastic system. That is a tragedy, for the idea of the spiritual director is highly applicable to the contemporary scene. It is a beautiful expression of divine guidance through the help of our brothers and sisters.

Spiritual directorship has an exemplary history. Many of the first spiritual directors were the desert Fathers and were held in high regard for their ability to 'discern spirits.' People would often travel for miles in the wilderness just to hear a brief word of advice, a 'word of salvation,' which summed up the will and judgment of God for them in their actual concrete situation. The *Apophthegmata* or 'Sayings of the Fathers' is an eloquent testimony to the simplicity and depth of this spiritual guidance. Also, many of the Cistercian laybrothers in twelfth-century England were distinguished for their ability to read and guide souls.

What is the purpose of a spiritual director? The seventeenth-century Benedictine mystic, Dom Augustine Baker, writes, 'In a word, he is only God's usher, and must lead souls in God's way, and not his own.'[4] His direction is simply and clearly to lead us to our real Director. He is the means of God to open the path to the inward teaching of the Holy Spirit.

His function is purely and simply charismatic. He leads only by the force of his own personal holiness. He is not a superior or some ecclesiastically appointed authority. The relationship is of an adviser to a friend. Though the director has obviously advanced further into the inner depths, the two are both learning and growing in the realm of the Spirit.

All this talk of 'soul' and 'spirit' might lead us to think that spiritual direction deals only with a small corner or compartment of our lives. That is, we would go to a spiritual director to care for our spirit the way we might go to an ophthalmologist to care for our eyes. Such an approach is false. Spiritual direction is concerned with the whole person and the interrelationship of all of life. Thomas Merton tells of a Russian spiritual director who was criticised for spending so much time earnestly advising an old peasant woman about the care of her turkeys. 'Not at all,' he replied, 'her *whole life* is in those turkeys.'[5] Spiritual direction takes up the concrete daily experiences of our lives and gives them sacramental significance. We learn 'the sacrament of the present moment' as Jean–Pierre de Caussade put it.[6] 'So, whether you eat or drink, or whatever you do, do all to the glory of God' (1 Cor. 10:31).

Spiritual direction is first born out of natural, spontaneous human relationships. A hierarchical, or even organisational, system is not essential to its function and is often destructive to it. The ordinary kinds of caring and sharing that belong to the Christian community are the starting point for spiritual direction. Out of them will flow 'kingdom authority' through mutual subordination and servanthood.

A spiritual director must be a person who has developed a comfortable acceptance of himself or herself. That is, a genuine maturity must pervade all of that person's life. Such persons are unmoved by the fluctuations of the times. They can absorb the selfishness and mediocrity and apathy around them and transform it. They are unjudging and unshakable. They must have compassion and commitment. Like Paul who thought of Timothy as his 'beloved child,' they must be prepared to take on certain parental responsibilities. Theirs must be a tough love that refuses to give approval to every whim. They should also know enough of the human psyche that they will not reinforce unconscious and infantile needs for authoritarianism.

Spiritual directors must be on the inward journey themselves and be willing to share their own struggles and doubts. There needs to be a realisation that together they are learning from Jesus, their ever-present Teacher.

How does such a relationship come about? As with all other things in the kingdom of God, it is arranged by prayer. Bringing and resting our case with God, we wait patiently for his way to be manifest. If he should invite us to speak to someone or make certain arrangements, we gladly obey. Such relationships can be formal as in some of the monastic orders, but they do not need to be. If we have the humility to believe that we can learn from our brothers and sisters and the understanding that some have gone further into the divine Centre than others, then we can see the necessity of spiritual direction. As Virgil Vogt of Reba Place Fellowship says, 'If you cannot listen to your brother, you cannot listen to the Holy Spirit.'[7]

Also, it is helpful to realise that there are many forms of spiritual direction. Preaching is a form of spiritual direction as is the ministry of many small groups. John Wesley established the 'class meetings' and the 'bands' as forms of spiritual direction. The Bible itself functions as spiritual direction, for as we read it prayerfully we are being formed more and more into the image of Christ.

In reflecting on the value of this ministry for centuries of Christians, Thomas Merton says that the spiritual director was something of 'a spiritual father who "begot" the perfect life in the soul of his disciple by his instructions first of all, but also by his prayer, his sanctity and his example. He was . . . a kind of "sacrament" of the Lord's presence in the ecclesiastical community.'[8]

THE LIMITS OF CORPORATE GUIDANCE

As we all know, dangers exist in corporate guidance as well as in individual guidance. Perhaps the most menacing danger is manipulation and control by leaders. If corporate guidance is not handled within the larger context of an all-pervasive grace, it degenerates into an effective way to straighten out deviant behaviour. It becomes a kind of quasi-magic formula through which leaders can impose their will upon individuals, an authorised system through which all differing opinions can be brought into line.

Such manipulative perversion results in the stifling of fresh spiritual vitality. The prophet Isaiah tells us that the coming Messiah 'will not break a bruised reed, or quench a smouldering wick' (Isa. 42:3; Matt. 12:20). It is not the way of Jesus to crush the weakest person or to snuff out the smallest hope. Tenderness towards each individual situation must inform all our deliberations. On one occasion George Fox was debating, and roundly defeating, one Nathaniel Stephens. Overwhelmed, Stephens declared that 'George Fox is come into the light of the sun, and now he thinks to put out my starlight.' Fox writes: 'But I said, "Nathaniel, give me thy hand"; then I told him I would not quench the least measure of God in any, much less put out his starlight.'[9]

There is also danger in the opposite direction. It is possible for a hard-hearted and stiff-necked people to hinder Spirit-inspired leaders. While leaders need the counsel and discernment of the believing community, they also need the freedom to lead. If God has called them to lead, they should not have to bring every detail of life to the community. We must never be seduced by Western democratic ideals into believing that every person must have an equal say about every triviality in the community's life. God appoints authoritative leadership in his Church so that his work may be done upon the earth.

Another danger is that corporate guidance will become

divorced from biblical norms. Scripture must pervade and penetrate all our thinking and acting. The one Spirit will never lead in opposition to the written Word that he inspired. There must always be the outward authority of Scripture as well as the inward authority of the Holy Spirit. In fact, Scripture itself is a form of corporate guidance. It is a way God speaks through the experience of the people of God. It is one aspect of 'the communion of the saints.'

Finally, we must recognise that corporate guidance is limited by our finitude. We are fallible human beings and there are times when, despite our best efforts, our own prejudices and fears keep us from a Spirit-led unity. Sometimes we simply see things differently. Paul and Barnabas, for example, could not agree on whether to take John Mark with them on their second mission-ary journey. Luke says 'a sharp contention' developed between them (Acts 15:39). We should not be surprised if we have the same experience in our ministry efforts.

If this happens, my counsel is that we be kind to each other. Ministry teams at times do part ways, and churches at times do split. Let us do all we can to make any such separation as gracious as possible. Let us pray for each other and ask God's blessing upon one another. Let us have the confidence of the apostle Paul that 'in every way, whether in pretence or in truth, Christ is proclaimed; and in that I rejoice' (Phil. 1:18).

Dallas Willard states, 'The aim of God in history is the creation of an all-inclusive community of loving persons, with Himself included in that community as its prime sustainer and most glorious inhabitant.'[10] Such a community lives under the immediate and total rulership of the Holy Spirit. They are a people blinded to all other loyalties by the splendour of God, a compassionate community embodying the law of love as seen in Jesus Christ. They are an obedient army of the Lamb of God living under the Spiritual Disciplines, a community in the process of total transformation from the inside out, a people determined to live out the demands of the gospel in a secular world. They are tenderly aggressive, meekly powerful, suffering, and over-coming. Such a community, cast in a rare and apostolic mould, constitutes a new gathering of the people of God. May almighty God continue to gather such people in our day.

FOR STUDY

Guidance is the most radical of the Disciplines because it goes to the heart of this matter of walking with God. Guidance means the glorious life of hearing God's voice and obeying His word.

The goal of guidance is not specific instructions about this or that matter but conformity to the image of Christ. Paul said, 'Those whom he foreknew he also predestined to be conformed to the image of his Son' (Rom. 8:29). Specific guidance in particular matters is a happy by-product of this goal having worked its way into our lives.

We make such a mystery out of the matter of the will of God. The surest sign that it is God's will for us to be where we are is that we are there! Now if we throw that away, we throw away the sovereignty of God over our lives. When we can come to the place where we understand that where we are is holy ground, we will begin to understand the meaning of guidance.

The will of God is discovered as we become acquainted with God, learn His ways, and become His friend. As we do this God will take us right where we are and produce in us the winsome fruit of 'love, joy, peace, patience, kindness, goodness, faithfulness, gentleness, self-control' (Gal. 5:22–23). As the friendship grows, as the conformity grows, we will know instinctively what actions would please Him, what decisions would be in accord with His way. Just as our intimate knowledge of and love for our wife or husband guides us to decisions we know they would approve, so our inward fellowship gives an inward knowledge of the ways of God.

There are, of course, the outward tests of God's guidance such as Scripture, the Christian community, divine providence working through circumstance, and our own personal integrity. There are also the exceptional means of guidance such as fleeces, dreams, visions, signs and angels. It is important for us to remember that God will not lead us in ways that are contrary to His known will. The Spirit that inspired the Scripture will lead us in ways consistent with the Scripture. Our understanding of God's ways is shaped and tempered by His self-revelation to us in the Bible.

We must also remember that there is such a thing as supernatural guidance that is not divine guidance. John the Beloved warns us to 'test the spirits to see whether they are of God' (1 John 4:1). There are principalities and powers who wage war against the Kingdom of God, and they are both real and dangerous.

And so we are not to listen to every voice that comes our way but only the voice of the true Shepherd. But here is the wonder of it all, for as Jesus reminded us He is the Good Shepherd and His sheep know His voice (John 10:4). We walk in the light, we fulfil His commandments, we put on the mind of Christ and as we do we find the voice of the true Shepherd quite different from all impostors. While Satan may push and condemn, Christ draws and encourages, and it is His voice that we obey.

Daily Scripture Readings

Sunday   — The pole star of faith. Hebrews 11
Monday   — The guidance of Divine Providence. Genesis 24:1–21
Tuesday   — The guidance of justice and obedience. Isaiah 1:17, 18–20
Wednesday — Led into all truth. Proverbs 3:5–6, John 14:6, 16:13, Acts 10:1–35
Thursday   — Closed doors, open doors. Acts 16:6–10, 2 Corinthians 2:12

Friday   — Listening or resisting? Acts 21:8–14
Saturday — The family likeness. Romans 8:14, 28–30

Study Questions

1 Is the idea of guidance as a *corporate* Discipline new or strange to you?

2 What do you think I mean by the term 'the Apostolic Church of the Spirit'? (Note: I am trying to give a rather different twist to the old concept of 'Apostolic Succession'.)

3 Do you believe that this Spirit-led, Spirit-intoxicated, Spirit-empowered people have already been gathered, or are yet to be gathered in our century?

4 Do you think that the notion of a people under the direct theocratic rule of God is workable or is it only an illusory pipe-dream? Am I reading the history of the early Church through rose-coloured glasses?

5 In what sense does the contemporary charismatic movement approximate to or fall short of this vision of a gathered people of the Spirit?

6 What are some of the dangers of corporate guidance?

7 What do you understand the idea of a 'spiritual director' to mean? Are there dangers to the idea? Are there advantages to the idea?

8 How should the idea of guidance influence the ways we carry on business in our churches? If we believed in guidance would it change our present church polity in any way?

9 Have you ever seen the idea of corporate guidance used in destructive ways? What lessons were you able to learn from that experience?

10 If living in guidance comes about mainly through entering into friendship with God so that we know and desire His ways, what should you drop from your life and what should you add to your life in order to deepen your intimacy with Christ?

Suggestions for Further Reading

Leech, Kenneth, *Soul Friend*, London: Sheldon Press, 1977.
Provides a superb history of Spiritual Direction and links it
to the best of contemporary psychology.

St John of the Cross, *The Dark Night of the Soul*, ed. Halcyon
Backhouse, London: Hodder & Stoughton, 1988. A classic on
the spiritual life, showing God's guidance and teaching in the
experiences of hiddenness and stillness.

13

The Discipline of Celebration

The Christian should be an alleluia from head to foot!
— Augustine of Hippo

Celebration is at the heart of the way of Christ. He entered the
world on a high note of jubilation: 'I bring you good news of a
great joy,' cried the angel, 'which shall come to all the people'
(Luke 2:10). He left the world bequeathing his joy to the
disciples: 'These things I have spoken to you that my joy may be
in you, and that your joy may be full' (John 15:11).

André Trocmé in *Jésus-Christ et la révolution non-violente* and
later John Howard Yoder in *The Politics of Jesus* go to some length
to demonstrate that Jesus began his public ministry by proclaiming the year of Jubilee (Luke 4:18, 19). The social implications
of such a concept are profound.* Equally penetrating is the
realisation that, as a result, we are called into a perpetual Jubilee
of the Spirit. Such a radical, divinely enabled freedom from
possessions and a restructuring of social arrangements cannot
help but bring celebration. When the poor receive the good
news, when the captives are released, when the blind receive

---

* Johannes Hoekendijk writes, 'Jubilee is exodus spelled out in terms
  of social salvation . . .' ('Mission – A Celebration of Freedom,' *Union
  Seminary Quarterly Review*, January 1966, p. 141).

their sight, when the oppressed are liberated, who can withhold the shout of jubilee?

In the Old Testament all the social stipulations of the year of Jubilee – cancelling all debts, releasing slaves, planting no crops, returning property to the original owner – were a celebration of the gracious provision of God. God could be trusted to provide what was needed. He had declared, 'I will command my blessing upon you' (Lev. 25:21). Freedom from anxiety and care forms the basis for celebration. Because we know he cares for us, we can cast all our care upon him. God has turned our mourning into dancing.

The carefree spirit of joyous festivity is absent in contemporary society. Apathy, even melancholy, dominates the times. Harvey Cox says that modern man has been pressed 'so hard towards useful work and rational calculation he has all but forgotten the joy of ecstatic celebration . . .'[1]

CELEBRATION GIVES STRENGTH TO LIFE

Celebration brings joy into life, and joy makes us strong. Scripture tells us that the joy of the Lord is our strength (Neh. 8:10). We cannot continue long in anything without it. Women endure childbirth because the joy of motherhood lies on the other side. Young married couples struggle through the first difficult years of adjustment because they value the insurance of a long life together. Parents hold steady through the teen years, knowing that their children will emerge at the other end human once again.

We may be able to begin tennis instruction or piano lessons by dint of will, but we will not keep at them for long without joy. In fact, the only reason we can begin is because we know that joy is the end result. That is what sustains all novices; they know there is a sense of pleasure, enjoyment, joy in mastery.

Celebration is central to all the Spiritual Disciplines. Without a joyful spirit of festivity the Disciplines become dull, death-breathing tools in the hands of modern Pharisees. Every Discipline should be characterised by carefree gaiety and a sense of thanksgiving.

Joy is part of the fruit of the Spirit (Gal. 5:22). Often I am inclined to think that joy is the motor, the thing that keeps everything else going. Without joyous celebration to infuse the other Disciplines, we will sooner or later abandon them. Joy produces energy. Joy makes us strong.

Ancient Israel was commanded to gather together three times a year to celebrate the goodness of God. Those were festival holidays in the highest sense. They were the experiences that gave strength and cohesion to the people of Israel.

THE PATH TO JOY

In the spiritual life only one thing will produce genuine joy, and that is obedience. The old hymn tells us that there is no other way to be happy in Jesus but to 'trust and obey.' The hymn writer received his inspiration from the Master himself, for Jesus tells us that there is no blessedness equal to the blessedness of obedience. On one occasion a woman in the crowd shouted out to Jesus, 'Blessed is the womb that bore you, and the breasts that you sucked!' Jesus responded, 'Blessed rather are those who hear the word of God and keep it!' (Luke 11:27, 28). It is a more blessed thing to live in obedience than to have been the mother of the Messiah!

In 1870 Hannah Whitall Smith wrote what has become a classic on joyous Christianity, *The Christian's Secret of a Happy Life*. The title barely hints at the depths of that perceptive book. It is no shallow 'four easy steps to successful living.' Studiously, the writer defines the shape of a full and abundant life hid in God. Then she carefully reveals the difficulties to this way and finally charts the results of a life abandoned to God. What is the Christian's secret of a happy life? It is best summed up by her chapter entitled 'The Joy of Obedience.' Joy comes through obedience to Christ, and joy results from obedience to Christ. Without obedience joy is hollow and artificial.

To elicit genuine celebration, obedience must work itself into the ordinary fabric of our daily lives. Without that our celebrating carries a hollow sound. For example, some people live in such a way that it is impossible to have any kind of happiness in their home, but then they go to church and sing songs and pray 'in the Spirit,' hoping that God will somehow give them an infusion of joy to make it through the day. They are looking for some kind of heavenly transfusion that will bypass the misery of their daily lives and give them joy. But God's desire is to transform the misery, not bypass it.

We need to understand that God does at times give us an infusion of joy even in our bitterness and hard-heartedness. But that is the abnormal situation. God's normal means of bringing his joy is by redeeming and sanctifying the ordinary junctures of human life. When the members of a family are filled with love and compassion and a spirit of service to one another, that family has reason to celebrate.

There is something sad in people running from church to church trying to get an injection of 'the joy of the Lord.' Joy is not found in singing a particular kind of music or in getting with the right kind of group or even in exercising the charismatic gifts of the Spirit, good as all these may be. Joy is found in obedience. When the power that is in Jesus reaches into our work and play and redeems them, there will be joy where once there was mourning. To overlook this is to miss the meaning of the Incarnation.

That is why I have placed celebration at the end of this study. Joy is the end result of the Spiritual Disciplines' functioning in our lives. God brings about the transformation of our lives through the Disciplines, and we will not know genuine joy until there is a transforming work within us. Many people try to come into joy far too soon. Often we try to pump up people with joy when in reality nothing has happened in their lives.

God has not broken into the routine experiences of their daily existence. Celebration comes when the common ventures of life are redeemed.

It is important to avoid the kind of celebrations that really celebrate nothing. Worse yet is to pretend to celebrate when the spirit of celebration is not in us. Our children watch us bless the food and promptly proceed to gripe about it – blessings that are not blessings. One of the things that nearly destroys children is being forced to be grateful when they are not grateful. If we pretend an air of celebration, our inner spirit is put in contradiction.

A popular teaching today instructs us to praise God for the various difficulties that come into our lives, asserting that there is great transforming power in thus praising God. In its best form such teaching is a way of encouraging us to look up the road a bit through the eye of faith and see what will be. It affirms in our hearts the joyful assurance that God takes all things and works them for the good of those who love him. In its worst form this teaching denies the vileness of evil and baptises the most horrible tragedies as the will of God. Scripture commands us to live in a spirit of thanksgiving in the midst of all situations; it does not command us to celebrate the presence of evil.

THE SPIRIT OF CAREFREE CELEBRATION

The apostle Paul calls us to 'Rejoice in the Lord always: and again I say, Rejoice' (Phil. 4:4 KJV). But how are we to do that? Paul continues, 'Have no anxiety about anything,' or as the King James Version puts it, 'Be careful for nothing.' That is the negative side of rejoicing. The positive side is 'in everything by prayer and supplication with thanksgiving let your requests be made known to God.' And the result? 'The peace of God, which passes all understanding, will keep your hearts and minds in Christ Jesus' (Phil. 4:6, 7).

Paul instructs us on how we can always rejoice, and his first word of counsel is to be 'full of care' for nothing. Jesus, of course, gives the same advice when he says, 'Do not be anxious about your life, what you shall eat or what you shall drink, nor about your body, what you shall put on' (Matt. 6:25). In both instances the same word is used, which we translate, 'anxious' or 'careful.' Christians are called to be free of care, but we find such a way foreign to us. We have been trained since we were two years old to be full of care. We shout to our children as they run to the school bus, 'Be careful,' that is, be full of care.

The spirit of celebration will not be in us until we have learned to be 'careful for nothing.' And we will never have a carefree indifference to things until we trust God. This is why the Jubilee was such a crucial celebration in the Old Testament. No one would dare celebrate the Jubilee unless they had a deep trust in God's ability to provide for their needs.

When we trust God we are free to rely entirely upon him to provide what we need: 'By prayer and supplication with thanksgiving let your requests be made known to God.' Prayer is the means by which we move the arm of God; hence we can live in a spirit of carefree celebration.

Paul, however, does not end the matter there. Prayer and trust by themselves are not adequate to bring us joy. Paul proceeds to tell us to set our minds on all the things in life that are true, honourable, just, pure, lovely, and gracious (Phil. 4:8). God has established a created order full of excellent and good things, and it follows naturally that as we give our attention to those things we will be happy. That is God's appointed way to joy. If we think we will have joy only by praying and singing psalms, we will be disillusioned. But if we fill our lives with simple good things and constantly thank God for them, we will be joyful, that is, full of joy. And what about our problems? When we determine to dwell on the good and excellent things in life, we will be so full of those things that they will tend to swallow our problems.

The decision to set the mind on the higher things of life is an act of the will. That is why celebration is a Discipline. It is not something that falls on our heads. It is the result of a consciously chosen way of thinking and living. When we choose this way, the healing and redemption in Christ will break into the inner recesses of our lives and relationships, and the inevitable result will be joy.

THE BENEFITS OF CELEBRATION

Far and away the most important benefit of celebration is that it saves us from taking ourselves too seriously. This is a desperately needed grace for all those who are earnest about the Spiritual Disciplines. It is an occupational hazard of devout folk to become stuffy bores. This should not be. Of all people, we should be the most free, alive, interesting. Celebration adds a note of gaiety, festivity, hilarity to our lives. After all, Jesus rejoiced so fully in life that he was accused of being a wine-bibber and a glutton. Many of us lead such sour lives that we cannot possibly be accused of such things.

Now I am not recommending a periodic romp in sin, but I am suggesting that we do need deeper, more earthy experiences of exhilaration. It is healing and refreshing to cultivate a wide appreciation for life. Our spirit can become weary with straining after God just as our body can become weary with overwork. Celebration helps us relax and enjoy the good things of the earth.

Celebration also can be an effective antidote for the periodic sense of sadness that can constrict and oppress the heart. Depression is an epidemic today and celebration can help stem the tide. In his Chapter titled 'Helps in Sadness,' François Fénelon counsels those who are bowed low with the burdens of life to encourage themselves 'with good conversation, even by making merry.'[2]

Another benefit of celebration is its ability to give us perspective. We can laugh at ourselves. We come to see that the causes we champion are not nearly so monumental as we would like to believe. In celebration the high and the mighty regain their balance and the weak and lowly receive new stature. Who can be high or low at the festival of God? Together the rich and the poor, the powerful and the powerless all celebrate the glory and wonder of God. There is no leveller of caste systems like festivity.

Thus freed of an inflated view of our own importance, we are also freed of a judgmental spirit. Others do not look so awful, so unspiritual. Common joys can be shared without sanctimonious value judgments.

Finally, an interesting characteristic of celebration is that it tends towards more celebration. Joy begets joy. Laughter begets laughter. It is one of those few things in life that we multiply by giving. Kierkegaard says that 'humour is always a concealed pair.'[3]

THE PRACTICE OF CELEBRATION

If celebration is primarily a corporate Discipline, and if it brings such benefit to the people of God, how is it practised? The question is a good one, for modern men and women have become so mechanised that we have snuffed out nearly all experiences of spontaneous joy. Most of our experiences of celebration are artificial, plastic.

One way to practise celebration is through singing, dancing, shouting. Because of the goodness of God, the heart breaks forth into psalms and hymns and spiritual songs. Worship, praise, adoration flow from the inner chambers. In Psalm 150 we see the celebration of the people of God with trumpet and lute and harp, with timbrel and dance, with strings and pipe and loud clashing cymbals.

What do little children do when they celebrate? They make noise, lots of noise. There is not a thing wrong with noise at the appropriate time, just as there is nothing wrong with silence when it is appropriate. Children dance when they celebrate.

When the children of Israel had been snatched from the clutches of Pharaoh by the mighty power of God, Miriam the prophetess led the people in a great celebration dance (Exod. 15:20). David went leaping and dancing before the Lord with all his might (2 Sam. 6:14, 16). The folk dance has always been a carrier of cultural values and has been used repeatedly in genuine celebration. Of course, dancing can have wrong and evil manifestations, but that is another matter entirely.

Singing, dancing, and noise-making are not required forms of celebration. They are examples only, to impress upon us that the earth indeed is the Lord's and the fullness thereof. Like Peter, we need to learn that nothing that comes from the gracious hand of God is inherently unclean (Acts 10). We are free to celebrate the goodness of God with all our viscera!

Laughing is another way we practise celebration. The old adage that laughter is the best medicine has a lot going for it. Indeed, Norman Cousins in his book, *Anatomy of an Illness*, discusses how he used the therapy of laughter to help him overcome a crippling disease. In his hospital bed Cousins watched old Marx Brothers films and 'Candid Camera' shows, and the genuine belly laughter he experienced seemed to have an anaesthetic effect and gave him pain-free sleep. Doctors even confirmed the salutary effect of laughter on his body chemistry.

Why not! Jesus had a sense of humour – some of his parables are positively comical. There is even such a thing as 'holy laughter,' a frequent phenomenon in various revival movements. Although I have not experienced holy laughter myself, I have observed it in others and its effects appear altogether beneficial. But whether God gives us this special grace or not, we can all experience times of wholesome laughter.

So poke fun at yourself. Enjoy wholesome jokes and clever puns. Relish good comedy. Learn to laugh; it is a discipline to be mastered. Let go of the everlasting burden of always needing to sound profound.

A third way to encourage celebration is to accent the creative gifts of fantasy and imagination. Harvey Cox observes that 'man's celebrative and imaginative faculties have atrophied.'[4] In another place he writes, 'There was a time when visionaries were canonised, and mystics were admired. Now they are studied, smiled at, perhaps even committed. All in all, fantasy is viewed with distrust in our time.'[5]

We who follow Christ can risk going against the cultural tide. Let's with abandon relish the fantasy games of children. Let's see visions and dream dreams. Let's play, sing, laugh. The imagination can release a flood of creative ideas, and it can be lots of fun. Only those who are insecure about their own maturity will fear such a delightful form of celebration.

Let us also relish the creativity of others. Those who create sculptures and paintings and plays and music are a great gift to us. We can organise art shows to display their work. We can sing their music in intimate gatherings and formal concerts. We can arrange for dramatic productions of our friend's works. We can have a family art show and feature the kids' paintings from school. Why not! It is great fun and builds community.

Another thing we can do is to make family events into times of celebration and thanksgiving. This is particularly true of the various rites of passage in our culture like birthdays, graduations, marriages, anniversaries. One couple I know plants a tree for every wedding anniversary. On their farm they now have a little forest of some forty trees that bear silent witness to their love and fidelity.

We can also celebrate lesser, but equally important events like finishing a major project, securing a job, receiving a raise. In addition, why not form regular rituals of celebration that are not connected with special events. Spend more time around the piano as a family and sing out! Learn the folk dances of various cultures and enjoy them together. Set up regular times to play games or watch movies or read books together. Turn visits to relatives into celebrations of your relationship. I am sure you can come up with many other ideas that belong to your family alone.

A fifth thing we can do is to take advantage of the festivals of our culture and really celebrate. What a great celebration we can make of Christmas. It does not have to have all the crass commercialism connected to it if we decide that we do not want it that way. Of course the giving of gifts is a great thing, but we can give many kinds of presents. Several years ago our young son Nathan, who was learning to play the piano at that time, gave every member of the family a special gift – playing a song he had learned. He had great fun gift wrapping huge boxes and trying to get everyone to guess what their gift was. And then when they opened it, a note said that he was going to play some little piece for them on the piano. How delightful, how fun!

And what about Easter? Forget the spring style show and celebrate the power of the resurrection. Make family Easter plays. Revive the May Day celebrations. Go pick flowers and deliver them to your neighbours and friends. Rejoice in the beauty of colour and variety. Why allow Halloween to be a pagan holiday in commemoration of the powers of darkness? Fill the house or church with light; sing and celebrate the victory of Christ over darkness. Let the children (and adults) dress up as biblical characters or as some of the saints through the centuries.

In the Middle Ages there was a holiday known as the Feast of Fools.[6] It was a time when all 'sacred cows' of the day could be safely laughed at and mocked. Minor clerics mimicked and ridiculed their superiors. Political leaders were lampooned. We can do without the excessive debauchery that often accompanied those festivities, but we do need occasions when we laugh at ourselves. Instead of chafing under the social customs of our day, we might do well to find ways to laugh at them.

We are not limited to established festivals; we can develop our own. One fellowship held a celebration night in appreciation of their pastors. Each family designed a homemade card. Various groups prepared skits, plays, readings, jokes. As one of those pastors, I can say that it was a hilarious night. Why do we wait until our pastors are ready to leave before we throw a party for them? If we will show our appreciation more often, they just might be encouraged to stay longer.

I know of one church that has a 'festival of lights' for Christmas. They have music, they have drama, and most of all they involve lots of people. I know of another group that meets quarterly to celebrate the foods of other countries. On one occasion they will have a Swedish meal, at another Irish, and at another Japanese.

Where I teach we have an annual event called 'Symphony of Spring,' and the good it does for the human spirit is impossible to calculate. It is the most anticipated event of the year. Music, costumes, colour – it is a mini-extravaganza with all the expertise of a professional production without the plastic superficiality. This event is not cheap. There is a considerable expense in time, energy, and money. But we all need such festivals of joy as together we seek the kingdom of God.

Celebration gives us the strength to live in all the other Disciplines. When faithfully pursued, the other Disciplines bring us deliverance from those things that have made our lives miserable for years which, in turn, evokes increased celebration. Thus, an unbroken circle of life and power is formed.

FOR STUDY

The Psalmist exclaimed, 'Our mouth was filled with laughter, and our tongue with shouts of joy' (Ps. 126:2). And St Augustine echoed Scripture's words with the declaration, 'A Christian should be an alleluia from head to foot.' Celebration is a happy characteristic of those who walk cheerfully over the earth in the power of the Lord.

The joy of the Lord is not merely a good feeling. It is acquainted with suffering and sorrow, heartache and pain. It is not found by seeking it. It does not come by trying to pump up the right emotions, or by having a cheery disposition, or by attempting to be an optimist.

Joy is the result of provision, place and personality functioning properly in the course of our daily lives. It comes as a result of the abundant life Jesus promised having taken over the ingrained habit patterns of our lives. It slips in unawares as our attention is focused upon the Kingdom of God.

Joy makes us strong. I'll never forget the day I heard the words of Agnes Sanford, 'On one of my most joyful and therefore most powerful days . . .' I do not remember the rest of the statement, but I never forgot the connection she made between joy and power. I have found this to be true, and I imagine you have also. On those days when the joy of the Lord seems to engulf us, there is an almost unhindered flow of God's life and power from us to others.

Celebration is a grace because it comes unmerited from the hand of God. It is also a Discipline because there is a work to be done. In Hebrews we are instructed to 'continually offer up a sacrifice of praise to God, that is, the fruit of lips that acknowledge his name' (Heb. 13:15). The sacrifice of praise is the work to which we are called. In the Old Testament there was a morning and an evening sacrifice. That, I think, is a good beginning for all New Testament priests, of which you are one. Begin the day with the morning sacrifice of praise, 'Lord, I love You, adore You, worship You, desire Your will and way . . .' Conclude the day with the evening sacrifice of thanksgiving. 'Thank You, Lord, thank You for Your love, Your presence, Your strength and grace . . .' And as we do this the fire will fall upon the sacrifice of our lips just as it did upon the altar of old. God's joy will come, and there will be dance and song and joy unspeakable and full of glory.

Before long we will find ourselves taking a 'thanksgiving' break rather than a coffee break at 10:00 and at 2:00. Soon so rich and full will be our experience that we will desire to be continually in His presence with thanksgiving in our hearts. And all of this will be occurring while we are carrying out the demands of our days – eating, working, playing, even sleeping. Belief in God turns into acquaintanceship and then into friendship. We look into the face of God until we ache with bliss, as Frank Laubach witnessed, 'I know what it means to be "God-intoxicated"'.

As noted before, this joy is beyond the pseudo gaiety of superficial religion. It is in no way connected with the 'smile if you love Jesus' froth of today. It is not even necessarily tied to spiritual ecstasy. Its source is found in the assurance of being rooted and grounded in God. It is the experience known to all the saints and confessed by Brother Lawrence, 'Lord, I am yours, dryness does not matter nor affect me!'

Daily Scripture Readings

Sunday	–	The Lord has triumphed gloriously. Exodus 15:1–2, 20–21
Monday	–	The joy of the Lord. 2 Samuel 6:12–19
Tuesday	–	Bless the Lord. Psalm 103
Wednesday	–	Praise the Lord. Psalm 150
Thursday	–	Hosanna! Luke 19:35–40, John 12:12–19
Friday	–	Walking and leaping and praising God. Acts 3:1–10
Saturday	–	Hallelujah! Revelation 19:1–8

Study Questions

1 Do you enjoy God?
2 There is a body of teaching which instructs us to praise God *for* all things, there is another which urges us to praise God *in* all things. Do you feel that the difference is significant and if so why?
3 Imagine some close friends in your church who have just

received the news that their eight-year-old daughter has been killed in an automobile accident. Should your attitude with them be: 'Weep with those who weep', or 'Rejoice in the Lord always: again I say, rejoice'?

4 Why do you think a wholesome evening of side-splitting laughter with friends does you so much good?

5 Why do you think human beings often find celebration so difficult?

6 Which do you like better: spontaneous bursts of joy or planned expressions of celebration? Why?

7 If you are in a study group would you be willing to devise together some hearty holy shout and try it out together before dismissing the meeting?

8 How about planning out a family non-holiday celebration this year?

9 Do you find it easy to laugh at yourself?

10 At the close of this study what covenant *must* you make with the Lord?

Suggestions for Further Reading

Castle, Tony, *Let's Celebrate!*, London: Hodder & Stoughton, 1984. Practical teaching on celebration in the church and in the lives of individual Christians.

Murphy-O'Connor, Cormac, *The Family of the Church*, London: Darton, Longman & Todd, 1984. The Bishop of Arundel & Brighton discusses whether and how the Church can be a family in today's world.

Ramon, Brother, *Fullness of Joy*, Basingstoke: Marshall Pickering, 1988. A study on the theme of joy; a pilgrimage of enquiry and devotion born of the author's varied ministry in churches and on hitchhikes around the country. Each chapter concludes with a meditation on some aspect of joy and a simple course of action to give it expression.

Notes

CHAPTER 1: THE SPIRITUAL DISCIPLINES: DOOR TO LIBERATION

1. John Woolman, *The Journal of John Woolman* (Secaucus, NJ: Citadel Press, 1972), p. 118.
2. Thomas Merton, *Contemplative Prayer* (London: Darton, Longman & Todd, 1973).
3. Heini Arnold, *Freedom from Sinful Thoughts: Christ Alone Breaks the Curse* (Rifton, NY: Plough Publishing House, 1973), p. 94.
4. Ibid., p. 64.
5. Ibid., p. 82.
6. Frank S. Mead, ed., *Encyclopedia of Religious Quotations* (London: Peter Davis, 1965), p. 400.

CHAPTER 2: THE DISCIPLINE OF MEDITATION

1. Morton T. Kelsey, *The Other Side of Silence: A Guide to Christian Meditation* (London: SPCK, 1977).
2. Madame Guyon, *Experiencing the Depths of Jesus Christ* (Goleta, CA: Christian Books, 1975), p. 3.
3. Timothy Ware, ed., *The Art of Prayer: An Orthodox Anthology* (London: Faber & Faber, 1966), p. 110.

4. Jeremy Taylor, *The House of Understanding: Selections from the Writings of Jeremy Taylor*, ed. Margaret Gest (Philadelphia: Univ. of Pennsylvania Press, 1954), p. 106.

5. Dietrich Bonhoeffer, *The Way to Freedom* (London: Fontana, 1972).

6. Guyon, p. 32.

7. Thomas à Kempis, *The Imitation of Christ* (London: Hodder & Stoughton, 1979).

8. Thomas Merton, *Contemplative Prayer* (London: Darton, Longman & Todd, 1973).

9. Morton Kelsey in *The Other Side of Silence* makes an excellent analysis of Eastern and Christian meditation.

10. Thomas Merton, *Spiritual Direction and Meditation* (St Albans: A. Clarke Books, 1975).

11. Merton, *Contemplative Prayer*.

12. William Penn, *No Cross, No Crown*, ed. Ronald Selleck (Richmond, IN: Friends United Press, 1981), p. xii.

13. Merton, *Contemplative Prayer*.

14. A. W. Tozer, *The Knowledge of the Holy* (Eastbourne: Kingsway, 1984).

15. Elizabeth O'Connor, *Search for Silence* (Waco, TX: Word Books, 1971), p. 95.

16. Merton, *Spiritual Direction and Meditation*.

17. Ibid.

18. Alexander Whyte, *Lord, Teach Us to Pray* (New York: Harper & Brothers, n.d.), p. 249.

19. As quoted in Lynn J. Radcliffe, *Making Prayer Real* (New York: Abington-Cokesbury Press, 1952), p. 214.

20. St Francis de Sales, *Introduction to the Devout Life*, ed. Peter Toon (London: Hodder & Stoughton, 1988).

21. Merton, *Contemplative Prayer*.

22. Merton, *Spiritual Direction and Meditation*.

23. Bonhoeffer.

24. Whyte, pp. 249–50.

25. Ibid., p. 251.

26. Evelyn Underhill, *Practical Mysticism* (New York: Dutton, 1943), p. 90.
27. Merton, *Spiritual Direction and Meditation*.

CHAPTER 3: THE DISCIPLINE OF PRAYER

1. E. M. Bounds, *Power Through Prayer* (Chicago: Moody Press, n.d.), p. 23.
2. Ibid., p. 38.
3. Ibid., pp. 38, 77.
4. Ibid., pp. 41, 54.
5. Ibid., p. 13.
6. Thomas Merton, *Contemplative Prayer* (London: Darton, Longman & Todd, 1973).
7. Søren Kierkegaard, *Christian Discourses*, trans. Walter Lowie (Oxford: Oxford University Press, 1940), p. 324.
8. Meister Eckhart, *Meister Eckhart*, trans. C. de B. Evans, Vol. 1 (London: John M. Watkins, 1956), p. 59.
9. As quoted in Lynn J. Radcliffe, *Making Prayer Real* (New York: Abington-Cokesbury Press, 1952), p. 214.
10. Frank C. Laubach, *Prayer the Mightiest Force in the World* (New York: Fleming H. Revell, 1946), p. 31.
11. Frank C. Laubach, *Learning the Vocabulary of God* (Nashville: Upper Room, 1956), p. 33.
12. Bounds, p. 83.
13. Thomas R. Kelly, *A Testament of Devotion* (London: Quaker Home Service, 1979).
14. Ibid., p. 35.
15. Bounds, p. 35.

CHAPTER 4: THE DISCIPLINE OF FASTING

1. John Wesley, *The Journal of the Reverend John Wesley* (London: Epworth Press, 1938), p. 147.
2. David R. Smith, *Fasting: A Neglected Discipline* (Fort

Washington, PA: Christian Literature Crusade, 1969), p. 6.

3. Arthur Wallis, *God's Chosen Fast* (Fort Washington, PA: Christian Literature Crusade, 1971), p. 25.

4. Dietrich Bonhoeffer, *The Cost of Discipleship* (London: SCM Press, 1964).

5. E. M. Bounds, *Power Through Prayer* (Chicago: Moody Press, n.d.), p. 25.

6. John Wesley, *Sermons on Several Occasions* (London: Epworth Press, 1971), p. 301.

7. Smith, p. 39.

8. Thomas R. Kelly, *A Testament of Devotion* (London: Quaker Home Service, 1979).

9. Wallis, p. 66.

10. Elizabeth O'Connor, *Search for Silence* (Waco, TX: Word Books, 1971), pp. 103, 104.

11. Wesley, *Sermons on Several Occasions*, p. 297.

CHAPTER 5: THE DISCIPLINE OF STUDY

1. Martin Buber, *Tales of the Hasidim: Early Masters* (New York: Schocken Books, 1948), p. 111.

2. André Gide, *If It Dies*, trans. Dorothy Bussey (New York: Random House, 1935), p. 83.

3. Evelyn Underhill, *Practical Mysticism* (New York: World, Meridian Books, 1955), pp. 93–94.

4. Fyodor Dostoevski, *The Brothers Karamazov* (London: Penguin, 1970).

5. Charles Noel Douglas, ed., *Forty Thousand Quotations* (Garden City, NY: Halcyon House, 1940), p. 1680.

CHAPTER 6: THE DISCIPLINE OF SIMPLICITY

1. Richard E. Byrd, *Alone* (New York: Putnam, 1938), p. 19.

2. Arthur G. Gish, *Beyond the Rat Race* (New Canaan, CT: Keats, 1973), p. 21.

3. Ibid., p. 20.
4. Søren Kierkegaard, *Christian Discourses*, trans. Walter Lowie (Oxford: Oxford University Press, 1940), p. 322.
5. Ibid., p. 27.
6. John Wesley, *The Journal of the Reverend John Wesley* (London: Epworth Press, 1938), Nov. 1767.
7. Ronald J. Sider, *Rich Christians in an Age of Hunger* (London: Hodder & Stoughton, 1978).
8. Kierkegaard, p. 344.
9. John Woolman, *The Journal of John Woolman* (Secaucus, NJ: Citadel Press, 1972), pp. 144–145.
10. Ibid., p. 168.
11. George Fox, *Works*, Vol. 8 (Philadelphia, 1831), p. 126, Epistle 131.

CHAPTER 7: THE DISCIPLINE OF SOLITUDE

1. Elizabeth O'Connor, *Search for Silence* (Waco, TX: Word Books, 1971), p. 132.
2. Dietrich Bonhoeffer, *Life Together* (London: SCM Press, 1954).
3. Catherine de Hueck Doherty, *Poustinia: Christian Spirituality of the East for Western Man* (London: Fount, 1977).
4. Thomas à Kempis, *The Imitation of Christ* (London: Hodder & Stoughton, 1979).
5. John Woolman, *The Journal of John Woolman* (Secaucus, NJ: Citadel Press, 1972), p. 11.
6. Bonhoeffer, *Life Together*.
7. Doherty.
8. St John of the Cross, *The Collected Works of St. John of the Cross*, trans. Kieran Kavanaugh and Otilio Rodriguez (Garden City, NY: Doubleday, 1964), p. 296.
9. Ibid., p. 363.
10. Ibid., p. 295.
11. Ibid., p. 364.

12. Ibid., p. 365.
13. Bonhoeffer, *Life Together.*
14. Thomas Merton, *The Sign of Jonas* (New York: Harcourt, Brace, 1953), p. 261.
15. Doherty.

CHAPTER 8: THE DISCIPLINE OF SUBMISSION

1. Thomas à Kempis, *The Imitation of Christ*, in an anthology entitled *The Consolation of Philosophy* (New York: Random House, 1943), p. 139.
2. *Hymns for Worship* (Nappanee, IN: Evangel Press, 1963), p. 248.
3. John Howard Yoder, *The Politics of Jesus* (Grand Rapids, MI: Eerdmans, 1972), pp. 181–82. (I am indebted to Yoder for several of the ideas that follow.)
4. Ibid., p. 181.
5. Ibid., p. 186.
6. Kempis.

CHAPTER 9: THE DISCIPLINE OF SERVICE

1. Thomas R. Kelly, *A Testament of Devotion* (London: Quaker Home Service, 1979).
2. St Francis of Assisi, *Selections from the Writings of St. Francis of Assisi* (Nashville: Upper Room Press, 1952), p. 25.
3. John Milton, *Poetical Works* (Oxford: Oxford University Press, 1966).
4. C. H. Dodd, quoted in William Barclay, *The Letters of John and Jude* (Philadelphia: Westminster Press, 1960), pp. 68, 69.
5. William Law, *A Serious Call to a Devout and Holy Life* (London: Hodder & Stoughton, 1987).
6. Thomas à Kempis, *The Imitation of Christ*, in an anthology entitled *The Consolation of Philosophy* (New York: Random House, 1943), p. 211.

7. Brother Ugolino di Monte Santa Maria, *The Little Flowers of St. Francis* (London: Hodder & Stoughton, 1985).

8. Dietrich Bonhoeffer, *The Cost of Discipleship* (London: SCM Press, 1964).

9. Jeremy Taylor, *The Rule and Exercises of Holy Living in Fellowship of the Saints: An Anthology of Christian Devotional Literature* (New York: Abingdon-Cokesbury Press, 1957), p. 353.

10. Dietrich Bonhoeffer, *Life Together* (London: SCM Press, 1954).

11. François Fénelon, *Christian Perfection* (Minneapolis: Bethany Fellowship, 1975), p. 34.

12. Ibid., p. 36.

13. Bernard of Clairvaux, *St. Bernard on the Song of Songs* (London: Mowbray, 1952), p. 70.

14. Bonhoeffer, *Life Together*.

15. Ibid.

CHAPTER 10: THE DISCIPLINE OF CONFESSION

1. Dietrich Bonhoeffer, *Life Together* (London: SCM Press, 1954).

2. Ibid.

3. Agnes Sanford, *The Healing Gifts of the Spirit* (New York: Holman, 1966), p. 110.

4. Bonhoeffer, *Life Together*.

5. St Alphonsus Liguori, 'A Good Confession,' in an anthology entitled *To Any Christian* (London: Burns & Oates, 1964), p. 192.

6. Douglas Steere, *On Beginning from Within* (New York: Harper & Brothers, 1943), p. 80.

7. Liguori, p. 193.

8. Geoffrey Chaucer, *The Canterbury Tales* (London: Penguin, 1970).

9. E. M. Bounds, *Power Through Prayer* (Chicago: Moody Press, n.d.), p. 77.

10. Liguori, p. 195.
11. Bonhoeffer, *Life Together* (The phrase 'living under the cross' is Bonhoeffer's.)
12. Sanford, p. 117.

CHAPTER 11: THE DISCPLINE OF WORSHIP

1. A. W. Tozer, *The Knowledge of the Holy* (Eastbourne: Kingsway, 1984).
2. Ibid.
3. Frank C. Laubach, *Learning the Vocabulary of God* (Nashville: Upper Room, 1956), pp. 22–23.
4. Brother Lawrence, *The Practice of the Presence of God* (London: Hodder & Stoughton, 1982).
5. Douglas Steere, *Prayer and Worship* (New York: Edward W. Hazen Foundation, 1942), p. 36.
6. Thomas R. Kelly, *The Eternal Promise* (New York: Harper & Row, 1966), p. 72.
7. Ibid., p. 74.
8. George Fox, Epistle 288 (1672), quoted in *Quaker Religious Thought 15* (Winter 1973–74): 23.
9. François Fénelon, *Christian Perfection* (Minneapolis: Bethany Fellowship, 1975), p. 4.
10. Thomas Merton, *Contemplative Prayer* (London: Darton, Longman & Todd, 1973).
11. As quoted in D. Elton Trueblood, *The People Called Quakers* (New York: Harper & Row, 1966), p. 91.
12. James Nayler, *A Collection of Syndry Books, Epistles, and Papers, Written by James Nayler, etc.* (London, 1716), p. 378.
13. Willard Sperry, 'Reality in Worship,' in *The Fellowship of Saints: An Anthology of Christian Devotional Literature*, ed. Thomas S. Kepler (New York: Abingdon-Cokesbury Press, 1963), p. 685.

CHAPTER 12: THE DISCIPLINE OF GUIDANCE

1. Brother Ugolino di Monte Santa Maria, *The Little Flowers of St. Francis* (London: Hodder & Stoughton, 1985).
2. Rufus M. Jones, *The Quakers in the American Colonies* (New York: Norton, 1921), p. 517.
3. John G. Whittier, ed., *The Journal of John Woolman* (London: Headley Brothers, 1900), p. 13.
4. Thomas Merton, *Spiritual Direction and Meditation* (St Albans: A. Clarke Books 1975).
5. Ibid.
6. Jean-Pierre de Caussade, *The Sacrament of the Present Moment*, trans. Kitty Muggeridge (London: Fount, 1981).
7. Dave and Neta Jackson, *Living Together in a World Falling Apart* (Carol Stream, IL: Creation House, 1974), p. 101.
8. Merton, *Spiritual Direction and Meditation*.
9. George Fox, *The Journal of George Fox* (London: Headley Brothers, 1975), p. 184.
10. Dallas Willard, 'Studies in the Book of Apostolic Acts: Journey into the Spiritual Unknown' (unpublished study guide available only from the author).

CHAPTER 13: THE DISCPLINE OF CELEBRATION

1. Harvey Cox, *The Feast of Fools* (Cambridge: Harvard University Press, 1969), p. 12.
2. François Fénelon, *Christian Perfection* (Minneapolis: Bethany Fellowship, 1975), p. 102.
3. D. Elton Trueblood, *The Humor of Christ* (New York: Harper & Row, 1964), p. 33.
4. Cox, p. 11.
5. Ibid., p. 10.
6. Ibid., p. 3.

A Brief Bibliography
of Recent Works

The notes in the back of this book, and the more extensive notes at the end of each chapter under the 'For Study' heading, are meant to provide you with resources for further exploration. In addition to those sources, I thought it would be helpful to give an update on books that have been published in more recent years. When I wrote *Celebration of Discipline*, the contemporary works on Spirituality were slim pickings indeed, especially among Protestants. But in the last few years a whole spate of new books have been written, some of them quite good, which is cause for rejoicing. Below is a sample listing of books that I hope can provide markings for your journey.

REFERENCE WORKS ON SPIRITUALITY

Many people have almost no sense of the history of Spirituality, or of the development of spiritual theology, or even of the major figures in the field. The volumes below will help to fill in any gaps you may feel in this regard.

Handley, Paul, Fiona MacMath, Pat Saunders, Robert Van Der Weyer, *The English Spirit*, London: Darton, Longman & Todd, 1988. A major new anthology of English spiritual writing from Caedmon to C. S. Lewis. The compilers are all members of the Little Gidding Community.

Jones, Cheslyn, Geoffrey Wainwright and Edward Yarnold, eds, *The Study of Spirituality*, New York: Oxford University Press, 1986. This volume provides an excellent sampling of writers from all of the major traditions in Spirituality. I am especially glad that an entire section is devoted to 'Pastoral Spirituality' since this emphasis has been sorely neglected in traditional programmes in Pastoral Theology.

Leech, Kenneth, *Experiencing God: Theology as Spirituality*, London: Sheldon Press, 1985. You may be acquainted with Kenneth Leech through his other books, *Soul Friend* and *True Prayer*. *Experiencing God* seeks to ground theology in its central role, which is the search for a transforming knowledge of God. The old writers used to speak of 'theology habitus', that is, a theology that transforms us at the most basic level of our habits. This is a substantial book that brings theology back into that tradition.

Ramsey, Boniface, *Beginning to Read the Fathers*, London: Darton, Longman & Todd, 1986. All those who have wanted to read the Early Church Fathers (including the Desert Fathers) but have felt intimidated by the cultural and linguistic gap will be encouraged by this book. It helps to clarify their varied positions on many themes from the 'human condition' to 'death and resurrection'. Fortunately, it has abundant quotations from the actual writings of the Fathers.

Seddon, Philip and Roger Pooley, *The Lord of the Journey*, London: Collins, 1986. A rich selection from Christian spiritual writings from the Early Church to the present day: a comprehensive introduction to the variety and depth of Christian thinking. The readings are arranged within a narrative structure, corresponding to the life-stages of a Christian's pilgrimage.

Wakefield, Gordon S., ed., *A Dictionary of Christian Spirituality*, London: SCM Press, 1988. A fascinating collection of articles, some about people and some about themes. It enables the reader to explore many aspects of spirituality. The information is presented in a clear and accessible way.

SPIRITUALITY AND PRAYER

Since prayer is at the heart of the spiritual life, it makes sense to give particular attention to this topic.

Anthony, Metropolitan, *Living Prayer*, London: Darton, Longman & Todd, 1980. Many popular misconceptions about prayer are dealt with in a simple yet profound way by Metropolitan Anthony, whose personal spirituality is deeply rooted in the Eastern Orthodox tradition.

Dalrymple, John, *Simple Prayer*, London: Darton, Longman & Todd, 1984. A small book on the nature and practice of prayer, which contains much insight drawn from the author's experience. The hallmarks of this book are authority, depth and lucidity.

Griffin, Emilie, *Clinging: The Experience of Prayer*, San Francisco: Harper & Row, 1984. Emilie Griffin knows God and so her warmly-felt invitation to the life of prayer can be taken seriously. This is a slender volume that is worth its weight in gold.

Mary Clare, Mother, *Encountering the Depths*, London: Darton, Longman & Todd, 1981. Wise, practical advice on developing the life of prayer. The problems encountered while seeking to grow in the spiritual life, in the context of the modern world, are presented as a challenge.

Ramon, Brother, *Deeper into God*, Basingstoke: Marshall Pickering, 1988. A joyful, enthusiastic challenge to explore spending time with God as a way of encountering Him afresh, and exposing ourselves more honestly to him.

GENERAL WORKS ON SPIRITUALITY

Some excellent books on Spirituality have come out in recent years. Below is a sample listing.

Colliander, Tito, *Way of the Ascetics: The Ancient Tradition of Discipline and Inner Growth*, trans. by Katherine Ferré, Oxford: Mowbray Books, 1983. If you have ever wanted to learn from the devotional masters of the Eastern Orthodox Church, this little book would be a good place to begin. It contains mainly succinct extracts from the writings of the Orthodox Church Fathers with brief commentary and practical applications for daily devotion.

England, Edward, *Keeping a Spiritual Journal*, Crowborough: Highland Books, 1988. Ten Christian writers explain the usefulness of keeping a spiritual journal, illustrating this through their own experience, and suggest general guidelines on how to go about it.

Foster, Richard J., *Money, Sex and Power: The Challenge of the Disciplined Life*, London: Hodder & Stoughton, 1985. While *Celebration of Discipline* is an attempt to describe how we live devotionally, this book is an attempt to describe how we live ethically – love of God, love of neighbour. In doing so, I present the monastic vows of poverty, chastity and obedience as a response to the issues of money, sex and power and seek to articulate contemporary vows of simplicity, fidelity and service.

Granberg-Michaelson, Wesley, *A Worldly Spirituality: A Call to Take Care of Life on Earth*, London: Harper & Row, 1984. This book calls for a new theological perspective that supports a caring, nurturing fellowship with the whole of God's creation. It seeks to apply the themes of Spirituality to the complex ecological problems we face today.

Hughes, Gerard, *God of Surprises*, London: Darton, Longman & Todd, 1985. A wise and lucid guide to the spiritual journey. It has much to say to those who are serious about encountering God, and also to those who have a love/hate relationship with the Church.

Jeff, Gordon, *Spiritual Direction for Every Christian*, London: SPCK, 1987. A handbook for anyone wanting to know about the skills of spiritual direction.

Jones, Alan, *Soul Making: The Desert Way of Spirituality*, London: SCM Press, 1986. This book encourages us to explore the heights and depths of human experience. The author seeks to show that we can come to understand more of God and His ways as we begin to live with the whole of our humanity.

Leckey, Dolores R., *The Ordinary Way: A Family Spirituality*, New York: Crossroad, 1982. The author attempts to apply the insights gained from the *Rule* of St Benedict to family life. It covers such issues as intimacy, equality, prayer, play, study, stability and hospitality.

McNeill, Donald P., Douglas A. Morrison and Henri J. Nouwen, *Compassion: A Reflection on the Christian Life*, London: Darton, Longman & Todd, 1982. Here is a book that seeks to apply the Christian virtue of compassion to the pressing social injustices of our day. The authors show how compassion is nurtured in a rightly ordered spiritual life and how it can move us into action on behalf of the bruised and broken.

Macy, Howard R., *Rhythms of the Inner Life: Yearning for Closeness with God*, Old Tappan, New Jersey: Fleming Revell, 1988. Using the Psalms as a basis, the author identifies seven movements of the heart that help to nurture the spiritual life: longing, waiting, trembling, despairing, resting, conversing and celebrating.

Nouwen, Henri J., *The Way of the Heart: Desert Spirituality and Contemporary Ministry*, London: Darton, Longman & Todd, 1981. Nouwen applies the insights of desert spirituality to the contemporary scene. He focuses particularly upon the Spiritual Disciplines of solitude, silence and prayer.

Tournier, Paul, *Creative Suffering*, London: SCM Press, 1982. One of the last books to be written by this great counsellor, and which grew out of a lifetime's experience, in which there had been much suffering.

Watson, David, *Discipleship*, London: Hodder & Stoughton, 1983. A call to be serious, faithful, disciplined followers of Christ. This book covers many aspects of the individual and corporate Christian life.

Willard, Dallas, *The Spirit of the Disciplines: Understanding How God Changes Lives*, San Francisco: Harper & Row, 1988. If I were to list the single most important book of this decade in Spirituality, this would be the book. It sets forth a clear theology for the Spiritual Disciplines as the means by which we are transformed into the likeness of Christ.

Scripture Index

Subject Index

Afterword by James Catford

Richard Foster has told me that he hates the expression 'a contemporary Christian classic', especially if it is attached to one of his own books. First it is hard to conceive of any contemporary book being a classic when it has hardly had the chance to stand the test of time. And then any truly seminal book is not a 'Christian classic' but simply a 'classic' as it has to stand up against the best in literature whatever the subject or idiom.

So let's settle for saying that *Celebration of Discipline* is as near to a classic as you can get in a book that's twenty-five years old and known by thousands of people as one of the greatest works they've ever read. I hope that this new edition will take it to a new generation – one that does not remember its first distinctive green cover or who never knew the Christian leader who wrote the foreword to the first British edition, David Watson.

The definitive Christian magazine *Christianity Today* has described Richard Foster as one of the mentors of a new movement within the Western Church sometimes called 'Emergent' or emerging church leaders. This informal group of younger Christian men and women have discovered that *Celebration of Discipline,* along with Richard Foster's other books, speak to our age just as much as they did a quarter of a century ago.

In our day of chilling out, being laid back and looking cool, it is surprising that what attracts people to *Celebration of Discipline* is just that – discipline. It's the remarkable discovery that by stepping into the classic disciplines of the Christian faith we can, entirely by the grace of God, take the first step to be changed into his likeness. The apostle Paul writes that he is in agony 'until Christ be formed in you' (Gal. 4:19). If Christianity is about anything then it's about the work of God to change us from the inside out.

But this process of renewal, or renovation of the heart as it has sometimes been called, is best done through the loving accountability of others who are also hungry for Christ to be formed within them. That's one of the reasons why, after writing *Celebration of Discipline*, Richard Foster set up Renovaré – pronounced *Ren-o-var-ay* and Latin for renewal – to introduce people to the resources that will help them experience this spirit-filled 'with-God life' for themselves.

One of the resources is the Renovaré spiritual formation group which comprises between two and eight people and meets informally every week or two. These special gatherings of like-minded people offer encouragement, support and mutual accountability in the context of much grace and mercy. They are easy to start up and a practical guide is available called *A Spiritual Formation Workbook* by James Bryan Smith and others.

It is worth pausing at this point to say that small groups also have the benefit of helping us avoid the dead hand of legalism on our lives. There seems to be something in many of us that wants to turn the grace and goodness of the Gospel into law, and then to go around putting it on other people. This must never happen. A group will watch out for any member coming out with a neat formula or ABC of Christian growth. This is how we help each other.

Another resource are the many books, both old and new, that describe the 'with-God life' that God intended for us and that deal with many common obstacles that we may encounter on the way. The impressive Hodder Christian Classics series is a good place to find many of these or you can try getting used copies via the web.

A third resource are the various Renovaré conferences and events that are arranged in Britain and Ireland as well as throughout the US and elsewhere. These experiences introduce Christians of all shapes and sizes, all ages and stages, to the various streams of the spiritual life that sit behind the teaching in *Celebration of Discipline*.

For more details of groups, books and events visit the Renovaré website either in Britain and Ireland at www.renovare.info or in the US at www.renovare.org

There are six streams, or dimensions of the Christian life, that Richard Foster has identified as forming a balanced vision for a disciple of Jesus Christ to follow. These are the *contemplative* or prayer-filled life, the *holiness* or virtuous life, the *charismatic* or Spirit-empowered life, the *social justice* or compassionate life, the *evangelical* or Word-centred life and the *incarnational* or sacramental life.

This balanced vision is explored more fully in the various Renovaré resources and on the website. Together the six streams are matched by a practical strategy to literally 'put on Christ' (Gal. 3:27) and are explored in *Celebration of Discipline*. And we need both parts of the equation. To have a practical strategy without a vision is about as useless as having a vision with no strategy. We need both.

May God richly bless our exploration of this 'with-God life' as we experience more and more fully our own celebration of discipline.

As the founding chair of Renovaré in the UK and Ireland, James Catford is also a member of the board of Renovaré in the US.

pw